T0214733

International Perspectives on Digital Media and Early Literacy

International Perspectives on Digital Media and Early Literacy evaluates the use and impact of digital devices for social interaction, language acquisition, and early literacy. It explores the role of interactive mediation as a tool for using digital media and provides empirical examples of best practice for digital media targeting language teaching and learning.

The book brings together a range of international contributions and discusses the increasing trend of digitalization as an additional resource in early childhood literacy. It provides a broad insight into current research on the potential of digital media in inclusive settings by integrating multiple perspectives from different scientific fields: (psycho)linguistics, cognitive science, language didactics, developmental psychology, technology development, and human–machine interaction. Drawing on a large body of research, it shows that crucial early experiences in communication and social learning are the basis for later academic skills. The book is structured to display children's first developmental steps in learning in interaction with digital media and highlight various domains of early digital media use in family, kindergarten, and primary schools.

This book will appeal to practitioners, academics, researchers, and students with an interest in early education, literacy education, digital education, the sociology of digital culture and social interaction, school reform, and teacher education.

Katharina J. Rohlfing is Professor of Psycholinguistics at Paderborn University, Germany.

Claudia Müller-Brauers is Professor for German Didactics at the Leibniz University Hannover, Germany.

Routledge Research in Early Childhood Education

This series provides a platform for researchers to present their latest research and discuss key issues in Early Childhood Education.

Books in the series include

Early Childhood Care and Education at the Margins
African Perspectives on Birth to Three
Edited by Hasina Banu Ebrahim, Auma Okwany and Oumar Barry

Attainment and Executive Functioning in the Early Years
Research for Inclusive Practice and Lifelong Learning
Hazel G. Whitters

Early Childhood Curriculum in Chinese Societies
Policies, Practices and Prospects
Weipeng Yang and Hui Li

Multiliteracies and Early Years Innovation
Perspectives from Finland and Beyond
Kristiina Kumpulainen and Julian Sefton-Green

Fröbel's Pedagogy of Kindergarten and Play
Modifications in Germany and the United States
Helge Wasmuth

International Perspectives on Digital Media and Early Literacy
The Impact of Digital Devices on Learning, Language Acquisition and Social Interaction
Edited by Katharina J. Rohlfing and Claudia Müller-Brauers

For more information about this series, please visit: www.routledge.com/education/series/RRECE

International Perspectives on Digital Media and Early Literacy

The Impact of Digital Devices on Learning, Language Acquisition and Social Interaction

Edited by Katharina J. Rohlfing and Claudia Müller-Brauers

Routledge
Taylor & Francis Group

LONDON AND NEW YORK

First published 2021
by Routledge
2 Park Square, Milton Park, Abingdon, Oxon OX14 4RN

and by Routledge
52 Vanderbilt Avenue, New York, NY 10017

Routledge is an imprint of the Taylor & Francis Group, an informa business

British Library Cataloguing-in-Publication Data
A catalogue record for this book is available from the British Library

Library of Congress Cataloging-in-Publication Data
A catalog record for this book has been requested

ISBN: 978-0-367-27904-2 (hbk)
ISBN: 978-0-429-32139-9 (ebk)

Typeset in Galliard
by Apex CoVantage, LLC

Contents

Figures

Tables

Contributors

Gökçe Elif Baykal is a postdoctoral researcher in Information Studies at Aarhus University. She holds her doctoral degree in Design, Technology and Society at Koç University. Her research focuses on child–computer interaction. She is interested in incorporating learning theories in cognitive development into research methods in human–computer interaction.

Jan M. Boelmann is a full professor and head of the Department of Literary and Media Didactics and the Centre for Didactic Computer Game Research at the Institute for German Language and Literature, University of Education Freiburg. His research interests are media didactics, text, images, multimedia, theory of narration, and youth/children's literature.

Karen Burstein is Chief Clinical Officer at iTether Technologies, Inc. in Phoenix, Arizona, where she develops and tests digital health education strategies and care coordination for population health management. She is Professor Emeritus of the School of Applied Language and Speech Sciences, and Communicative Disorders at the University of Louisiana.

Adriana G. Bus is Professor Emeritus of Leiden University, Netherlands; a professor at the University of Stavanger, Norway; and an honorary professor at ELTE Eötvös Loránd University, Budapest, Hungary. She aims at designing new digital book formats that benefit not only children's meaning-making of narratives but also their enjoyment of literature.

Simone C. Ehmig received her Ph.D. degree in communication studies from Johannes Gutenberg University Mainz in 2000. Since 2009, she has been the head of the Institute for Research on Reading and Media of the German Reading Foundation (Stiftung Lesen). She has been an honorary professor at the University of Mainz since 2019. Her research interests are factors influencing reading socialization in the early years, especially the role of reading aloud.

Tilbe Göksun is Associate Professor of Psychology at Koç University. She received her Ph.D. in psychology from Temple University in 2010 and did postdoctoral work in neuropsychology at the University of Pennsylvania between 2010 and 2013. Her research interests include language and cognitive development and language–thought interaction in different populations.

Susanne Grassmann received a Ph.D. degree in psychology from the University of Leipzig in 2009. She has held several senior researcher positions at universities in the Netherlands and in Switzerland. Since 2017, she has been developing digital learning applications. Her mission is to boost the effectiveness of (digital) educational media.

Angela Grimminger received her Ph.D. degree in psycholinguistics from Paderborn University in 2017. She is interested in young children's use of multimodal means of communication and individual differences in its development.

Lukas Heymann holds a degree in education from Johannes Gutenberg University Mainz. Since 2008, he has been a research associate at the Institute for Research on Reading and Media of the German Reading Foundation (Stiftung Lesen). Among his main research interests are the development of reading motivation and digital media concepts to encourage children and adolescents.

Junko Kanero is Assistant Professor of Psychology at Sabancı University. Junko received her Ph.D. degree in developmental psychology and neuroscience from Temple University in 2016. Her research interests include language development in childhood, the use of technology in language education, and interaction between language and non-linguistic cognition.

Aylin C. Küntay is Professor of Psychology at Koç University. She received her Ph.D. in psychology from the University of California, Berkeley in 1997. Her research is on language and communicative development of children and their social interactions, including with technology.

Juliane Leinweber received her Ph.D. degree in theoretical medicine from the RWTH Aachen University in 2014. Since 2019, she has been a full professor of therapy science at the HAWK Hildesheim/Holzminden/Göttingen University of Applied Sciences. Her research interest is new technologies in speech and language therapy.

Ulrich J. Mertens received his master's degree in sport science from Bielefeld University, with a focus on intelligence and motion. Since 2018, he has been a Ph.D. student at Paderborn University, working in the interdisciplinary project "Empirical and computational study of iconic gesture-speech integration and its development in preschool children."

Christiane Miosga received her Ph.D. degree in Educational Linguistics from Hannover University in 2002. Since 2016, she has been an apl. professor in the Department of Speech and Language Pedagogy & Therapy at Hannover University. Her research interests are conversational analysis and didactics of multimodal interaction in school, daycare, and therapy.

Claudia Müller-Brauers completed her doctoral studies at Dortmund Technical University in 2012. Since 2018, she has been a full professor and head of the Department of Didactics of Symbol Systems – German at Leibniz University Hannover. Her research interests are early literacy processes, digital children's literature, and the evaluation of language promotion concepts.

Nicole Najemnik is a Ph.D. student in the multidisciplinary graduate program "Online Participation". In her doctoral thesis, she analyzes influencing factors on women's involvement in local e-participation procedures using Bourdieu's theory of social action. Her research interests are digital divides and e-democracy.

Frank Niklas received his Ph.D. in psychology from the Julius-Maximilians-University Würzburg in 2010. Since 2019, he has been a full professor of educational psychology and family studies at the Ludwig-Maximilians-University Munich. His research focuses on children's learning and development in the context of the home learning environment.

Cansu Oranç is a researcher at the Max Planck Institute for Human Development. She received her Ph.D. in psychology from Koç University. Her research focuses on children's learning with technology and their understanding of digital sources of information.

Ines Potthast M.A., B.A. is a research assistant in the Department of Didactics of Symbol Systems – German at the Institute for Special Education of Leibniz University Hannover. Her research interests are interactions of hearing-impaired children and their families, language acquisition, and multilingualism.

Ute Ritterfeld is a trained speech and language pathologist (1983, Heidelberg) and received her Ph.D. in psychology (1995, TU University Berlin). As a full professor at TU Dortmund University, she has been heading the department of language and communication within the Rehabilitation Sciences since 2010. Her research in the overlapping areas of health and education has a strong focus on technology.

Katharina J. Rohlfing received her Ph.D. degree in linguistics from Bielefeld University in 2002. Since 2015, she has been a full professor of psycholinguistics and the head of SprachSpielLabor at Paderborn University. Her research interests are young children's acquisition of language, and how it can be scaffolded in social interaction.

Kathleen Roskos studies the design and use of digital books as teaching and learning resources that support early literacy development and promote early literacy skills. She is a professor emerita of the Department of Education and School Psychology at John Carroll University, Cleveland, Ohio.

Scarlet Schaffrath is a Ph.D. student in the interdisciplinary research program "Digital Society", funded by the State of North Rhine-Westphalia, Germany. In her doctoral thesis, she focuses on visions of educational robots and child–robot interactions from a techno-social perspective. She is interested in innovation processes and methods to describe these processes.

Anja Starke is a rehabilitation pedagogue and clinical linguist. She received her Ph.D. in rehabilitation sciences at the TU Dortmund University in 2015. Since 2019, she has been a full professor of inclusive education, focusing on children with speech, language, and communication needs. In her research, she focuses on the use of new media in speech therapy and speech promotion, as well as on the professionalization of pedagogical professionals.

Nils F. Tolksdorf is a Ph.D. fellow of the interdisciplinary research program "Digital Society", funded by the State of North Rhine-Westphalia, Germany, and works at Paderborn University. He received his B.A. and M.A. degrees in linguistics from Paderborn University. His research focuses on how social robots can support children's language learning.

Astrid Wirth holds a master's degree in psychology from the Johannes Gutenberg University Mainz, Germany. She currently works as a research associate at the Ludwig-Maximilians-University Munich and is writing her dissertation on the impact of early shared reading and the home literacy environment on children's linguistic and socioemotional competencies.

Britta Wrede is head of the Medical Assistance Systems group at Bielefeld University. She received her Ph.D. in computer science in 2002 and has been working in human–machine interaction since then. Her research is inspired by cognitive models of interaction, especially those derived from parent–child interaction.

Isabel Zorn has been a professor of media education at TH Köln University of Applied Sciences, Germany. She is a member of the Institute of Media Research and Media Education and the director of the research cluster "Digital Technologies in Social Services". Isabel's research interests are the interlink of technology design, education, and social work.

Introduction to international perspectives on digital media and early literacy

Katharina J. Rohlfing and Claudia Müller-Brauers

For today's children, the early learning environment is no longer characterized by paper-based books and games. Increasingly, it is tablets, smartphones, apps, and software that are shaping their young lives and conveying not only media experiences but also modified access to (early) literacy. Accordingly, more and more e-books, apps, and software are being designed specifically for educational purposes, taking strong advantage of the fact that children can use digital devices on their own without assistance or supervision. In addition, researchers are investigating social robots as potential learning partners because their physical presence can be used to embed interaction in a real environment. Current research (e.g., Anwar, Bascou, Menekse, & Kardgar, 2019; Vulchanova, Baggio, Cangelosi, & Smith, 2017; Barr & Nichols Linebarger, 2017; see also Chapter 7) strongly suggests that the benefits of these devices certainly vary, and that the application of digital media should be considered individually for each specific child – that is, with respect to her or his specific abilities, skills, and social environment.

With this book, we aim to provide insights into current research on the impact of digital devices on language and literacy learning and on the role of interactive mediation. We align ourselves with the internationally confirmed finding that language and literacy are key to economic, academic, and social well-being. We therefore propose that it is important to recognize these new possibilities for fostering language and literacy and to study them both closely and constantly. Together with Pempek and Lauricella (2017, p. 68), we consider it to be imperative for researchers to continue to examine how the devices emerging within this trend toward ever more digitalization can both support and hinder the interaction that is at the core of language and literacy acquisition. In line with this imperative, the following contributions target empirically based examples of best practice that can encourage teachers in both kindergartens and elementary schools to use digital media systematically in support of early literacy skills. We do this by including both novel empirical studies and the experience-based perspectives of professionals working in the field of (early) childhood education. Hence, the contributions in this volume are divided into two parts: (1) interaction with digital devices (Chapters 1 to 5) and (2) literacy learning with digital media (Chapters 6 to 10). Although learning is clearly a topic in both parts of the book, the latter part focuses more strongly on evaluating the effects on learning.

Our book pursues the following hypotheses: (1) the use of digital media is changing the ways in which humans interact, and this is affecting adult–child practices and (2) combining the use of digital media and social interactions with adults will promote (early) literacy and learning more successfully than letting children use digital devices by themselves. From an educational perspective, however, such a combination of adults and digital media requires not only a new and systematic division of interactive roles, tasks, and time for activities but also a careful consideration of its didactic implications.

When addressing these hypotheses, the first part of the book highlights research examining how digital media is changing familiar media practices, together with longitudinal studies or reviews addressing the value of particular characteristic features of digital media and the effects they have on language learning. The first chapter, by **Adriana G. Bus, Kathleen Roskos, and Karen Burstein**, provides an extensive review of current studies and longitudinal results on learning with "digital additions." The authors argue that there are some specific cases in which interaction with digital devices might be more beneficial than interaction with traditional picture books. Next, **Christiane Miosga's** chapter aims to show how familiar interaction formats, such as traditional picture book reading, are changing through the increasing use of digital media. The study demonstrates that traditional media (e.g., books) generally seem to have more beneficial effects for early literacy than the e-books and iPad apps used by older children because they focus on interactive scaffolding in the form of emotional attunement. The chapter by **Scarlet Schaffrath, Nicole Najemnik, and Isabel Zorn** addresses the question of whether an interaction with tablets has the "inclusive potential" to bring children of kindergarten age together. Presenting their results, the authors argue that digital media in the form of tablets create occasions for communication in which differently abled children initiate attempts to engage in mutual play. However, they also make greater demands on educators, who need to ensure that they create and foster inclusive play settings.

In their chapter, **Katharina J. Rohlfing, Angela Grimminger, and Britta Wrede** also demonstrate how interactive roles are being transformed by the use of digital media. They show that when interacting with a robot, caregivers have an important role to play in encouraging the child and explaining the technology. Studies in child–robot interaction therefore need to include adults as interpreters of what is (currently) nonadaptive technology. This is especially important because robots have still not been adjusted to the way children communicate in social interactions – as the chapter by **Nils F. Tolksdorf and Ulrich J. Mertens** reveals so clearly. These authors analyze children's multimodal communication and alert us to the fact that if technology is to become inclusive, adaptive, and accessible to young children, it needs to be designed to better perceive the multimodal ways in which they interact.

In the second part of the book, we aim to point out how the use of digital media can be modified for language teaching and learning, and how digital media can have an inclusive potential for all children in kindergarten settings. **Astrid Wirth, Simone C. Ehmig, Lukas Heymann, and Frank Niklas** argue that digital media offer access to target groups that are more difficult to reach with printed media. Hence, in this respect, digital media seem to possess an "inclusive potential" that can be used beneficially in our society. The chapter by **Cansu Oranç, Gökçe Elif Baykal, Junko Kanero, Aylin C. Küntay, and Tilbe Göksun** goes beyond e-books and reports results from a recently completed European Union (EU) project on social robots and children's language learning. Going beyond social robots, the authors systematically compare digital devices in terms of their learning effects. They point out that new devices such as social robots, virtual peers, and tangible user interfaces offer novel possibilities of interaction, also for children with special needs. The chapter by **Anja Starke, Juliane Leinweber, and Ute Ritterfeld** provides concrete guidelines that designers need to consider when developing digital products to promote children's (second) language learning. A theoretical model for the analysis of picture-book apps according to their potential for story comprehension is provided in the chapter by **Claudia Müller-Brauers, Jan M. Boelmann, Christiane Miosga, and Ines Potthast**. Using a particular app, the authors demonstrate ways of promoting language more systematically, and they discuss both potentials and limitations when designing digital literature for children. The final chapter by **Susanne Grassmann** is a short report on a webpage that has been developed to foster cross-situational language learning by providing educators with pictures across different contexts.

Each chapter closes with three key considerations for parents, educators, and producers. Through its broad approach, this book offers education students, preschool teachers, and elementary school teachers **didactic know-how** that they can apply in various ways: In developing language education programs that are based on digital media, in reflecting over and providing training on interactive strategies when applying digital media in learning settings, or in sharing experiences with parents. Based on expertise in education and interaction, the chapters also provide concrete suggestions for technological improvements for producers.

Clearly, the different parts of our book reflect the differences in the state of the art. It offers not just one but many answers regarding the effects of digital media on language skills and literacy. These answers call for careful consideration not only in terms of children's individual skills but also in the settings and the type of social interaction in which digital media should be applied. Through the contributions and the different answers provided in this book, we aim to persuade parents, teachers, and producers that they should keep an eye on contemporary research so that they can apply it in the educational context, and thereby make their own contribution to actively, meaningfully, and responsibly shaping technological developments.

As a final note, we wish to thank all the reviewers who spent their time providing valuable suggestions to the individual contributions. We also wish to express our gratitude to Jonathan Harrow; his feedback and detailed comments on language supported us tremendously in improving the readability and coherence of the individual contributions being gathered together for international perspectives.

References

Anwar, S., Bascou, N. A., Menekse, M., & Kardgar, A. (2019). A systematic review of studies on educational robotics. *Journal of Pre-College Engineering Education Research (J-PEER)*, *9*(2), 1–15. doi:10.7771/2157-9288.1223

Barr, R., & Nichols Linebarger, D. (Eds.). (2017). *Media exposure during infancy and early childhood: The effects of content and context on learning and development.* New York, NY: Springer.

Pempek, T. A., & Lauricella, A. R. (2017). The effects of parent-child interaction and media use on cognitive development in infants, toddlers, and preschoolers. In F. C. Blumberg & P. J. Brooks (Eds.), *Cognitive development in digital contexts* (pp. 53–74). London, England: Academic Press.

Vulchanova, M., Baggio, G., Cangelosi, A., & Smith, L. (2017). Editorial: Language development in the digital age. *Frontiers in Human Neuroscience, 11*, 447.

Part I

Learning and interaction with digital devices

Chapter 1

Promising interactive functions in digital storybooks for young children

Adriana G. Bus, Kathleen Roskos, and Karen Burstein

Introduction

When first introduced about 30 years ago, digital picture storybooks seemed so promising. Stories enlivened with animations, music, and sounds seemed to be an exciting development that opened up new possibilities for actively engaging children with stories. Digital storybooks, however, have yet to realize their promise, although the ubiquity of digital media virtually guarantees their growing presence in early childhood. This confronts us with a pressing question: Which digital book format immerses children in stories and benefits not only children's meaning-making of narratives but also their sheer enjoyment of literature?

In this chapter, we address this question by sorting out the interactive affordances of digital book reading. We first look at interactivity in early first-generation digital books in which digital enhancements were enjoyable, but additions often missed the mark of supporting children's comprehension of the story. We then describe some theoretical drivers of interactivity that may help explicate the greater efficacy of some techniques over others. Building on this work, we explore efforts to improve and advance interactive designs in digital storybooks that increase engagement and deepen children's early literacy and literary experiences. We close the chapter with a long view of the potential benefits of digital books in children's literacy development and a call for collaboration that will bring together book app creators/authors and researchers to build a stronger knowledge base around digital books in early childhood.

One aside before we start: Digital books are indeed *new, innovative* books. Hence, as has become current practice, it is risky to simply migrate or recycle paper books to interactive app formats – an effort akin to the horse designed by a committee that turns out to be a camel. Linda Labbo (personal communication) compares the new books with kitchen machines – shapeshifters that can slice, dice, or mash. Thus, there are a variety of possibilities that make the outcome uncertain and sometimes unrecognizable as a narrative experience.

Digital storybooks version 2.0

Interactivity in first-generation digital books

Early digital storybook designs were often additive, the objective being to *add technology to* the paper book, mostly by including user-activated visual and sound effects as mechanisms for engaging children. The user taps an object, animal, or person to elicit a sound (e.g., snore, laugh, scratch) or perform an action (e.g., fall, jump, laugh). In many cases, this interaction had no relevance to the story, except that it allowed the children to "interact" with the illustration (Zhao & Unsworth, 2017). In brief, the design goal was to include interactive functions that invite the child to explore these mechanisms as objects in the book. However, the risk is that performing these actions will lead to less exploration of narrative meanings. Those with computer expertise had a heavy hand in the early designs of these books, evidenced by their (naïve) belief that by making reading sessions more interactive, children would be more motivated – an assumption that probably guided their choices of which technology to add to books. First-generation digital storybooks such as *Just Grandma and Me* (Mayer, 1983) and *P. B. Bear's Birthday Party* (Davis, 1994) are examples of this design approach. In *Just Grandma and Me*, the successive screens present the same defining features of paper picture books: on each screen, a section of text and an illustration. When opening a new screen, the text is read aloud automatically, and story events explained in the narration are animated. However, this does not occur simultaneously. After the oral narration finishes, we see what the narration explained – for instance, a boy building a sandcastle and a big wave destroying the castle. After the oral rendition and animation, the user can activate ten or more hotspots in the frozen screen and elicit visual and/or sound effects, almost all incongruent with the storyline: a blob in the sand turning into a fountain; a little beetle hurrying away through the sand; a prehistoric spear thrower in bearskin running by.

Although such interactive enhancements are designed to be motivating (Ricci & Beal, 2002), adding these to a multimedia presentation may distract children from the storyline and diminish meaning-making. Albeit novel and exciting, irrelevant information quickly overloads the human capacity to learn (Renninger, 1992). Outcomes of studies testing the effects of these early digital book designs on children's narrative comprehension were indeed generally negative. Labbo and Kuhn's (2000) case study of *Arthur's Teacher Trouble* (Brown, 1994) concluded that children trying to integrate all available information in the narration – hence, also the incoherent gimmicks – fail to make meaning of the story. For example, they do not succeed in integrating the prehistoric spear thrower into the story of Little Critter on the beach with his grandma. Furthermore, quantitative studies support the adverse effects of cognitive overload on comprehension. Instead of immersing young children in stories, the designs seem to distract them from the storyline and result in lower scores on comprehension (Parish-Morris, Mahajan, Hirsh-Pasek, Golinkoff, & Collins, 2013). Bus, Sarı, and Takacs (2019) concluded that activating many hotspots unrelated to the storyline distorted meaning-making. Focusing on the number of pages on which the story that the child retold was similar to the original story, children's score decreased by more than 25% when unrelated hotspots were added to the storyline. A meta-analysis of these and other early studies reaffirmed the design pitfalls of digital additions that introduce extraneous information. Nonetheless, there were not enough studies to make a clear-cut distinction between problematic and possibly promising interactivity in stories (Takacs, Swart, & Bus, 2015).

In brief, research on first-generation digital books yielded some valuable insights into the design of interactivity in digital storybooks. The interactions that digital books afford can work for or against story comprehension as a cornerstone of early literacy. Realizing the digital promise in New Age storybooks therefore requires a more fine-grained analysis of digital additions that promote literate thinking in storybook reading. A closer inspection of what works and why it works will allow us to identify which digital storytelling techniques support the design and development of quality digital storybooks in early childhood literature.

Theory and principles of interactivity in 2.0 digital books

Multimedia learning theories

Second-generation (version 2.0) digital books shift the design focus to digital additions with potential for supporting young children's narrative comprehension skills (Bus, Takacs, & Kegel, 2015; Bus et al., 2019; Korat & Shamir, 2008; Parish-Morris et al., 2013; Roskos, Brueck, & Lenhart, 2017; Roskos, Brueck, & Widman, 2009). We refer to these broadly as digital storytelling techniques that may include adding materials such as a dictionary, embedding motion and camera movements in illustrations, adding music and sounds, or asking story-related questions. In our own research, we aim to develop interactive 2.0 designs that are more explicitly theory-driven than first-generation digital books (see Figure 1.1 for an overview of the theoretical cornerstones essential to version 2.0 designs).

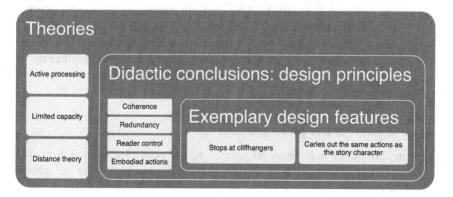

Figure 1.1 Theoretical cornerstones, didactic conclusions, and exemplary design features

Grounded in assumptions that underlie theories of multimedia learning (Mayer, 2009), the following theories are particularly relevant:

Active processing: Humans are not passive processors who seek to add as much information as possible to memory (Mayer, 2005a). They are active processors who seek to make sense of new information. This typically includes paying attention, selecting from all incoming information, and integrating information with their prior knowledge (Gopnik & Meltzoff, 1997). The child applies cognitive processes to incoming narrative and other information to make sense of the storyline (Glenberg, Gutierrez, Levin, Japuntich, & Kaschak, 2004). We do not want children to lean back and listen; we want them to actively make attempts to interpret the presented information – the main reason to add interactive functions. Interactivity is a strength of digital media that, if intertwined with a narrative, may be a strong tool to promote effective problem solving.

Capacity theory: However, the interactive embedded content may come at a cost for performance. Because the human information processing system has a limited capacity, distributing cognitive resources across both the narrative and the embedded content may be problematic. A person's ability to process both simultaneously depends on how much capacity separate sources require. Adverse outcomes may result from limited resources being available for processing both narrative and embedded content (Kahneman, 1973). When the embedded content is tangential to the narrative, the two parallel processes of comprehension compete for limited resources in working memory. The result may be that the narrative cannot be processed as deeply as it might otherwise be, and that children may attend to only part of it, thus potentially distorting understanding of the narrative content and resulting in less detailed representations (Yokota & Teale, 2014).

Distance theory: However, outcomes may be different when interactive functions are intertwined with the narrative. By studying educational television content, Fisch (2000) introduced the idea that distance between the narrative and embedded content will contribute to clear-cut distinctions between problematic and promising embedded content, suggesting that if the distance between the narrative and the embedded content in digital books is small, these elements can complement one another rather than compete for resources, thereby functioning to increase meaning-making of the narrative.

Do's and don'ts of interactive quality design

Version 2.0 books may draw on several design principles derived from the assumptions underlying theories of multimedia learning in order to achieve beneficial interactivity. In the following sections, we briefly describe four principles that seem particularly important for interactive digital books. The do's and don'ts of digital storytelling techniques are intended to support children's active engagement in digital books and meaning-making. Previous publications (e.g., Bus et al., 2015; Sarı, Asûde Başal, Takacs, & Bus, 2019) describe the temporal contiguity and modality principles. Both are demonstrably relevant for digitizing picture storybooks but are not related to this chapter with its focus on interactive functions.

Coherence principle: It is important that children are involved only in the interactive functions striking the very core of the narrative, and that we bypass interactive functions related only to story themes that would risk introducing extraneous material that might distract children from the storyline. For instance, we may expect adverse effects on story comprehension when an on-demand dictionary provides word definitions. However useful word definitions may be for vocabulary learning, cognitive load theory warrants concern when embedding dictionaries in narratives because additional processing may reduce the amount of attention available for understanding narrative content. Processing word definitions reduces the available resources in working memory for processing the narrative, thereby raising the risk that children will not understand the story or miss important details. Only when interactive functions highlight the organization of the narrative do we expect children to comprehend narratives better.

Redundancy principle: It might be tempting to add interactive functions that are core to the storyline but do not add much to the process of meaning-making. Mayer's (2005b) redundancy principle predicts that children comprehend more from a nonredundant story because the addition of redundant information requires additional extraneous processing. For instance, Mayer (2005b) found that people learn more deeply from graphics and narration than from graphics, narration, *and* on-screen text. Digital books may include reader-activated effects that are related to the narrative but do not add new information. For instance, in a story about balloons, the child can click on the balloons to see them rise. Assuming that young children are familiar with balloons, such interactive functions do not add to the static picture. Hence, they are redundant, and may unnecessarily tax the meaning-making system, easily resulting in cognitive overload.

Reader-control principle: To promote attention, select from all incoming information, and integrate information with prior knowledge, it may be supportive for multimedia material to be presented in segments over which the learner has control. Presenting the story as a continuous flow of information (Mayer, 2009) may not elicit active processing of the material. A simple way to enable control is to ensure that new information (e.g., a new illustration or a camera movement within an illustration) does not appear automatically, but only after the user activates it. Figure 1.2, for example, presents three screenshots from an interactive digital book. Each time the camera moves and a new perspective appears within the same illustration, the narrative stops and an action by the reader (child or adult) is required to continue the story. Readers can indicate whether or not they have integrated all incoming information and are ready for a new segment of information. The intuitive appeal of reader control is that readers have the opportunity to adapt the story to their own (processing) speed to an even greater extent than that possible with traditional paper books (Lawless & Brown, 1997). The hypothesis is that reader control is an important principle: when children have more control over story processing, this may promote paying attention, organizing new information, and integrating new information into story comprehension (Gopnik & Meltzoff, 1997).

Figure 1.2 Screenshots demonstrating the stops on one of the screens in a story called *Lightning*

Source: Permission granted by *Het Woeste Woud*, NL

Figure 1.2 (Continued)

Embodied actions principle: Several developers and researchers have suggested that one promising form of interaction may be *embodied action*. Such action places the viewer/reader in a position to physically engage in an action similar to that of a character on the screen (Kucirkova, 2019; Mangen, Hoel, & Moser, 2018). Version 2.0 books provide opportunities for users to *interact physically with the story's characters* (Zhao & Unsworth, 2017). They may position readers within digital storylines, thus rendering the dimensions of stories more explicit and salient. The hypothesis is that this virtual *as-if* mode of experience will amplify empathy by aligning the reader with the actions of the character (Kucirkova, 2019). Sargeant (2015), for instance, developed the app *How Far is Up?* in which children can move a toy rocket around a scene by tilting the device or by dragging a finger across the screen. She assumes that users experience the bodily feeling of moving an object in fictional space, which may enable them to empathize more with the story characters. Such interactive functions may afford the experience of perceiving the world from the perspective of the story character, thus deepening comprehension of the storyline (Mangen et al., 2018). Empirical evidence from studies of story enactment corroborates the potential cognitive and emotional benefits of assuming an *as-if* stance in narrative comprehension in terms of understanding literary elements such as character motivation and feelings (see, e.g., Lillard et al., 2013; Nicolopoulou, Schnabel Cortina, Ilgaz, Brockmeyer Cates, & de Sá, 2015). Research on the effects of this design principle on literary understanding is very new and open to testing the effects on understanding character actions, and to developing an empathetic stance in young children.

Recent research on 2.0 designs

Several studies have tested digital book designs by contrasting versions with and without specific user-activated interactivity features such as a dictionary or questions. A recent content analysis of commercially available storybook apps examined how the user-activated effects are intertwined with the storyline (Korat & Falk, 2017). A similar content analysis carried out ten years earlier confirmed that storybook CD-ROMs are usually overloaded with reader-activated animations or sounds that are, at best, peripheral to the storyline but are mostly not related to the story (e.g., a tea towel turning into a dove; a fast-growing flower making music). Korat and Falk's recent update that analyzed randomly selected storybook apps revealed similar findings: Reader-activated animations and sounds are still dominant in storybook apps, but nowadays, they are aligned more coherently with the narrative themes than before. Nonetheless, interactive functions are not integrated successfully with the narrative storyline.

To date, a robust body of studies has shed light on digital affordances, as seen in v2.0 designs that make the digital promise clearer and more attainable. In general, they suggest that interactive functions make digital books more engaging than books without these features (e.g., Richter & Courage, 2017; Strouse & Ganea, 2017; Willoughby, Evans, & Nowak, 2015). Nonetheless, the same studies report evidence on the adverse effects that such interactive affordances may have on making meaning of the narratives, showing that children get sidetracked by such features (e.g., Chiong, Ree, Takeuchi, & Erickson, 2012; Moody, Justice, & Cabell, 2010; Richter & Courage, 2017; Strouse & Ganea, 2017). Several studies have illustrated that reader-activated animations and sounds – the kind of interactivity that is abundantly available in commercial storybook apps – neither promote nor inhibit children's story comprehension (Lauricella, Barr, & Calvert, 2014; Richter & Courage, 2017). Unfortunately, much of the research thus far is fraught with methodological issues. For instance, in many studies, children read the story only once or twice in one session, and this is probably insufficient to show positive or negative effects of particular affordances (Penno, Wilkinson, & Moore, 2002).

In sum, research on second-generation digital book design shows that the most common forms of interactive technology in storybook apps – namely, reader-activated visual or sound effects – are engaging and often informative (e.g., why people are sitting in the doctor's waiting room), but do not complement the narrative flow of the story (Lauricella et al., 2014; Richter & Courage, 2017). In reality, most interactive functions in version 2.0 designs do match the *coherence* principle, but our impression is that they often do not match the *redundancy* principle. Key to more effective interactive functions is that they probably engage children more deeply with the thematic content while maintaining the integrity of the story. However, due to a lack of prototypes using basic principles of *reader control* and *embodied actions*, there is still little evidence regarding the efficacy of these principle-attuned affordances.

Improving the interactivity function

Since the early days of CD-ROM books, considerable progress has been made in the design quality of digital storybooks for young children. Spurred on by the emergence and technical quality of tablet technologies, the production of interactive picture storybook apps has accelerated (Kucirkova & Littleton, 2016). Yet, dominated by classic forms of interaction (e.g., version 1.0), most do not reflect the influence of theories that take into account the *sensorimotor contingencies* (Mangen et al., 2018, p. 5) of children's social-emotional and cognitive engagement with storybooks. Still missing from the design toolset of quality digital storybooks is an *embodied cognition perspective* that includes carrying out the same actions of the story characters to promote empathy and, thereby, narrative comprehension.

Well-placed interactive affordances may contribute significantly to children's early meaning-making of narrative text, but few experiments to date have included such books. Nonetheless, several researchers have described prototypes of interactive books that might be beneficial for children's engagement in stories and making meaning of the narration (e.g., Paciga, 2015; Yokota & Teale, 2014). In these prototypes, children carry out small actions that are in line with the narration, thus providing readers with opportunities to engage more deeply with the thematic content while maintaining the integrity of the story (Yokota & Teale, 2014, p. 581). Instead of features that cause young readers to lose sight of the main storyline, these apps successfully integrate interactivity with the narrative line.

A promising example mentioned by Yokota and Teale is the story *The Monster at the End of This Book* (Callaway Digital Arts, 2010), in which Grover, one of the Sesame Street characters, ties knots, nails up boards, and builds a brick wall. A reader is able to break through each of these barriers by touching hotspots, thereby moving the story forward. Similar examples are rare. Among the abundance of digital books with playful interactivity, few integrate interactivity with the narrative as in *The Monster at the End of This Book* to strengthen children's engagement and deepen story comprehension (Yokota & Teale, 2014).

Along with avoiding redundancy, improving the interactivity of digital books involves embodied actions that may simulate gestures in meaning-making and stimulate empathy with story characters (cf. Paciga, 2015; Sargeant, 2015; Zhao & Unsworth, 2017). This can be illustrated by the previously mentioned app, *How Far is Up?* (Sargeant, 2014), in which users can move a toy rocket around a scene by tilting the hardware device or by dragging a finger across the screen. Such an exploratory activity aims to help users experience the bodily feeling of moving an object in a fictional space, thus promoting perspective taking and affording the experience of perceiving the world from the perspective of another person (Kucirkova, 2019). In brief, embodiment theory predicts that virtually experiencing like another person might be superior to just imagining that experience (Robbins & Aydede, 2009).

We hypothesize that embodied actions realized with the help of digital affordances will increase the empathy-building potential of narratives. Some evidence for this assumption can be found in research showing that students remember a text better if they can physically manipulate toy objects referred to in it (Glenberg et al., 2004). Other evidence comes from thematic fantasy paradigm studies in play research (Roskos, in press).

The Dutch app developer Christiaan Coenraads (Het Woeste Woud) has experimented with forms of interactivity to promote children's reflection on story events and deepen story comprehension. In line with the *user-control* principle, his prototype does not advance the story automatically but is user-paced, thereby providing time to pay attention, select from incoming information, and integrate information with prior knowledge. His *stops* take place at crucial moments in the storyline and are very suggestive of themes for discussion. Preferably the *stops* are cliffhangers – plot devices in fiction in which the main character is in a precarious or difficult dilemma or is confronted with a shocking revelation. See Figure 1.2, in which the boy (main character) in the story is eager to go to school; the story is interrupted, so the user can reflect on this and maybe guess why the character is so eager. To prompt the narrative to continue, the user must take action by clicking on an on-screen icon.

This prototype, which is user-paced as well as aligned with the *embodied actions* principle, prompts users to replicate the actions of the character. For instance, after the character has borrowed his father's weather-making machine, he has to find the correct button on the dashboard because he wants to make lightning. We first see the character sitting, puzzled, in front of the dashboard (see Figure 1.3). Then the camera zooms in on the dashboard, so the user sees the dashboard in the same way as the character does. One of the buttons lights up while the text paraphrases the boy: "Hmmm, which is the button for lightning? Maybe this one?" The story continues only after the user has clicked on or touched the button that lights up, even though it is clear that the character has selected the wrong button. This interaction, when interleaved into the natural flow of the story, may stimulate the user's empathy with the character's doubts and feelings, potentially deepening story comprehension. The reader may also feel *as if* she or he is complicit with the experience of the character and events.

Figure 1.3 The story advances only after the user has pressed the button selected by the story character; this button lights up (second screenshot)

Source: Permission granted by *Het Woeste Woud*, NL

Figure 1.3 (Continued)

Anstadt and Bus (2019) conducted a randomized controlled trial with different versions of this storybook app to test the effects of the interactive functions in *Lightning*. The trial, involving 77 4- to 6-year-old children, revealed a positive effect of the interactive functions in this app on engagement and story comprehension. The children were more attentive and successful in making meaning when they were in control, as compared to a version of the same story that advanced automatically, thereby simulating the experience of watching a film rather than that of reading a book. To assess attention during book reading, the researchers coded children's responsivity to two distractive events by looking away from the screen: (1) a pen dropped by the researcher and (2) a phone making noise. Comprehension was assessed by a retelling of main events prompted by key pictures.

Because reader control over pace coincided with carrying out the same actions as the story characters, Anstadt and Bus were unable to conclude which is more important from the trial. The researchers reported a high amount of verbal engagement due to the stops. Even though the session did not include an adult interacting with the child, children spontaneously brought up personal experiences or prior knowledge related to the story content to the examiner, suggesting that children use the stops to mentally organize information about the story. Many children started to hypothesize what would happen next ("The dad may wake up") and suggest the valence of the action ("His dad will be angry"). This format seems to promote children's reflection on story events by not continuing the story until they understand events and integrating these events with previous events. This format may reduce the risk of cognitive overload due to "missing links" (cf. Zhou & Yadav, 2017). In the same vein, children took much more time to read the story when it included *stops* as compared to the version that advanced automatically.

When adults and children share story apps, built-in *stops* may also promote opportunities for adult–child interactivity related to the story content in a very natural way. When *stops* take place at crucial moments in the story, preferably cliffhangers, they may provoke discussion suggestive of story themes. Supportive of this format is Kim and Anderson's (2008) finding that giving parent and child control over the pace of the story resulted in more interactions compared to a closed format in which pages turned automatically. So far, we notice that at these *stops*, children often start talking to the adult sitting next to them and look for confirmation of their responses and feelings about the story events (disbelief, uncertainty, involvement). Our first experiences with parents who have been directed to share storybook apps containing stops with their children are promising, suggesting that the type of presentation (stops instead of automatic advances) sets adults and children in a lean-forward (engaged) mood rather than that of laid-back (passive) listeners (Bus, unpublished data). These interruptions seem to promote the necessary interactive approach in a target group of 3-year-olds for whom most narratives are complex and who are in need of help in understanding.

In sum, findings suggest that it might be helpful to interrupt stories each time new information appears, thereby giving learners control over the pace at which new information is made available and meeting their need for processing time. Findings also suggest that making meaning of narratives can be enhanced when children carry out the same actions as the story characters, thereby stimulating empathy with them. The hypothesis is that the *virtual "as-if"* mode of experience will amplify empathy and align the reader with the emotional life of the character. Empirical evidence from studies of story enactment corroborates the potential cognitive and emotional benefits of assuming an *"as-if"* stance in narrative comprehension and understanding literary elements (see, e.g., Lillard et al., 2013; Nicolopoulou et al., 2015). Research on the effects of this design principle on literary understanding is very new and open to testing for effects on understanding a character's actions and developing an empathetic stance in young children. We suggest that this area is open for exciting research into information processing in young children, as well as into the design and quality of literature that facilitates comprehension across ages, contexts, and differences in children.

Realizing the digital promise in storybooks

Storybook apps are at the cutting edge of innovation in early childhood literature. High-quality digital designs with more complex interactives interleaved in stories may increase child engagement and improve not only narrative comprehension but also book-based vocabulary. Digital designs may also enhance children's abilities to grasp a character's motives for actions including feelings, thus enabling them to experience stories from different perspectives that nurture social-emotional understanding, namely empathy. Due to the technology, digital books may, in this respect, be more helpful than paper books shared with an adult who explains story events. Even though the American Academy of Pediatrics urges caution in digital-book reading with young children, research is building up support for its proper place in family literacy and early literacy educational practices.

Benefits of digital picture storybooks in literacy development

There is growing evidence that storybook apps can be powerful shapers of the reading habits and skills of young readers. The most interesting finding is that the technology, unique to storybook apps, can enhance story comprehension. As discussed, different features built into digital books may not only support but also hinder story comprehension. We discussed a selection of well-designed studies that have tested how children benefit from mindfully enhanced digital books. We hypothesize that a new generation of digital storybooks enriched with digital storytelling techniques may even be more profitable to young children than regular storybook reading. A promising expectation is that storybook apps may challenge children cognitively and emotionally to empathize with story characters, and thus promote a better understanding of characters' motives and emotions. Apps may become mainstays of storybook reading, taking appropriate advantage of features of the digital world that go beyond what is possible with paper books. However, despite growing evidence in support of this hypothesis, more direct evidence based on new ways of testing is required to fine-tune the format and make such a radical "leap of faith." It seems important to assess whether books that promote carrying out the same actions as story characters do indeed stimulate empathy and, as a result, increase story comprehension. In other words, in addition to common tests that assess book-based story comprehension and vocabulary, we need tests that assess a child's ability to understand the story characters' feelings and emotions. Unfortunately, such additions are rarely available in commercial storybook apps, and to date, have rarely been tested.

Benefits of digital picture storybooks in understanding literary texts

We now know that it is possible to build in interactive functions that attract children's attention to literary elements in stories and support narrative comprehension. For instance, in the recent app *Lightning*, designed by Christiaan

Coenraads, the narrative text is often in conflict with what the illustrations show: Paraphrasing the boy, the narrative emphasizes that his father "trusts" him and allows him to use the weather machine without having to ask for permission. The illustrations, on the other hand, show that his father does not allow this. They show an oversized lock connected to the machine and the father keeping a key in his hand while asleep. Technology can be used to make children aware of such contradictions between narration and illustrations and make them reflect on what this says about the boy's intentions and the relationship with his father, thus deepening extratextual understanding of the intent and behaviors of the characters.

Making books appropriate for parents/teachers who are sharing stories with a child

So far, research on parent–child interaction with digital books has shown only negative effects (e.g., Chiong et al., 2012). Apps reveal interactions that are less related to the story content, and talk focuses more on technology. The main reason for this is probably that the books are not built to stimulate adult–child interaction. It is a challenge to design new books that include features that will promote this interaction. However, observations of *stops* in books, preferably adjacent to cliffhangers, suggest that these may be helpful because they make adults aware of story events that may benefit from discussion, and they may promote reflection by and comments from children. For instance, we observed parents sharing a story with their toddler about a bird teaching a cat how to fly. The story appeared to be more complex than parents thought because for most toddlers, it is not obvious that cats cannot use their paws as wings to fly with. The app might build in *stops* where an explanation is needed to better understand story events; and it may even include suggestions for questions or embodiment by a parent that could increase the quality of explanations.

Supporting collaboration between app designers and researchers

To fully employ the potential of technology in storybook apps, there is an urgent need to experiment with book formats that are not just interactive but also aligned with the theoretical underpinnings of multimedia learning theory. New research should not focus solely on interactive book apps. These are abundantly available on the commercial market, but often are created and authored without any input from experts in cognition and literacy. The findings presented in this chapter demonstrate how theory- and evidence-based approaches to the interactive design of storybook apps can contribute to improving education. We discussed some promising interactive designs, but unfortunately such designs are rare in the commercial market to date.

A collaborative process can integrate the expertise of app developers, computer specialists, literacy educators, and specialists in multimedia learning to create and author high-quality digital books. Collaboration is indispensable if we are to develop digital picture storybooks that integrate the best of literary features and emerging digital affordances. To make optimal use of technology in storybooks, it seems vital to start collaboration at an early stage in the design process and to engage in close dialogue from the start.

Meaningful innovation, however, depends on a diversity of ideas, methods, and strategies. Greater research interdisciplinarity is essential to broaden theoretical frameworks and blur the boundaries between competing methodological paradigms in order to deliver broader and deeper accounts of digital influence on early reading experiences (Mangen et al., 2018). Furthermore, open exchange between scholars is needed to address research problems adequately, to share data, and to create networks for contributing theoretical, methodological, and pedagogical expertise (Kucirkova, 2019). So far, few studies have described the outcomes of such productive collaborations that integrate the expertise of app developers, computer specialists, and early literacy educators in order to create and author high-quality digital books that will ultimately be tested under experimental conditions (e.g., Anstadt & Bus, 2019).

Concluding statement

Improvements in digital storybooks for young children have been made since they arrived on the market in the 1980s. However, we argue that their potential has yet to be fully explored. Digital picture storybooks are mostly recycled paper books that include some technology – but mostly not intertwined with the storyline. Grounded in Mayer's multimedia learning theory, we described essential principles that need to be taken into account when attempting to make the best use of the digital storybook format for storytelling. We assume that a close collaboration between authors, technicians, designers, and learning experts can result in technology-enhanced books that will include new digital techniques to tell the story. This might even result in a new kind of children's literature including, apart from traditional storytelling techniques – that is, a literary text, illustrations, and how text and illustration relate to each other – brand new technologically based techniques to make story events comprehensible and empathize with the emotions, motives, and feelings of the characters. Authors, app designers, and educators need to join forces to make this happen.

Three key considerations for parents, educators, and producers

- Every year, young children spend increasing amounts of time on smartphones and tablets. As such, it is important that this time is well spent and includes book reading – a primary source of language and literacy development.
- Parents, educators, and media producers should be aware of the promise of digital storybooks for young children. Well-designed digital books

could be more supportive of children's learning than traditional picture storybooks due to technologically based storytelling techniques that help young readers to comprehend storylines and recognize complex elements of literary stories, such as irony and suspense.

- Particularly promising are interactive storytelling techniques that enable the reader to embody the actions of the story characters. They amplify the readers' empathy with story characters – a core component of meaning-making.

References

Anstadt, R., & Bus, A. G. (2019). Bliksem! Een experiment met digitale verteltechnieken [Lightning! An experiment with digital storytelling techniques]. In E. Seegers & R. Van Steensel (Eds.), *Lekker lezen: het belang van leesmotivatie* (pp. 219–231). Delft, Netherlands: Eburon.

Bus, A. G., Sarı, B., & Takacs, Z. (2019). The promise of multimedia enhancement in children's digital storybooks. In J. E. Kim & B. Hassinger-Das (Eds.), *Reading in the digital age: Young children's experiences with e-books* (pp. 45–58). Cham, Switzerland: Springer.

Bus, A. G., Takacs, Z. K., & Kegel, C. A. T. (2015). Affordances and limitations of electronic storybooks for young children's emergent literacy. *Developmental Review, 35,* 79–97. doi:10.1016/j.dr.2014.12.004

Chiong, C., Ree, J., Takeuchi, L., & Erickson, I. (2012). *Comparing parent-child co-reading on print, basic, and enhanced e-book platforms: A Cooney center quick report.* Retrieved from www.joanganzcooneycenter.org/wp-content/uploads/2012/07/jgcc_ebooks_quickreport.pdf.

Fisch, S. M. (2000). A capacity model of children's comprehension of educational content on television. *Media Psychology, 2,* 63–92. doi:10.1207/S1532785XMEP0201_4

Glenberg, A. M., Gutierrez, T., Levin, J. R., Japuntich, S., & Kaschak, M. P. (2004). Activity and imagined activity can enhance young children's reading comprehension. *Journal of Educational Psychology, 96,* 424–436. doi:10.1037/0022-0663.96.3.424

Gopnik, A., & Meltzoff, A. N. (1997). *Learning, development, and conceptual change: Words, thoughts, and theories.* Cambridge, MA: MIT Press.

Kahneman, D. (1973). *Attention and effort.* Englewood Cliffs, NJ: Prentice-Hall.

Kim, J. E., & Anderson, J. (2008). Mother-child shared reading with print and digital texts. *Journal of Early Childhood Literacy, 8,* 213–245.

Korat, O., & Falk, Y. (2017). Ten years after: Revisiting the question of e-book quality as early language and literacy support. *Journal of Early Childhood Literacy, 19,* 206–223. doi:10.1177/1468798417712105

Korat, O., & Shamir, A. (2008). The educational electronic book as a tool for supporting children's emergent literacy in low versus middle SES groups. *Computers & Education, 50,* 110–124. doi:10.1016/j.compedu.2006.04.002

Kucirkova, N. (2019). How could children's storybooks promote empathy? A conceptual framework based on developmental psychology and literary theory. *Frontiers in Psychology, 10,* 121. doi:10.3389/fpsyg.2019.00121

Kucirkova, N., & Littleton, K. (2016). *The digital reading habits of children: A national survey of parents' perceptions of and practices in relation to children's reading for pleasure with print and digital books.* Retrieved from www.booktrust. org.uk/news-andblogs/news/1371

Labbo, L. D., & Kuhn, M. R. (2000). Weaving chains of affect and cognition: A young child's understanding of CD-ROM talking books. *Journal of Literacy Research, 32,* 187–210. doi:10.1080/10862960009548073

Lauricella, R. A., Barr, R., & Calvert, S. L. (2014). Parent-child interactions during traditional and computer storybook reading for children's comprehension: Implications for electronic storybook design. *International Journal of Child-Computer Interaction, 2,* 17–25. doi:10.1016/j.ijcci.2014.07.001

Lawless, K. A., & Brown, S. W. (1997). Multimedia learning environments: Issues of learner control and navigation. *Instructional Science, 25,* 117–131.

Lillard, A. S., Lerner, M. D., Hopkins, E. J., Dore, R. A., Smith, E. D., & Palmquist, C. M. (2013). The impact of pretend play on children's development: A review of the evidence. *Psychological Bulletin, 139,* 1–34. doi:10.1037/a0029321

Mangen, A., Hoel, T., & Moser, T. (2018). *Technologies, affordances, children, and embodied reading: A case for interdisciplinarity.* In N. Kucirkova, J. Rowsell, & G. Falloon (Eds.), *The Routledge handbook of learning with technology in early childhood* (pp. 235–248). New York, NY: Routledge.

Mayer, R. E. (2005a). Cognitive theory of multimedia learning. In R. E. Mayer (Ed.), *The Cambridge handbook of multimedia learning* (pp. 31–48). Cambridge, England: Cambridge University Press.

Mayer, R. E. (2005b). Principles for reducing extraneous processing in multimedia learning: Coherence, signalling, redundancy, spatial contiguity, and temporal contiguity principles. In R. E. Mayer (Ed.), *The Cambridge handbook of multimedia learning* (pp. 183–200). Cambridge, UK: Cambridge University Press.

Mayer, R. E. (2009). *Multimedia learning.* Cambridge, England: Cambridge University Press.

Moody, A. K., Justice, L. M., & Cabell, S. Q. (2010). Electronic versus traditional storybooks: Relative influence on preschool children's engagement and communication. *Journal of Early Childhood Literacy, 10,* 294–313. doi:10.1177/1468798410372162

Nicolopoulou, A., Schnabel Cortina, K., Ilgaz, H., Brockmeyer Cates, C., & de Sá, A. B. (2015). Using a narrative- and play-based activity to promote low-income preschoolers' oral language, emergent literacy, and social competence. *Early Childhood Research Quarterly, 31,* 147–162. doi:10.1016/j.ecresq.2015.01.006

Paciga, K. A. (2015). Their teachers can't be an app: Preschoolers' listening comprehension of digital storybooks. *Journal of Early Childhood Literacy, 14,* 1–37. doi:10.1177/1468798414552510

Parish-Morris, J., Mahajan, N., Hirsh-Pasek, K., Golinkoff, R. M., & Collins, M. F. (2013). Once upon a time: Parent-child dialogue and storybook reading in the electronic era. *Mind, Brain, and Education, 7,* 200–211. doi:10.1111/mbe.12028

Penno, J. F., Wilkinson, I. A. G., & Moore, D. W. (2002). Vocabulary acquisition from teacher explanation and repeated listening to stories: Do they overcome the Matthew effect? *Journal of Educational Psychology, 94,* 23–33. doi:10.1037/0022-0663.94.1.23

Renninger, K. A. (1992). Individual interest and development: Implications for theory and practice. In K. A. Renninger, S. Hidi, & A. Krapp (Eds.), *The role of interest in learning and development* (pp. 361–376). Hillsdale, NJ: Erlbaum.

Ricci, C. M., & Beal, C. R. (2002). The effect of interactive media on children's story memory. *Journal of Educational Psychology, 94*, 138–144. doi:10.1037//0022-0663.94.1.138

Richter, A., & Courage, M. L. (2017). Comparing electronic and paper storybooks for preschoolers: Attention, engagement, and recall. *Journal of Applied Developmental Psychology, 48*, 92–102. doi:10.1016/j.appdev.2017.01.002

Robbins, P., & Aydede, M. (2009). A short primer on situated cognition. In P. Robbins & M. Aydede (Eds.), *The Cambridge handbook of situated cognition* (pp. 3–10). New York, NY: Cambridge University Press.

Roskos, K. (in press). The book-play paradigm in early literacy pedagogy. In M. Han & J. Johnson (Eds.), *Play & culture studies: Play and literacy* (Vol. 16). Falls Village, CT: HamiltonBook.

Roskos, K., Brueck, J., & Lenhart, L. (2017). An analysis of e-book learning platforms: Affordances, architecture, functionality and analytics. *International Journal of Child-Computer Interaction, 12*, 37–45. doi:10.1016/j.ijcci.2017.01.003

Roskos, K., Brueck, J., & Widman, S. (2009). Developing analytic tools for e-book design in early literacy learning. *Journal of Interactional Online Learning, 8*. Retrieved from www.ncolr.org/jiol

Sargeant, B. (2015). What is in an ebook? What is a book app? And why should we care? An analysis of contemporary digital picture books. *Children's Literature in Education, 46*, 454–466. doi:10.1007/s10583-015-9243-5

Sarı, B., Asûde Başal, H., Takacs, Z. K., & Bus, A. G. (2019). A randomized controlled trial to test efficacy of digital enhancements of storybooks in support of narrative comprehension and word learning. *Journal of Experimental Child Psychology, 179*, 212–226. doi:10.1016/j.jecp.2018.11.006

Strouse, G. A., & Ganea, P. A. (2017). Toddlers' word learning and transfer from electronic and print books. *Journal of Experimental Child Psychology, 156*, 129–142.

Takacs, Z. K., Swart, E. K., & Bus, A. G. (2015). Benefits and pitfalls of multimedia and interactive features in technology-enhanced storybooks. *Review of Educational Research, 85*, 698–739. doi:10.3102/0034654314566989

Willoughby, D., Evans, M. A., & Nowak, S. (2015). Do ABC eBooks boost engagement and learning in preschoolers? An experimental study comparing eBooks with paper ABC and storybook controls. *Computers & Education, 82*, 107–117. doi:10.1016/j.compedu.2014.11.008

Yokota, J., & Teale, W. H. (2014). Picture books and the digital world: Educators make choices. *The Reading Teacher, 67*, 577–585. doi:10.1002/trtr.1262

Zhao, S., & Unsworth, L. (2017). Touch design and narrative interpretation: A socio-semiotic approach to picture book apps. In N. Kucirkova & G. Falloon (Eds.), *Apps, technology and younger learners, international evidence for teaching* (pp. 87–98). London, England: Taylor & Francis.

Zhou, N., & Yadav, A. (2017). Effects of multimedia story reading and questioning on preschoolers' vocabulary learning, story comprehension and reading engagement.

Educational Technology Research and Development, 65, 1523–1545. doi:10.1007/s11423-017-9533-2

Digital books mentioned in this chapter

Brown, M. (1994). *Arthurs teacher trouble* [Computer software]. Novato, CA: Random House-Broderbund.

Callaway Digital Arts. (2010). *The monster at the end of this book* (Version 3.3) [Mobile application software]. Retrieved from http://itunes.apple.com

Coenraads, C., & de Wijs, L. (2017). *Bliksem!* [Lightning]. Groningen, NL: Het Woeste Woud.

Davis, L. (1994). *PB Bear's birthday party.* London, UK: Dk Pub.

Mayer, M. (1983). *Just grandma and me.* Novato, CA: Brøderbund.

Sargeant, B. (2014). *How far is up?* (Version 1.2). Retrieved October 20, 2014 from https://itunes.apple.com/app/how-far-is-up/id860628627?mt=8

Chapter 2

Cognitively activating and emotionally attuning interactions

Their relevance for language and literacy learning and teaching with digital media

Christiane Miosga

It is well known that early experiences with books predict later reading success (Bus, van Ijzendoorn, & Pellegrini, 1995). However, the quality of these early experiences with reading is also important because an interactive, dialogically shared reading and storytelling style is likely to foster emergent literacy (Fletcher & Reese, 2005; Noble et al., in press). Recently, more and more e-books and picture book apps have been produced to teach preschoolers preliteracy skills (Kucirkova & Littleton, 2016), but research has yet to explore the impact of these types of books on shared reading interactions and positive literacy outcomes in any systematic manner. The research presented here fills this gap with two studies investigating the effects of dialogic multimodal style on children's story comprehension in analogue and digital adult–child reading situations. Whereas the first study points to critical changes that take place during reading interaction in a digital setting, the second study aims to investigate whether training can provide important impulses to help practitioners cope with these changes.

The potential of shared reading and storytelling interaction for (early) language and literacy learning

Shared reading can promote early literacy skills. Theoretically, potential benefits of (early) language and literacy learning can emerge in both the *reader* and the *medium*. Studies from reading research have sufficiently emphasized the potential benefits of adults' dialogic reading style for children's cognitive and language development (e.g., Whitehurst et al., 1988). A few studies show positive effects on narrative skills (Grolig, Cohrdes, Tiffin-Richards, & Schroeder, 2019) and especially on the comprehension of the story, when joint engagement is characterized by important thematic dimensions of the narrative and when verbal strategies are combined with nonverbal ones such as engaging children in enacting stories (Pesco & Gagné, 2017). Research on *intuitive parental didactics* (Papoušek &

Papoušek, 1989) and on *multimodal motherese* (see Gogate, Bahrick, & Watson, 2000; Jungmann, Miosga, Fuchs, & Rohlfing, 2009) also points to the potential benefits of the multimodality of parental reading styles. Parents' intuitive multimodal action modification supports children in structuring linguistic and motor actions (Rohlfing, Fritsch, Wrede, & Jungmann, 2006); in directing or (re)establishing attention; in emphasizing important or new aspects of an utterance or action; and in expressing, evaluating, challenging, and activating emotions. In everyday language support, increasing attention is being paid to the responsiveness of early childhood professionals (e.g., Gutknecht, 2012; Remsperger, 2011). These professionals also use multimodal responsive strategies to support children's language acquisition processes by adapting their own language, gestures, facial expressions, prosody, or gaze sensitively to the needs and interests of the child. Within the framework of interaction formats such as *sustained shared thinking* (Siraj-Blatchford, 2007), *shared attention*, and *shared intentionality* (Tomasello & Carpenter, 2007), adults model activities in the *zone of proximal development* (Vygotsky, 1987) and stimulate cognitive and linguistic development. Within the framework of multimodal "communing attunement" (Stern, 2000, p. 148), which is also called *emotionese* here, the adult caregiver is in tune with the child's need to establish "togetherness" and thus creates the motivating basis for the language teaching and learning process (see Jungmann et al., 2009).

The communication pattern of "affect attunement" (Stern, 2000, p. 137) can be observed in parent–child communication from about 9 months of age onward. Instead of imitating the child's emotional expression directly, as in communication settings with younger infants, mothers now reproduce the child's expression in a modified form by taking up qualities of intensity, timing, and rhythm; and they shape and "translate" these into other modalities of expression. Stern (2000) assumes that this indirect mirroring of emotions assures the child that she or he is not just being imitated, but actually understood. A rhythmic arm movement of the child can, for example, be reproduced by a rhythmically similar sound expression.

The processes of cognitive and emotional stimulation, modeling, and adjustment constitute essential resources in shared reading interactions. The studies presented here examine how these adjustment processes are influenced by the resources available in the digital medium. Alongside verbal devices, the qualities of multimodal motherese and emotionese (Jungmann et al., 2009; Miosga, 2017) such as facial expression, motion, gestures, voice, and prosody, along with the "cross-modal attunement" (Stern, 2000, pp. 141, 148) needed to establish shared inner images, thoughts, and feelings, are essential categories for analyzing cognitively activating and emotionally attuning interactions. The following categories are important for capturing *emotional attunement* and *cognitive activation* as well as creating prerequisites and conditions for successful language and literary learning processes:

1 **Involvement** of the dialogue partners (children and adults) – that is, attentiveness, interest, attention, productive or receptive activity, liveliness, and presence (cf. also Remsperger, 2011, p. 84, "entanglement interactions").

2   **Child orientation** – that is, the responsiveness or the reactions of the adult person to the dialogue offers made by the child along with the references to everyday life, to previous knowledge, and to the interests of the child through so-called "distancing prompts" (Zevenbergen & Whitehurst, 2003, p. 180), so-called "professional responsivity" (Gutknecht, 2012, p. 22), and "sensitive responsivity" (Remsperger, 2011, p. 125) in early childhood education. Responsive language-promoting strategies such as *scaffolding* (Bruner, 1983), conversation-controlling *conditional relevancies* (Schegloff & Sacks, 1973), or *interactive demands* (Hausendorf & Quasthoff, 2005) encourage children through sustained shared thinking to engage in activities within the *zone of proximal development* (Vygotsky, 1987).

3   **Structuring** of story and dialogue by the caregiver or dialogue partner to promote story comprehension and storytelling.

Use and effectiveness of digital children's literature for language and literacy learning

Today, digital devices are an important part of early childhood reality (Chaudron, Di Gioia, & Gemo, 2018; Ofcom, 2018). Even young children are using smart-phones or tablets (69% of 3- to 4-year-olds in Ofcom, 2018; 58.2% in Billington, 2016). Although research in early childhood education suggests that there are many settings in which digital technology is rarely used (Billington, 2016), picture book apps are particularly popular with young children's caregivers (Kucirkova & Littleton, 2016). However, up to now, findings on the efficacy of digital children's literature for language acquisition are heterogeneous (Reich, Yau, & Warschauer, 2016). Many studies confirm that both parents and children differ in their interactive behavior when reading either conventional books or stories based on a digital picture book (Chiong, Ree, Takeuchi, & Erickson, 2012; Rvachew, Rees, Carolan, & Nadig, 2017), but no differences have been found in relation to the acquisition of various aspects of literacy (Kelley & Kinney, 2017). Nonetheless, some studies do report positive effects of the use of digital books on the development of early literacy skills – for example, on word recognition when children operate the medium autonomously and explore it self-motivatedly (Zipke, 2017); and on story comprehension when the app shows a close congruency between verbal and nonverbal information (e.g., Korat & Shamir, 2007; see also Bus, Takacs, & Kegel, 2015).

In contrast, other studies have found that the excessive use of *hot spots* in *enhanced e-books* makes it difficult to understand the story, with attention and concentration being lost on games and other distracting factors (see De Jong & Bus, 2003; see also Bus et al., 2015). A study by Parish-Morris, Mahajan, Hirsh-Pasek, Michnick Golinkoff, and Fuller Collins (2013) with children 3.5 to 6.5 years of age also showed that parents take a different interactive approach to reading e-books out loud in comparison to conventional books. When reading conventional books out loud, parents involve their children more in the interaction, increase their conversation contributions, or ask more questions in order to trigger their child's thought processes. In addition, results show that particularly when young children were read a story in e-book form, they were less able to penetrate the narrative structure semantically and bring events into a coherent sequence. One possible factor influencing this is considered to be the accompanying interactive activities linked to the operation of the e-book. These affect parent–child communication and the reception process (see also Chiong et al., 2012). Further comparative studies confirm these results: In a study with 3- to 5-year-olds, Reich et al. (2019) found that children's talk when reading print books dialogically with an adult was more about the story plot, whereas when the digital book itself read the story to them, their talk centered on the technological aspects of the iPad. Krcmar and Cingel (2014) also found increased comprehension in children when using the traditional book format, but that this was related closely to parents' increased distraction talk when sharing the digital book.

The concepts of joint engagement developed at the beginning of this chapter can be summarized as follows: it is known that adults act intuitively to promote language in dialogic reading, and the concepts of emotional attunement or sustained shared thinking discussed here create the basic conditions for this. However, the following questions arise: What influence do digital resources have on joint engagement? Are the digital potentials of picture book apps also used to stimulate children cognitively and attune them emotionally? Are the readers themselves stimulated by the digital possibilities to act in a language-promoting way? And how successful is reading with an app in terms of early literacy learning and teaching?

Therefore, the aim of the following two studies was to explore the potential of picture book apps and app-based reading situations for children's literacy skills – on the one hand, in order to create a basis for a deeper understanding of the teaching and learning conditions in dialogic reading in connection with digital media, and on the other hand, to formulate implications for practice on how best to exploit the potential for language and literacy learning of digital children's literature. It is assumed that reading children's digital literature will benefit early literacy only if the digital resources support or are used in the language-promoting repertoire of the dialogic reading interaction between adults and children (e.g., Miosga, 2017, 2019; Parish-Morris et al., 2013).

Study 1: The impact of using digital media in shared reading and storytelling interaction on the child's story comprehension

This study examined whether there are differences in the interaction between child and caregiver when reading a conventional picture book compared to an app. How does the dialogic adjustment change depending on the medium? And does the medium affect children's story comprehension?

Method

Participants

Twelve adult–child dyads were recruited via a questionnaire assessing the use of digital media in families and early childhood institutions in the greater Hannover area of North Germany. All adults and children were monolingual German speakers with normal hearing and language abilities according to parents' reports. The 12 children (five boys and seven girls) were 2–3 years of age (mean age: 36.33 months; range: 24–43; SD = 6.6 months).

The ten adult participants were the children's caregivers (five mothers, two fathers, and three educational professionals). This selection was chosen specially for a follow-up study assessing any potential differences in behavior. All participants reported using tablets regularly, and that they were familiar with traditional shared reading practices as well as the picture book app format.

Materials

Materials included a printed story book and an iPad with the interactive picture book *7 grummelige Grömmels und ein kleines Schwein* [Seven grumpy Grömmels and a little pig] by Iris Wewer (2012), from the app Tigerbooks (https://tiger.media/tigerbooks/). This is a narrative picture book app highlighting the topics of family and friendship. During a nighttime trip the main protagonist, the little pig, discovers a house inhabited by the hairy, terribly scary, and voracious Grömmel family.

The app permits a typical page-turning reading experience (swiping) and provides additional technical features such as buttons that can be switched on and off to activate the text or sounds, as well as interactive visual and audio animations that make it possible to see motions and lightning, to hear the sounds and literal speech of the protagonists, and so forth. In addition to interactive narrative animations that pick up the story directly, there are also illustrative animations to click on repeatedly. These are pointed out by flashing dots, so-called "hot spots." Sounds accompany the app.

Procedure

The children shared the storybook with an adult reader. They were asked to look at the story as they usually do. A within-subject design was chosen for the study: each adult–child dyad shared the same paper book and a picture book app under three conditions:

1 Traditional paper book: **Analogue**
2 iPad picture book app with interactive features: **Digital 1**
3 iPad picture book app with interactive features and audio text (iPad reads book to dyad): **Digital 2**

Adult–child dyads were randomly assigned to read either the traditional version (Analogue) or the app version (Digital 1) first. After reading, each child was asked about her or his story comprehension only once. This was assessed on the basis of a semistructured conversation stimulus. At the end of reading, caregivers asked questions about understanding the story (in terms of factual information extraction, inference formation, and adaptations of the picture book input) by addressing, for example, the protagonists or the action motives (*Who is taking part in the story? Who lives in the house? What is the pig doing in the Grömmels' house? Why does the Grömmel want to eat the pig? Why is the pig allowed to stay with the Grömmels? Whom are the Grömmels afraid of?*).

The shared reading interactions were videotaped for later transcription and coding. The children's answers to the questions on story comprehension were noted and recorded.

Coding

The shared reading interactions were transcribed in each condition with GAT2 (see Selting et al., 2009) and documented using images and frame comics (Schmitt, 2016). These were analyzed and coded by two independent observers using a specially developed category system. The variables coded were the total book reading duration, the speaking rate (number of utterances of the adult and number of utterances of the child), and the types of utterances by adults. An utterance was defined as each phrase uttered by the adult or the child, not including reading the text.

The types of utterance produced by the adult were coded as being either content- or behavior-related. Examples of content-related utterances are *What's that pig doing? Who's hiding there?* Examples of behavior-related utterances are *Press it here! Wait, don't press it yet* (when hot spots appear)*!* Speaking rate and utterance type were coded for approximately 5 minutes of parent–child interaction in each condition.

In addition, the style of interaction, characterized as *joint engagement*, was coded with the subcategories *emotionally attuning interactions* and *cognitively activating interactions*, which were counted as interrelated turns. An adult or child's turn was defined as a related pair of utterances or actions initiated by the adult speaker and responded to by the child, or vice versa.

Emotionally attuning interactions address the cross-modal transformation of emotions and attitudes, the establishment of common inner images and feelings, and moments of shared attention such as taking over the intensity of the child's prosody or mutual tracking of gaze and pointing gestures together with the child's corresponding reactions.[1] Cognitively activating interactions refer to the processes of cognitive cooperation and sustained shared thinking: going beyond the here and now, verbalizing inner processes, making up own assumptions, appreciating the child's questions, using *positive questioning* ("I don't know, what do you think?") or using *making sense words* ("I think . . . " "I wonder . . . ") (see Siraj-Blatchford, 2007), *open-ended prompts* ("What's happening in this picture?"), *recall prompts* ("Do you remember what happened to the little pig in this story?" "What do you think, why . . . ?" "What if . . . ?"), *Wh- prompts*, and so forth together with the child's corresponding reactions (Zevenbergen & Whitehurst, 2003).

Both initiations and responses were coded. Coders were blind to the study hypotheses, and 20% of transcripts were recoded for reliability. The intercoder agreement was 75.36% (Krippendorf's alpha). The quantitative data were supplemented by qualitative interaction analyses in order to describe the multimodal interpersonal adjustment processes step by step.

To capture the differences between the media conditions (Analogue and Digital 1) in story comprehension, children's answers were assessed in terms of the proportion of correctly answered, incorrectly answered, and unanswered questions. In addition, answers were analyzed qualitatively with regard to their relation to the media features, linguistic adaptations, the type of question (interference question, factual information), and how differentiated they were.

Results

Time and number of utterances

First, results in Table 2.1 show that the digital interaction time was longer than the analogue interaction time (Digital 1: mean transcription = 15.23 min; Analogue: mean transcription = 11.38 min; $t = -4.19$, $p < .01$).[2] Reading the digital picture book often took more time because children wanted to activate the sound effect on each page before moving to the next page.

However, there was a large interindividual variance of 5–22 minutes. Furthermore, an inspection of individual reading durations also revealed that a relatively long or short interaction time remained stable regardless of the medium. It is possible that the reading styles of the caregivers (short or extensive), independent of the medium, were similar in every setting, so that their impact on the duration of interaction was more decisive than that of the medium itself.

At the same time, the number of utterances by the adult and the child decreased in the digital setting. Table 2.2 shows, in particular, that more child utterances ($M = 17.55$, $SD = 12.36$) were observed in the analogue setting than in the digital setting (Digital 1: $M = 7.64$, $SD = 6.17$; Digital 2: $M = 9.91$, $SD = 8.20$).

Table 2.1 Total book reading duration

Variant	M	SD	Min	Max
Analogue	11.38 min	2.29	07.30 min	14.24 min
Digital 1	15.23 min	2.18	12.40 min	18.42 min
Digital 2	14.31 min	4.35	05.15 min	22.27 min

Table 2.2 Number of utterances per setting

Variant	M	SD	Variant	M	SD
Child Analogue	17.55	12.36	**Adult Analogue**	26.36	14.78
Child Digital 1	7.64	6.17	**Adult Digital 1**	20.82	6.69
Child Digital 2	9.91	8.20	**Adult Digital 2**	18.64	8.74

Table 2.3 Types of utterance of the adult reader per setting

Type of utterance	M	SD	Type of utterance	M	SD
Story-related Analogue	23.45	12.1	**Behavior-related Analogue**	2.91	3.36
Story-related Digital 1	11.09	5.87	**Behavior-related Digital 1**	9.73	6.47
Story-related Digital 2	11.73	7.70	**Behavior-related Digital 2**	6.91	4.70

The difference from Analogue to Digital 1 ($t = 2.43$, $p = .03$) was significant, whereas the difference from Analogue to Digital 2 ($t = 1.59$, $p = .14$) failed to attain significance.

Similarly, as can be seen in Table 2.2, more utterances in the adult reader were observed during the interaction with the analogue medium ($M = 26.36$, $SD = 14.78$) than in the interaction with the digital medium (Digital 1: $M = 20.82$, $SD = 6.69$; Digital 2: $M = 18.64$, $SD = 8.74$). However, both differences between Analogue and Digital 1 ($t = 1.05$, $p = .32$) and between Analogue and Digital 2 ($t = 1.41$, $p = .19$) failed to attain significance.

Quality of utterances

The quality of utterances also varied under different media conditions (see Table 2.3). Paired sample t tests revealed that the analogue setting prompted more story-related utterances in adults (Analogue to Digital 1: $t = 3.27$, $p = .01$, Cohen's $d = 1.30$; Analogue to Digital 2: $t = 2.89$, $p = .02$, Cohen's $d = 1.16$) than the digital setting. In contrast, the digital setting prompted more behavior-related utterances in adults than the analogue setting (Digital 1 to Analogue: $t = 2.64$, $p = .02$, Cohen's $d = 1.32$; Digital 2 to Analogue: $t = 1.89$, $p = .09$, Cohen's $d = 0.98$, summarized in Table 2.3).

In the analogue setting, the adult frequently and predominantly used content-related utterances: *What's the pig doing? Who's hiding there?* In the digital setting, behavior-related utterances (in relation to the medium) were dominant: *Press this button. Wait, don't press this button yet. I think it blinked on the slipper, too. Press on it once there* (when hot spots appear). *Don't wipe it yet. Back again* (in relation to technical side activities). This technical focus of comments has also been

Table 2.4 Number of emotionally attuning and cognitively activating interactions per setting

Emotionally attuning interactions	M	SD	Cognitively activating interactions	M	SD
Analogue	29	7.10	**Analogue**	19.09	15.03
Digital 1	19.18	8.42	**Digital 1**	7.55	4.57
Digital 2	12.27	9.52	**Digital 2**	8.09	5.65

reported in other studies (Chiong et al., 2012; Muratović, 2014; Parish-Morris et al., 2013). The children also appeared to be very reluctant to produce content-related utterances to the picture book app. Their frequently short remarks referred particularly to hot spots (*There* [when hot spots appear]. *Look.*) that distracted from the story and interrupted the reading process. The qualitative analysis also showed that the analogue setting also prompted considerably more turn taking.

Emotional attunement and cognitive activation

Focusing on the quality of interaction and the promotion of language development through emotionally attuning interactions and cognitively activating interactions, there were even clearer differences between the storybook formats (see Table 2.4). In the interaction with the traditional book, both emotionally attuning interactions (Analogue to Digital 1: $t = 5.19$, $p < .001$; Analogue to Digital 2: $t = 8.23$, $p < .001$, summarized in Table 2.4) and cognitively activating interactions (Analogue to Digital 1: $t = 2.81$, $p = .018$; Analogue to Digital 2: $t = 2.65$, $p = .02$, summarized in Table 2.4) could be observed much more frequently.

Qualitative multimodal analysis

These findings were supplemented by carrying out qualitative multimodal interaction analyses of language-promoting or language-inhibiting interactions and responsive strategies in conversation excerpts. The idea was to describe the multimodal interpersonal adjustment processes step by step (see excerpts and analysis in Miosga, 2017, 2019). Here, it was not only the action of the caregiver that was relevant, but also the child's corresponding reaction – that is, the *mutual* focus of attention on a common goal as described in the previously mentioned interaction formats of sustained shared thinking, joint attention, shared intentionality, and emotional attunement. Moments of involvement, child orientation, and story structuring as discussed at the beginning of the chapter were identified.

The analysis showed that the analogue interaction format favored the characteristics of multimodal motherese and emotionese in dialogic reading: Compared to the app-based interaction, the analogue interaction was characterized by an involved, child-oriented, and content-structuring speech formation (see Miosga, 2017). Joint **involvement** and shared attention were reflected in referential eye contact; in matching of facial expressions; in monitoring of gaze; in pointing gestures, pauses, and accents; in mutual mirroring of nodding the head and smiling; and in imitating intonation contour and timbre. Common images and emotional experiences were shared and confirmed in this way. The **orientation toward the themes and intentions of the child** was evident in distancing prompts; in physical attention; in the nonverbal prompt reaction to turn-taking signals of the child; in signs of listening such as *hmm* or signs of misunderstanding such as frowning; and in the prosodical, gestural, and facial imitation, synchronization, and modification of the child's utterances. Wh-questions were developed from the concrete context and were oriented toward the child's themes and intentions. In this way, adult and child shared their thoughts for several turns. **Structuring of the story** was reflected in changes in pitch, volume, and tempo and in the use of pauses and gestures in reading. The change from reading to narration was marked prosodically by a change in volume and tempo.

In the Digital 1 setting, Wh- questions were also asked: *<<f> ha,> what's THERE,>* or *<<p> what's he doing THERE,> (points to the hot spot)*. However, these did not encourage the child to share her or his thinking or to continue the content-related topic, but instead stimulated the child to activate the technical features of the medium. Especially in combination with action-initiating verbs such as *look where the green pOInt is, TOUCH it, maybe something's hAppened,* they signaled to the child which media-related activities were expected. In the digital setting, the child's verbal and multimodal conversational shares were low. There was hardly any turn taking, so no dialogues either. Hot spots often interrupted the reading process, so that the caregiver read faster and tried repeatedly to attract attention through pointing gestures and final accentuation with rising cadence. There were considerably fewer prosodic variations, especially in the transition from reading to dialogue and in the marking of literal speech. The reading style of the caregiver showed an isotonic intonation contour; and in dialogue, the prosodic marking through initial and final accentuation was dominant and served to (re)create attention (see Miosga, 2017). Joint attention focused on technology and not on common themes and emotional states.

It can therefore be assumed that the child's story comprehension – measured by answering questions at the end of the reading – was lower than that when using a traditional picture book (Table 2.5):

Table 2.5 Results on story comprehension

Analogue setting	M	SD	Digital 1 setting	M	SD
Correct answer	3.83	2.23	Correct answer	1.33	1.86
Incorrect answer	0.17	0.41	Incorrect answer	1.00	0.63
No answer	2.00	2.28	No answer	3.83	1.47

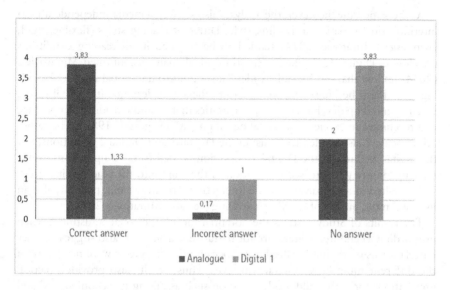

Figure 2.1 Number of responses in analogue versus digital reading interaction

Figure 2.1 shows that children participating in the analogue setting gave significantly more correct answers than children who looked at the picture book digitally ($t = 2.71$, $p = .04$); and, vice versa, significantly more incorrect answers were given after the app-based reading interaction ($t = 5.00$, $p = .004$).

In terms of quality, it was particularly inference questions that were answered incorrectly or not at all. Questions about the factual intake of information were mainly answered with additional information referring to the illustrative animations (e.g., secondary protagonists such as the dog, which is animated as a sausage-eating hot spot but does not play a role in the story). The reading text contained repetitions typical of the format and age, such as "Am nächsten Morgen war das kleine Schwein noch da. . . . [The pig was still there the next morning. . . .]" (Wewer, 2012). Linguistic adaptations in both formats were similar.

Summary

Results suggest that the intuitive use of a caregiver's repertoire for language learning and literacy practices was affected negatively by the presence of technical features. Child utterances, story comprehension, and adult scaffolding strategies were low in the app-based interaction. The characteristics of multimodal motherese, attunement, and cognitively and emotionally activating interactions were more observable in the analogue condition than in the app format.

At the same time, however, the analyses also showed a media-independent high interindividual variation in reading style. Different reading styles (flexible, rigid, changing) (Muratović, 2014) tended to be retained in all reading conditions (Analogue, Digital 1, Digital 2). Interindividual analyses confirmed Muratović's (2014) finding that the "flexible reader," analogous to traditional storybook reading, could also be judged to be the most efficient in dealing with digital media when opening up developmental opportunities that promote reading competence and reaching the "zone of proximal development" (Vygotsky, 1987). The rather "rigid reader" also tended to persist in the Digital 1 and Digital 2 conditions, but the digital medium in the Digital 2 condition tended to open up new room for maneuvering (e.g., increased integration of the child into the reading situation). This resulted in an expansion of the interaction (structure) and, possibly, also an increase in the quality of storybook reading (see also Muratović, 2014).

The results of Study 1 stress the potential for interpersonal adjustment when using (digital) children's literature for narrative learning but also suggest quality criteria for using digital picture books, because the caregivers were not aware of the different multimodal interaction style. Thus, results also provide practical implications for early childhood education such as raising preschool carers' and educators' awareness of and sensitivity toward app-based interaction. This also includes knowledge about how the technical features can be used in a reflective, guided, and inclusive way when using apps in educational settings.

Study 2 reports on how practitioners can apply such a reflective kind of use of digital children's literature.

Study 2: Using digital picture books in kindergarten and preschool

The second study examined how educational practitioners develop their professional responsiveness from a first to a second data point through training in how to deal with the picture book app and coaching with video-based multimodal interaction analysis. It was assumed that the reconstruction and reflection of attitudes (Nentwig-Gesemann, Fröhlich-Gildhoff, Harms, & Richter, 2011) and overriding concepts such as *sustained shared thinking* (Hildebrandt, Scheidt, Hildebrandt, Hédervári-Heller, & Dreier, 2016; Siraj-Blatchford, 2007) and *emotional attunement* (Miosga, 2019; Stern, 2000) would enable more successful adjustment processes in digital dialogic reading.

Method

Participants

In this study, participants were 10 early-years practitioners and 29 children aged 2–3 and 5–6 years from a German kindergarten (5 of these children were multilingual: L1 Spanish, Polish, Greek, and Russian). According to voluntary information given by the practitioners, all adult participants used media such as tablets and smartphones on a regular basis in their everyday lives, but some of them expressed concerns about implementing tablets in kindergarten.

Procedure

The practitioners responded to a questionnaire on usage behavior and attitudes toward digital media – in particular, picture book apps – in early education. Each practitioner read a picture book app with a group of 2–4 children using a tablet at two measurement dates (T1 and T2). Both T1 and T2 were videotaped. Test materials consisted of the app version of two picture books that were available in the participating kindergarten. After T1, practitioners participated in a one-day training in which they were introduced to inhibiting and supportive strategies for picture book reading and familiarized with a reflective use of the picture book app. Furthermore, after the training, successful moments of adjustment and inhibiting and supportive use of the app features were identified from the video data and reconstructed together with the individual practitioners. Two weeks later, at a second measurement date after qualification, an app-based shared reading interaction was videographed again (T2). The interactions (pre T1 and post T2) were compared in order to investigate how professional responsiveness had developed in dealing with the app.

Coding

Media-related actions, content-related utterances, and utterances related to the child's own experiences were coded and counted. Furthermore, utterances regarding media-related actions were differentiated into utterances referring to the content of the story or utterances referring to technical actions and distracting side activities. In addition, the interactions regarding the use of the digital features for involvement, child orientation, and structuring were analyzed by Conversation Analysis (Deppermann, 2008) and, with a focus on multimodal resources, by multimodal interaction analysis (Mondada, 2013; Schmitt, 2015) in order to identify successful moments of attunement and inhibiting and supportive use of the app features.

Results

Explorative analyses of professional responsiveness in dealing with the app in the comparison from T1 to T2 showed that the interaction patterns of the practitioners after the intervention (workshop, self-assessment, and video analysis) developed individually. Looking at the evaluation of the questionnaire on attitudes toward digital media, the practitioners benefited from the training in very different ways depending on their original attitude toward the use of digital media: Practitioners with a neutral to negative attitude toward the use of digital media especially tended to avoid the use of app features at T1. At T2, they showed a targeted use of the features for cognitively and emotionally activating interactions, as well as for stimulating the imagination for shared inner images and moods. Practitioners with a positive attitude toward the use of digital media showed a differentiated use of digital features at T2. They changed from an intuitive inflationary use of all features with many distracting technical side activities, to deliberately targeted medium-related actions that referred to the content and/or involved either individual or all children. This will be illustrated in a case study.

Case study

The reading interactions at both measurement dates took place between an early-years practitioner and two children (a boy and a girl, both 3.0 years of age) with the picture book app *Ein Tag auf dem Bauernhof* [A day on a farm] (Rudel, 2011). In the questionnaire, the practitioner had shown an open-minded attitude toward the use of digital media in early education.

Comparative analyses showed that the interaction duration increased from T1 (8:57 minutes) to T2 (11:28 minutes). Figure 2.2 shows that also, utterances related to content and to the children's everyday lives increased from T1 to T2. Medium-related actions, on the other hand, decreased by one-half in favor of content and the relation to the children's everyday lives. Qualitative analyses showed that the medium-related actions at T1 referred largely to technology-related side activities (swiping, turning pages, pressing all hot spots: e.g., *press, you press THERE ne? Everywhere*) and led to long pauses between reading passages, whereas hardly any medium-related actions referring to the content were observed.

With respect to T2, the utterances related to content- and everyday-life increased significantly. In addition, a large proportion of the medium-related actions at T2 referred to the content. The digital features were used specifically to involve the children in the characters, moods, and spaces; to relate to the children's everyday lives; and to structure the storyline. In addition, the practitioner reacted promptly to the animations and sounds activated by the children and linked them to content aspects of the story such as plot development, narrative means, or book characters' beliefs, intentions, and emotions.

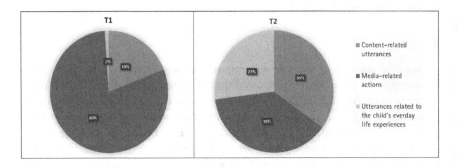

Figure 2.2 Responsiveness of practitioner, before (T1) and after the training (T2)

In order to establish **involvement** of both or one of the children in the story, the sound function was used in a supportive way, stimulating the involvement in the scene in such a way that one hears the chickens cackling when arriving at the farm or the rustling of the leaves in the wind while searching in the bushes. The practitioner specifically used animations and sounds at the end of units of meaning to initiate processes of shared attention and multimodal attunement:

Visiting the chickens (P: Practitioner, B: Boy, G: Girl, *Reading text in italics*)

```
01 P:      << behaucht, p> ↑GUCK mal die sUchen ↑NE, >
           (.) =
           <<breathy,p>   look   they're   searching
           right, >
→          = ((presses hot spot, searching arm move-
           ment is visually animated))
02 B:         [((imitates arm movement))]
03 G:              [((imitates arm movement))]
04 P:      ((looks at B and imitates the arm movement))
           <<l, f> SO: macht sie mit den Händen, NE, >
           (.)
           so she does it with her hands, right,
           <<p> die sucht Überall im Gebüsch, >
           she searches everywhere in the bushes,
→05 P:     ((switches on the noises, the rustling of
           the leaves while searching sounds))
06 G:      ((presses hot spot, repeats arm movement,
           looks at B))
07 B+G:    ((repeat the arm movements together, laugh,
           and look at P.))
08 P:      die dicke BERta sucht immer neue verSTECKe;
           the fat berta is always looking for new
           hiding places;
           ENDlich finden wir ihre EIer. (.)
           finally we find her eggs.
           <<h, :-) > das ist ja fast wie Ostern; >(.)
           kichert Lena;
           it's almost like easter; (.) giggles Lena;
           ((looks first at B. then at G., presses
           turn page))
```

The practitioner also involved the children through the targeted use of hot spots and encouraged them to imitate animal voices:

In the cowshed

→01 P: ((looks at the tablet and presses the hot spot to animate the audio animation of the cow))

→02 P: könnt ihr AUCH MUHN? (.)
         can you moo too?

  03 B: <<f> MUH::>
          moo ((looks at G))

---

and to trace feelings:

Visit to the goats

  01 P: auch die ZIEgen bekommen etwas BrOt.
          also the goats get some bread.
          <<h> OH gUck mal.> sie lEcken mir mit ihrer rAUen zunge die FInger ab.
          <<h> oh look.> they lick the fingers with their rough tongue.

→02 P: ((animates movement and sound of the goat's tongue))

→03 P: ↑HIlfe das kItzelt;
          Help that tickles;

  04 G: ((giggles, pulls shoulders up))

Through a targeted use of hot spots, the practitioner was also increasingly **child-oriented**. She reacted promptly with questions such as *mögt ihr AUch ↑hImbeeren/* [do you also like raspberries?] or *könnt ihr AUCH MUHN/* [can you moo too?] to the activating of the animation by the children, and thereby took up the topics, activities, and intentions of the child. She also used the hot spot as an opportunity to respond to the child's verbal reaction by mirroring and confirming the child's intention and expanding it linguistically to link it to the plot of the story:

```
  01 G:    <<p> ein schmetterLING.>
           a butterfly.
→02 P:     ((presses hot spot to animate the movement of
           the butterfly))
           <<len, :-), hell> EIN schmetterLING fliegt
           über den GeMÜSEgarten GEnau;>
           a butterfly flies over the vegetable garden
           right;
```

To **structure** the storyline, the practitioner used pauses for structuring and longer pauses for processing at the end of units of meaning. With the use of hot spots, the practitioner marked the change from reading to narration (line 8), but also the end of a page or a section of meaning (line 05).

Grandma's garden

```
  01 P:      <<h, f> ZUerst besuchen wir MEIne ↑O:ma,> (.)
             first of all we'll visit my grandma, (.)
  02 P:      <<h,f> Oma kümmert sich UM die [↑!HÜH!:ner
             und ↓!GÄN!se.> (.)]=
             grandma takes care of the [chicken and
             geese.]
  03 G+B:                           [((children are monitoring
                                    the animals by gaze))]
  04 P:      = <<l, f> UND um unseren !GROß!:en O:bst
             und geMÜsegarten.>(-)
             and of our big fruits- and vegetable
             garden.
→05 P:       ((animates sounds of the garden))
  06 P:      <<h,f, :-)> wie !LUS!tig sagt Lena-> (.)=
             how funny says Lena-
  07 P:      = <<h,f> bei EUch laufen die ↑!HÜH:!ner
             frei herUM und die
             BLU:men müssen hinter dem ZAUn blei↓ben.>
             at yours the chickens run around freely and
             the flowers need to stay behind the fence.
→        ((animates motion and sounds of the
             chicken))
→08 P:       <<l,p> die habens GUT (.)die HÜHner;>
             the chickens are doing well
```

This led to an understanding of contexts and to a clarification of focal points of meaning. The hot spot replaced or prolonged pauses in order to structure the plot development and thus lead through the story in an orderly way.

Similar interaction patterns could also be found in further analyses. By reconstructing and reflecting on attitudes and superordinate concepts such as sustained shared thinking and emotional attunement, all practitioners developed increasingly successful adjustment processes in dialogical reading with the app. In addition, the use of the digital features changed from an intuitive, technology-focused use to a targeted use of the app's features with the aim of involvement, everyday-life orientation, and story structuring.

Discussion and practical implications

The results suggest that parents' and practitioners' intuitive use of a repertoire for language learning and literacy practices was affected negatively by the presence of technical features. Child-initiated communication, story comprehension, and adult scaffolding strategies were low in the app-based interaction. The characteristics of multimodal motherese, attunement, and cognitively and emotionally activating interactions were observed more in the analogue condition than in the app format.

With regard to Study 1, note that it covers only a small sample from a similar social milieu in just one recent situation. Therefore, to better understand children's literacy learning and adults' reading behavior with picture book apps, future research should adopt a dynamic evaluative framework instead of a comparative design. It remains to be seen whether caregivers can learn to use the digital features of apps to promote language development over time (see also Chapter 1). Furthermore, more attention needs to be paid to differences in milieu. Finally, long-term studies are needed to record social and individual changes in the use and handling of digital media and to take these results into account in app development.

At the same time, the results of Study 2 suggest that reflective use has great potential for language and literacy support. Reconstructing and reflecting on attitudes and the targeted use of digital features with overriding concepts such as sustained shared thinking and emotional attunement enables more successful adjustment processes in digital dialogic reading.

Picture book apps also offer opportunities for prevention and inclusion. A German study (Stiftung Lesen, 2012) has shown that boys (see also Kucirkova & Littleton, 2016; Liu & Huang, 2008), fathers, and parents from an educationally disadvantaged background could be reached more easily through digital reading. Moreover, apps make it possible to include different languages and individual linguistic, cognitive, and social requirements (Zorn, Justino, Schneider, & Schönenberg, 2016, see also Chapters 6 and 9), thereby also enabling participation in shared reading interactions for children with disabilities. The use of digital literature can support the establishment of either community or difference. Digital features can offer opportunities for participation by involving and encouraging all or individual children in differentiated ways, or by making reading a *gemeinsame Sache* [common matter] for all (Naugk, Ritter, Ritter, & Zielinski, 2016, p. 52).

At the same time, results point to the potential of picture book apps not only through a conscious use of the technical features but also through the design of the app itself. The potential of the medium lies in the interactive, multimedia functions of apps such as the touchscreen for interactive viewing, the reading function in different languages, or the visual and auditory animation of individual images and background noises. These support receptive and productive narrative skills as long as they do not distract from the story, and as long as the animations correspond to the story and can be activated in a way complementary to it.

The technical side of activities is an especially inhibiting factor when the app is overloaded with technical features and animations that distract from the story and cannot be deactivated. Because there is still no overriding evaluation system or seal of approval for the market, how apps are used depends strongly on the app itself, on the receptive and productive skills of the children, and on the family media usage habits of children and caregivers.

Müller-Brauers, Boelmann, Miosga, and Potthast (see Chapter 9) report on how apps need to be developed and designed so that they will encourage parents and practitioners to engage in cognitively activating and emotionally attuning interaction. Some researchers have already worked out these potentials (e.g., Knopf, 2018). The results highlight the need to analyze apps in terms of their levels of structure and genre, of the embedding of animations, and of the types of conversation they initiate.

Results should be incorporated into the formulation of quality criteria for the design of picture book apps, into language didactic concepts for digital children's literature in kindergartens, and into educational and counseling concepts for practitioners and parents. Practitioners and caregivers need opportunities to learn and practice new forms of pedagogy with digital technology and to use video-based analyses and reflections on the multimodal interaction design that support or inhibit language learning.

Three key considerations for parents, educators, and producers

For parents

- Be aware of the implicit changes brought about by distractive digital features when dealing with a picture book app, so that you can include the animations consciously in the dialogic adjustment and the story.

For educators

- Familiarize yourself with the digital features of picture book apps and with the story. Choose apps that encourage you and the children to use the animations dialogically to support involvement, an everyday-life orientation, and story comprehension. Use video-based coaching or collegial case studies to reconstruct and reflect on attitudes when dealing with app-based reading interactions, so that you will be able to exploit their potential for inclusive language and literacy support.

For app producers

- Cooperate with developmental psychologists and education scientists in developing apps and integrate a guidebook specifying how to handle the digital features. Apps should be developed and designed so that they encourage parents and practitioners to engage in cognitively activating and emotionally attuning interactions.

Notes

1 Due to the multifunctionality of nonverbal and paraverbal modalities, the coding of this category was not always clear. Problems and shortcomings in its coding might have arisen from the subjectivity of the interpretation. Therefore, the category was defined in a differentiated way and confirmed by four independent raters. The category was distinguished from simple imitation of child behavior, selective attunement, misattunement, tuning, and nonauthentic attunement (Stern, 2000, pp. 138–161). Although purposeful misattunement can also be functional and meaningful in order to challenge and support the child, this was not included in this category.
2 Paired t tests were used throughout the study to test differences in interaction for significance.

References

Billington, C. (2016). *How digital technology can support early language and literacy outcomes in early years settings: A review of the literature.* London, England: National Literacy Trust.

Bruner, J. (Ed.). (1983). *Child's talk: Learning to use language.* New York, NY: Norton.

Bus, A. G., Takacs, Z. K., & Kegel, C. A. (2015). Affordances and limitations of electronic storybooks for young children's emergent literacy. *Developmental Review, 35,* 79–97.

Bus, A. G., van Ijzendoorn, M. H., & Pellegrini, A. D. (1995). Joint book reading makes for success in learning to read: A meta-analysis on intergenerational transmission of literacy. *Review of Educational Research, 65,* 1–21.

Chaudron, S., Di Gioia, R., & Gemo, M. (2018). Young children (0–8) and digital technology: A qualitative study across Europe: EUR 29070. *Education Futures for the Digital Age: Theory and Practice, 68*(3). Retrieved from https://ojs.cuni.cz/pedagogika/article/view/1308

Chiong, C., Ree, J., Takeuchi, L., & Erickson, I. (2012). Print books vs. e-books: Comparing parent-child co-reading on print, basic, and enhanced e-book platforms. *The Joan Ganz Cooney Center*, New York, NY. Retrieved from www. joanganzcooneycenter.org/wp-content/uploads/2012/07/jgcc_ebooks_quickreport.pdf

De Jong, M. T., & Bus, A. G. (2003). How well suited are electronic books to supporting literacy? *Journal of Early Childhood Literacy*, 3(2), 147–164.

Deppermann, A. (Ed.). (2008). *Gespräche analysieren. Eine Einführung.* Wiesbaden, Germany: Springer VS.

Fletcher, K. L., & Reese, E. (2005). Picture book reading with young children: A conceptual framework. *Developmental Review*, 25(1), 64–103.

Gogate, L., Bahrick, L., & Watson, J. (2000). Study of multimodal motherese: The role of temporal synchrony between verbal labels and gestures. *Child Development*, 71(4), 878–894.

Grolig, L., Cohrdes, C., Tiffin-Richards, S. P., & Schroeder, S. (2019). Effects of preschoolers' storybook exposure and literacy environments on lower level and higher level language skill. *Reading and Writing*, 32(4), 1061–1084.

Gutknecht, D. (Ed.). (2012). *Bildung in der Kinderkrippe. Wege zur professionellen Responsivität, Entwicklung und Bildung in der frühen Kindheit.* Stuttgart, Germany: Kohlhammer.

Hausendorf, H., & Quasthoff, U. M. (Eds.). (2005). *Sprachentwicklung und Interaktion. Eine linguistische Studie zum Erwerb von Diskursfähigkeiten.* Radolfzell, Germany: Verlag für Gesprächsforschung.

Hildebrandt, F., Scheidt, A., Hildebrandt, A., Hédervári-Heller, É., & Dreier, A. (2016). Sustained shared thinking als Interaktionsformat und das Sprachverhalten von Kindern. *Frühe Bildung*, 5(2), 82–90.

Jungmann, T., Miosga, C., Fuchs, A., & Rohlfing, K. J. (2009). Konzeption eines Elterntrainings auf der Grundlage der Befunde aus der Multimodalen Motherese-Forschung. In U. de Langen-Müller, M. Hielscher-Fastabend, & B. Kleissendorf (Eds.), *Sprachtherapie lohnt sich?! Zum aktuellen Stand der Evaluations- und Effektivitätsforschung in der Sprachtherapie* (p. 234). Köln, Germany: ProLog. Retrieved from www.ifs.uni-hannover.de/fileadmin/ifs/Abteilungen/Sprach-Paedagogik_und_-Therapie/Projekte/Emotionale_Abstimmung/Poster_Multimodales_Motherese_Miosga-1.pdf

Kelley, E. S., & Kinney, K. (2017). Word learning and story comprehension from digital storybooks: Does interaction make a difference? *Journal of Educational Computing Research*, 55(3), 410–428.

Knopf, J. (2018). Literarisches Lernen im Kindergarten. Zum Potential digitaler Medien am Beispiel von Bilderbuch-Apps. In D. Henle & P. Nauwerck (Eds.), *Sprachenlernen konkret!* (pp. 46–59). Baltmannsweiler, Germany: Schneider Verlag Hohengehren.

Korat, O., & Shamir, A. (2007). Electronic books versus adult readers: Effects on children's emergent literacy as a function of social class. *Journal of Computer Assisted Learning*, 23(3), 248–259.

Krcmar, M., & Cingel, D. P. (2014). Parent-child joint reading in traditional and electronic formats. *Media Psychology*, 17(3), 262–281.

Kucirkova, N., & Littleton, K. (2016). *The digital reading habits of children.* A national sur-vey of parents' perceptions of and practices in relation to children's reading for plea-sure with print and digital books. London, England: BookTrust. Retrieved from www.booktrust.org.uk/news-and-blogs/news/1371

Liu, Z., & Huang, X. (2008). Gender differences in the online reading environment. *Journal of Documentation, 64*(4), 616–626.

Miosga, C. (2017). Stimme und Leseverhalten in Eltern-Kind-Interaktionen mit Bilder-büchern und/oder digitalen Medien? In K. Hannken-Illjes, K. Franz, E. M. Gauß, F. Könitz, & S. Marx (Eds.), *Stimme-Medien-Sprechkunst* (pp. 174–188). Baltmannsweiler Hohengehren, Germany: Schneider Verlag.

Miosga, C. (2019). "Come together" – Multimodale Responsivität und Abstimmung im Spracherwerb und in der Sprachförderung. In I. Bose, S. Kurtenbach, & K. Hannken-Illjes (Eds.), *Kinder im Gespräch – mit Kindern im Gespräch* (pp. 149–174). Berlin, Germany: Frank & Timme.

Mondada, L. (2013). Multimodal interaction. In C. Müller, A. Cienki, E. Fricke, S. Ladewig, D. McNeill, & S. Tessendorf (Eds.), *Body-language-communication: An international handbook on multimodality in human interaction* (pp. 577–589). Berlin, Germany: de Gruyter.

Muratović, B. (Ed.). (2014). *Vorlesen digital: Interaktionsstrukturierung beim Vorlesen ge druckter und digitaler Bilderbücher* (Vol. 11). Berlin, Germany: de Gruyter.

Naugk, N., Ritter, A., Ritter, M., & Zielinski, S. (Eds.). (2016). *Deutschunterricht in der in- klusiven Schule. Perspektiven und Beispiele*. Weinheim, Germany: Beltz Nikolo.

Nentwig-Gesemann, I., Fröhlich-Gildhoff, K., Harms, H., & Richter, S. (2011). Professionelle Haltung – Identität der Fachkraft für die Arbeit mit Kindern in den ersten drei Lebensjahren. *WiFF Expertisen, 24*, 57–84.

Noble, C., Sala, G., Lowe, M., Lingwood, J., Rowland, C., Gobet, F., & Pine, J. (in press). The impact of shared book reading on children's language skills: A meta-analysis. *Educational Research Review*. Retrieved from https://psyarxiv.com/cu7bk/

Ofcom. (2018). *Children and parents: Media use and attitudes report*. Retrieved from www.ofcom.org.uk/__data/assets/pdf_file/0024/134907/Children-and-Parents-Media-Use-and-Attitudes-2018.pdf

Papoušek, H., & Papoušek, M. (1989). Intuitive parenting: Aspects related to educational psychology. *European Journal of Psychology of Education, 4*(2), 201–210.

Parish-Morris, J., Mahajan, N., Hirsh-Pasek, K., Michnick Golinkoff, R., & Fuller Collins, M. (2013). Once upon a time: Parent-child dialogue and storybook reading in the electronic era. *Mind, Brain, and Education, 7*, 200–211.

Pesco, D., & Gagné, A. (2017). Scaffolding narrative skills: A meta-analysis of instruction in early childhood settings. *Early Education and Development, 28*(7), 773–793.

Reich, S. M., Yau, J. C., & Warschauer, M. (2016). Tablet-based ebooks for young children: What does the research say? *Journal of Developmental & Behavioral Pediatrics, 37*(7), 585–591.

Reich, S. M., Yau, J. C., Xu, Y., Muskat, T., Uvalle, J., & Cannata, D. (2019). Digital or Print? A comparison of preschoolers' comprehension, vocabulary, and engagement from a print book and an e-book. *AERA Open, 5*(3), 1–16. Retrieved from https://journals.sagepub.com/doi/pdf/10.1177/2332858419878389

Remsperger, R. (Ed.). (2011). *Sensitive Responsivität. Zur Qualität pädagogischen Handelns im Kindergarten*. Wiesbaden, Germany: Springer VS.

Rohlfing, K. J., Fritsch, J., Wrede, B., & Jungmann, T. (2006). How can multimodal cues from child-directed interaction reduce complexity in robots? *Advanced Robotics, 20*(10), 1183–1199.

Rudel, I. (Ed.). (2011). *Pixi-Buch: "Ein Tag auf dem Bauernhof"*. Hamburg, Germany: CARLSEN Verlag GmbH. Retrieved from www.appsfactory.de

Rvachew, S., Rees, K., Carolan, E., & Nadig, A. (2017). Improving emergent literacy with school-based shared reading: Paper versus ebooks. *International Journal of Child-Computer Interaction, 12*, 24–29.

Schegloff, E. A., & Sacks, H. (1973). Opening up closings. *Semiotica, 8*(4), 289–327.

Schmitt, R. (2015). Positionspapier: Multimodale Interaktionsanalyse. In U. Dausendschön-Gay, E. Gülich, & U. Krafft (Eds.), *Ko-Konstruktionen in der Interaktion. Die gemeinsame Arbeit an Äußerungen und anderen sozialen Ereignissen* (pp. 43–51). Bielefeld, Germany: Transcript.

Schmitt, R. (2016). Der "Frame-Comic" als Dokument multimodaler Interaktionsanalysen. In H. Hausendorf, R. Schmitt, & W. Kesselheim (Eds.), *Interaktionsarchitektur, Sozialtopographie und Interaktionsraum* (pp. 189–224). Tübingen, Germany: Narr.

Selting, M., Auer, P., Barth-Weingarten, D., Bergmann, J. R., Bergmann, P., Birkner, K., Couper-Kuhlen, E., et al. (2009). Gesprächsanalytisches Transkriptionssystem 2 (GAT 2). *Gesprächsforschung – Online-Zeitschrift zur verbalen Interaktion, 10*, 353–402.

Siraj-Blatchford, I. (2007). Creativity, communication and collaboration: The identification of pedagogic progress in sustained shared thinking. *Asia-Pacific Journal of Research in Early Childhood Education, 1*, 1–14.

Stern, D. N. (Ed.). (2000). *The interpersonal world of the infant: A view from psychoanalysis and development psychology* (2nd ed. with new introduction). New York, NY: Basic Books.

Stiftung Lesen. (Ed.). (2012). *Vorlesestudie 2012. Digitale Angebote – neue Anreize für das Vorlesen*. Mainz, Germany: Author. Retrieved from www.stiftunglesen.de/download.php?type=documentpdf&id=752

Tomasello, M., & Carpenter, M. (2007). Shared intentionality. *Developmental Science, 10*, 121–125.

Vygotsky, L. S. (1987). Thinking and speech. In *The collected works of LS Vygotsky* (Vol. 1, pp. 39–285). Boston, MA: Springer.

Wewer, I. (Ed.). (2012). *7 grummelige Grömmels und ein kleines Schwein* from the app "Tigerbooks". Retrieved from https://tiger.media/tigerbooks/

Whitehurst, G. J., Falco, F. L., Lonigan, C. J., Fischel, J. E., DeBaryshe, B. D., Valdez-Menchaca, M. C., & Caulfield, M. (1988). Accelerating language development through picture book reading. *Developmental Psychology, 24*(4), 552–559.

Zevenbergen, A. A., & Whitehurst, G. J. (2003). Dialogic reading: A shared picture book reading intervention for preschoolers. In A. van Kleeck, S. A. Stahl, & E. B. Bauer (Eds.), *On reading books to children: Parents and teachers* (pp. 177–200). Hillsdale, NJ: Lawrence Erlbaum.

Zipke, M. (2017). Preschoolers explore interactive storybook apps: The effect on word recognition and story comprehension. *Education and Information Technologies, 22*(4), 1695–1712.

Zorn, I., Justino, J., Schneider, A., & Schönenberg, J. (2016). Potentials of digital technology for participation of special needs children in kindergarten. In K. Miesenberger, C. Bühler, & P. Penaz (Eds.), *Computers helping people with special needs: 15th International Conference, ICCHP* (pp. 301–304). Cham, Germany: Springer.

Chapter 3

Exploring media practices in inclusive early childhood settings

Scarlet Schaffrath, Nicole Najemnik, and Isabel Zorn

Introduction

Because learning in early childhood takes place mostly through play, inclusion in early childhood education can be understood as the possibility for differently abled children to play together. Like many other types of play, inclusive play requires communication – be it verbal or nonverbal. Moreover, communicative skills can be considered to be a protective factor against exclusion from early childhood onward because they serve to express one's own needs, to communicate with others, and to be perceived as an attractive play partner (German Youth Institute [DJI], 2016). For this reason, promoting literacy skills is a central task in early childhood education and care (ECEC). In the early years, literacy is referred to as competencies in verbal communication, phonological awareness, and written text. With respect to verbal communication, the training of language skills in German kindergartens[1] has been integrated into everyday life (German: *Alltagsintegrierte Sprachbildung*[2]) for a few years now as a consequence of the inclusive course adopted by policymakers (Ministry of Family Affairs, Children, Youth, Culture, and Sports [MFKJKS], 2014).

However, the fact that promoting literacy skills is tightly linked to play in early education places new demands on educational professionals. It confronts them with the task of fashioning communication settings in ways that address the children's individual interests, needs, and abilities while also being suitable for group settings in which all children are able to participate. In this sense, it is important to promote children's early literacy skills along with various materials that are suitable for typical settings. However, the potential for fostering literacy skills using digital media with a high call character as materials has yet to be well explored. So far, little is known about what effects digital media may have on communication within a group setting and therefore on inclusive play (Stephenson & Limbrick, 2015). We addressed this research gap in two inclusive kindergartens in the state of North Rhine-Westphalia, Germany, with an exploratory study designed to look at the possibilities of activities with digital media for inclusive playing and communication settings. In line with the criteria of promoting common play and creating occasions for communication between differently abled children, as well as between children with German as their mother tongue and children with another mother tongue, we investigated the opportunities and challenges of using tablets to design inclusive play and learning situations. Assuming that in ECEC, the use of digital media as a source for shared interest creates additional occasions for communication and interaction between differently abled children, we conducted nonparticipatory observations of activities with tablets in five kindergarten groups. Our aim was to contribute to the discourse over the use of digital media in ECEC through findings on their aptness for communication and participation processes in inclusive early childhood settings.

Our chapter is structured as follows: Aiming to answer the question how the use of tablets in inclusive settings shapes communication and interaction among diverse children (children with or without a disability, children with or without German as a mother tongue), we first discuss concepts in early childhood education that relate to participatory practices, the role of early literacy skills, and (digital) media use in ECEC. We look at how these three areas are intertwined and then present our study. Drawing on our findings, we argue that depending on the pedagogical design of play and learning situations and the professionals' interactions with differently abled children, there is a risk of excluding children with disabilities. We conclude that implementing (digital) media in education curricula also requires media training for the professionals concerned so that they can use suitable media in a pedagogically valuable way.

Theoretical background: a sociocultural approach to learning and its implications for inclusion

To explore the potential of tablet apps for fostering communication and participation in ECEC, we draw on a sociocultural approach to learning (Rogoff, 2003) and an understanding of early childhood education as being situated in social contexts and supportive of the children's development of learning dispositions.

Early childhood settings aim to promote children's agency (Vandenbroeck & Bouverne-De Bie, 2006). This approach regards children as competent social actors and empowers them to take part actively in their own educational processes. Following situated learning theory (Lave & Wenger, 1991), educational processes take place in social contexts and are embedded in a community of practice with many learners of different levels working, playing, learning together, and thus participating in an activity. Lave and Wenger (1991) point to the relevance of social formations for learning in which participants interact with each other, and they argue that "legitimate participation" lays the ground for meaningful learning activity (ibid., pp. 27–29). In practice, these ideas are sometimes contradicted by isolating children with special needs and placing them in special learning and therapy situations that will allow specific treatment in concentrated learning spaces that address their specific skills. The ideas on legitimate participation also seem to be contradicted when early childhood education is embedded in contexts of measurement and standardization, thereby furthering a focus on diagnosis, therapy, separation, and control; and children with special needs are especially at risk of being subjects to such therapy and separation approaches (Dahlberg, 2004). We assume that tendencies in this direction may still be found even under enacted "inclusion" conditions. Against these tendencies, Lave and Wenger (1991) point out that in communities of learning, each learner has something to contribute, and that learning takes place by communicating and sharing meaningful tasks.

Can digital media foster the contribution of each learner? Assuming that inclusive settings aim for legitimate participation by all children involved, we were looking for an approach that would explain why and how ECEC can include children in inclusive settings in joint motivating activities – and why, among others, digital media may even play an important role in bringing children together for meaningful play. We should highlight that this question contradicts a common view on the integration of digital media as being legitimized only when they promise a special solution for a specific learning issue such as learning numbers, words, and so forth.

Building on empirical findings in early childhood settings in New Zealand, Carr's (2001) approach centers around learning dispositions. Learning dispositions are a repertoire of learning strategies and motivations with the help of which a child perceives, selects, or creates learning opportunities. Through learning efforts, a child's repertoire is constantly expanded. The relation between dispositions and action taking is referred to as the behavioral, cognitive, and social abilities for regarding, searching for, or creating situations as learning environments (Ritchhart, 2002). According to Carr (2001), these important dispositions are:

1   *Taking an interest* in an activity or topic can be shown by children in the form of verbal expressions or body posture
2   *Getting involved* in an activity or topic can be observed by a deep engagement with an object, theme, or person or by a status of "flow" – that is, being immersed in the situation and not easily distractible
3   *Persisting with uncertainty and challenges* during an activity or an interaction – that is, not giving up but rather searching for solutions to a given problem
4   *Expressing ideas and feelings* in the form of classic communication with others but also through singing, acting, or drawing
5   *Taking responsibility* within an activity in order to contribute to a certain goal by, for example, giving advice and helping others but also by holding oneself back so that others have a chance to participate

These dispositions should be looked at as a series of stages. For instance, taking an interest is often a prerequisite for the motivation of achieving a goal (Renninger, Hidi, & Krapp, 1992), whereas getting involved in an activity is a sign that challenges and skills are balanced insofar as a learner feels able to achieve a goal (Csikszentmihalyi, 1997). Within each of these dispositions, Carr (2001) differentiates between three levels of perceiving situations as learning environments:

being ready, being willing, and *being able.* The educator's task is to detect signs of these dispositions in children and to assess which level they are on. By observing and fostering these learning dispositions, ECEC aims to support children's underlying needs. These are their feeling of *belonging* to and being appreciated by others; emotional and physical *well-being;* and their (perceived) possibility for *exploration* of their environment; for verbal, nonverbal, and symbolic *communication;* and for *contribution* and participation within social learning situations. Again, these needs should be looked at as being built one upon another, with participation being the final goal of educational processes. Carr (2001) presents these needs as being at the bottom of an iceberg – (almost) invisible. Yet, the learning dispositions she describes can be observed and give hints about the satisfaction of children's needs under the assumption that learning dispositions (i.e., actions taken such as the persistence shown in an activity) are a consequence of being satisfied, for instance, regarding the possibility to explore an environment or a material. With respect to criteria for suitable materials, they should elicit children's curiosity (Haas, 2012).

We argue that digital media might be suitable materials due to their interactive character, and that they might be especially suitable for children with disabilities whose needs, and thus prerequisites for learning, are at risk of being neglected. In conclusion, Carr's concept emphasizes two important aspects: First, learning dispositions – especially the ability to take responsibility – are not only important for educational processes but also a prerequisite for participation in social contexts. Second, these educational processes depend on communication skills, especially when looking at the last two dispositions: expressing ideas and feelings and taking responsibility.

We consider that it is especially the needs of children with disabilities that may not be satisfied sufficiently in ECEC settings, despite the inclusive approach that is now taken in Germany. This is due to a two-group thinking about children with and children without disability (Heimlich, 2013) and resulting processes of separation as well as a focus on diagnosing and treating disabilities as if they were illnesses (Dahlberg, 2004). Such practices and foci can be a risk for children's development, because underlying needs must first be satisfied before educational processes can be initialized and learning dispositions become apparent. Therefore, we argue that Carr's approach should be given special consideration when looking at inclusive early childhood settings, also because it arose out of the idea of fostering diversity and intercultural communication between people of indigenous and nonindigenous heritage in New Zealand (German Youth Institute [DJI], 2005).

Current research on digital media in inclusive early childhood settings

So far, little research has been conducted at the intersection between the use of digital media, the support of early literacy skills, and practices of participation in inclusive early childhood settings. These areas are often looked at separately.

However, some studies do point to the potential of using digital media to support either early literacy skills or participatory practices in early childhood settings.

The use of digital media for early literacy skills

Regarding the potential of using digital media to support early literacy skills, a case study from Norway indicates the potential of apps to support different types of conversation within a multicultural and multilingual group of 5-year-old children (Sandvik, Smørdal, & Østerud, 2012). These findings seem valuable because unrecognized disorders or delays in children's language development can also affect their later cognitive, emotional, and social development (Rice, 1993). As described earlier, both educational processes and the opportunity to participate depend strongly on communicative skills. Therefore, promoting literacy skills is a central task in German ECEC. It is assumed that children learn language best through close interactional loops and through role models in personal contact (German Youth Institute [DJI], 2016). Furthermore, literacy skills have been fostered mostly within activities such as shared picture book reading (Shanahan & Lonigan, 2010; Wirts, Egert, & Reber, 2017). Children with disabilities, however, are less exposed to early literacy activities than their peers (Hallbauer, 2014). We argue that promoting literacy skills in ECEC is not only relevant for successful learning in a child's educational career but might also be a key to more participation. Digital media might be suitable materials to promote communication, especially when developed according to the principles of universal design that enable equal access to technology for a diversity of people without further adjustments having to be made (Preiser & Ostroff, 2001). Such technologies might help not only children with disabilities but also children with a migrant background whose mother tongue is not German.

The use of digital media for participation

With respect to potential of participation, a study project addressing a child with multiple disabilities in Germany points to reduced boredom, a decline in antisocial behavior, and an extended attention span when engaging in a tablet activity. These aspects are even stronger when other children play with the child on the tablet (Zorn, Justino, Schneider, & Schönenberg, 2016). Furthermore, research from Finland points to the potential of digital media to create occasions for communication in participatory learning settings to which differently abled children can contribute (Leinonen & Sintonen, 2014). In these settings, digital media serve as a source for joint attention (Jones & Carr, 2004). In Germany, (digital) media are regarded as beneficial for supporting language skills (Ministry of Family Affairs, Children, Youth, Culture, and Sports [MFKJKS], 2014) and inclusion. Schluchter (2015) regards the use of media as an opportunity to strengthen inclusive structures because they can promote children's (perceived) self-efficacy, agency, and ability to communicate, and provide opportunities for letting differently abled children participate in educational activities. This potential, however, seems to depend strongly on the skills and practices of early childhood professionals.

Up to now, the media equipment in German early childhood settings has been restricted mostly to books, cassettes, and CD players. Digital media such as digital cameras, computers, and tablets are not widely available (Feierabend, Plankenhorn, & Rathgeb, 2015). The media equipment corresponds with the use of media in German kindergartens. Around one-third of kindergarten employees do not feel competent enough to implement media education (Meister, Friedrichs-Liesenkötter, Keller, Pielsticker, & Temps, 2012) or may hesitate to embrace the potential value of digital media for educational purposes (Friedrichs-Liesenkötter, 2016). This is all the more problematic because families with low socioeconomic status (SES) especially regard professionals in kindergarten as being responsible for their children's media education (Feierabend et al., 2015; German Institute for Trust and Security on the Internet [DIVSI], 2015). In turn, many professionals regard digital media as a danger for children's development (German Institute for Trust and Security on the Internet [DIVSI], 2015; Six & Gimmler, 2007) and feel more responsible for other areas of education such as language learning. In conclusion, there is a need for more research on digital media education for inclusive settings in ECEC (Zorn, 2019).

Tablet activities in inclusive early childhood settings: an exploratory study

To gain further knowledge about the potential of activities with digital media to support participatory practices and communication in inclusive early childhood settings, we conducted an exploratory study in two inclusive kindergartens in the German state of North-Rhine Westphalia in 2016.

Objective and research question

Within the scope of the research project, we asked the following question from the perspective of media education and the social sciences: *How do communication and interaction between differently abled children, as well as children with another mother tongue than German, take place when using digital tablet games?*

Aiming to cast light on the challenges of using digital media for participation and common learning and play in inclusive ECEC settings, we assumed that there is a synergy between the use of digital media and early literacy skills, and that both are relevant to children's chances of participation. As shown in Figure 3.1, digital media offer additional occasions for communication and interaction by enabling children not only to interact *with* the technology but also to talk *about* the technology and the content. Referring to the former, digital media such as tablets are interactive and "respond" to children's actions. This might raise their interest not only in the device but also in the (learning) content. We argue that interacting

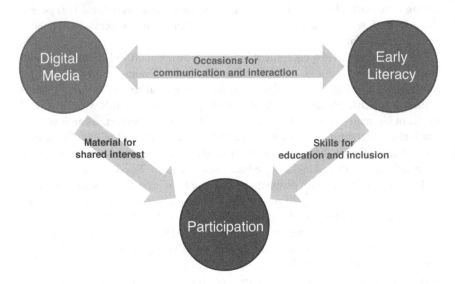

Figure 3.1 Synergy between media use and literacy skills for the purpose of participation

Source: (Schaffrath, Najemnik, & Zorn)

with digital media can foster early literacy skills when apps are chosen that match the targeted areas of early literacy – that is, verbal communication, phonological awareness, and written texts. Because digital media address multiple senses with their auditory and visual cues, they seem to be particularly suitable for children with a mother tongue other than German as well as for children with disabilities. Moreover, children often show interest in activities in which digital media are used (Biermann, Daveri, & Eder, 2015). Referring to the latter, digital media might function as material for encouraging a shared interest and offer occasions for communication over the content (What is the game about? Do you know the game's protagonists?), the device (How does the tablet work? How can I switch between games?), and especially the negotiation processes within the social context of a group activity (Whose turn is it? Which game do we want to play?). Therefore, digital media can be regarded as a suitable material for fostering practices of participation by letting children contribute to an activity that asks them to persist when facing uncertainty and challenges, express ideas and feelings, and take responsibility (for themselves, other children, and the device).

Sample and methods

The target group for the exploratory study included professionals from ECEC with proven expertise in caring for differently abled children, and the children in their care. In order to meet a broad concept of inclusion, we focused on groups containing children with disabilities and/or with a migrant background, which, in many cases, goes along with multilingualism. Inclusion here is understood as social participation that requires not only being open to the diversity of children but also actively reducing barriers so that all children are empowered and enabled to contribute to a group activity (German Youth Institute [DJI], 2013). The two integrative kindergartens (Kindergarten A and Kindergarten B) in the study are located in residential areas in Cologne. These areas are inhabited by families with lower SES. The generally high proportion of persons with a migration background in these areas was also represented in the two kindergartens by the number of children whose mother tongue was not German. Both kindergartens are providing inclusive care to children with German as their mother tongue, German as a second language, with disabilities, and without disabilities.

In Kindergarten A, the inclusive character of the institution was particularly evident in the experience with augmentative and alternative communication (AAC), for which one of the professionals had attended further training. However, digital media were not part of this training. The kindergarten was in regular contact with external experts on speech and language development and was supported on a regular basis within the institution by a speech therapist and a physiotherapist. In Kindergarten B, one of the professionals had been trained in the concept of language learning in everyday life. She had taken on the role of mediator and passed on her knowledge to her colleagues. Furthermore, Kindergarten B had hired a speech therapist on a half-day basis and a specialist for psychomotor education who supported nonverbally communicating children both individually and in group settings. Until the study was conducted, both kindergartens had rarely used digital media with children. Therefore, in the week prior to the observations, we gave an onsite introduction in both kindergartens to the tablet and its functions, as well as to the apps that would be used during the tablet activity. To enable the professionals to further familiarize themselves with the tablet functions and the apps, the tablets were left with them until the day of the observations.

For the study, we conducted nonparticipatory observations of five groups during a one-hour tablet activity. The groups contained a total of 50 differently abled children, including children with German as their mother tongue and children with German as their second language, together with 10 professionals. Each group consisted of about 8 to 12 children and was cared for by two professionals. Observations took place in mixed groups without prior knowledge about the disabilities or language issues of the participating children. However, observers quickly found out obvious disabilities, such as trisomy 21 (also known as Down syndrome), or other mother tongues than German. Because the study focused on practices of inclusion and separation, we do not find it necessary to identify specific diagnoses in the sample, but rather explain practices of separation and inclusion in terms of the observation results.

During the tablet activities, we observed the behavior of children and professionals with a semistructured record sheet based on Carr's learning dispositions. On this sheet, we made notes about (a) the communication and interaction of professionals with differently abled children and children with a mother tongue other than German, in terms of their reactions to children's attempts to play on the tablet and their supporting strategies, such as giving hints and encouraging children to explore the tablet; (b) the communication and interaction between differently abled children in terms of verbal and nonverbal behavior, signs of shared interest, and common play; (c) children's emotions during the activity, such as obvious signs of boredom or happiness; and (d) further observations relating to the practicability of a tablet activity within a group, and preliminary interpretations such as the dependency of children's communicative behavior on the pedagogical setup of the mediated activity. Three of the five groups (two in Kindergarten A and one in Kindergarten B) were observed by two researchers during the tablet activity, whereas the other two groups in Kindergarten B were observed by only one researcher due to a lack of personnel resources. We subjected the record sheets to Mayring's (2015) structuring qualitative content analysis in order to filter the data according to previously set criteria. In our case, these criteria were inspired by Carr's learning dispositions and functioned as deductive categories for the analysis. The categories related to the initiation and maintenance of children's interaction and communication, their interest in the tablet activity, and their involvement and persistence during the activity. Another focus was on the strategies educational professionals used to accompany the activities of children and thus to enable or prevent exploration, communication, and contribution.

In the following, we will explain how and why we decided to use tablets and apps for the purpose of inclusive play and learning settings in kindergarten.

Media selection: hardware and software

With respect to the inclusive approach taken in German early childhood settings, appropriate materials in learning environments should address multiple sensory channels, have a high call character, and be accessible to all children (German Youth Institute [DJI], 2013). We argue that tablets might meet these requirements because they are interactive and, due to their intuitive design, they might be even easier to access for children as well as for professionals who have limited experience with the pedagogical use of digital media within ECEC. Therefore, we provided the kindergartens with two tablets each. Because the apps for the iOS operating system were rated better than the Android-based games, we used iPads for the research project.

Against the background of the study's objective and the context of playing and learning in inclusive settings, apps for the tablets were selected on the basis of the following criteria: They should have a focus on early literacy, be accessible for children with disabilities, be comprehensible for children between the ages of 3 and 6 years so that they could use them by themselves, and be able to be played in a group of children. With respect to aspects of data security, we also attached importance to the possibility of using the apps without internet access. Furthermore, the apps should be affordable. Five promising apps were selected after an expert interview with a speech therapist who recommended focusing on apps that are fun to use and elicit children's interest, rather than on therapy for children with developmental speech delays or other anomalies. To select the final two out of five apps, we conducted a user test with students from the program "Early Childhood Education and Family Studies" at the Technical University of Applied Sciences Cologne who, according to their training, can be regarded as potential future users of such technology in ECEC settings. Android- and iOS-based tablets were rated in terms of their look and feel (How appealing does the user interface seem to be for children?), usability (Does the user interface seem to be intuitive for children aged 3 to 6 years?), interactivity (Do the apps seem to foster children's reactions or are they designed only to consume content?) and the possibility of using them with several children (Do the apps seem suitable for group settings?). In this regard, we found that apps categorized as educational or developed as tools for AAC in the app stores are more expensive than those categorized as gaming apps. The two apps used in the kindergartens were "MIXIMAL" by *YATATOY* and "I spy with Lola" by *BeiZ Oy*.

1   "MIXIMAL" is an app that promotes phonological awareness. It reminds users of an analogue flap book that allows children to swap body parts of animals and put them together on three levels. They swipe left or right on the tablet and can hear the name of the created animal by tapping the corresponding icon on the screen. The name of the animal is divided both auditorily and visually into three syllables, as shown in Figure 3.2a. The aim of the game is to put the body parts together correctly so that the animal conducts an activity such as brushing its teeth, as shown in Figure 3.2b. In addition, the body parts move individually as soon as a child taps on them. The app can be downloaded from the Apple Store and costs 2.99 euro. It is categorized there as an educational app and is recommended from the age of 4 onward.

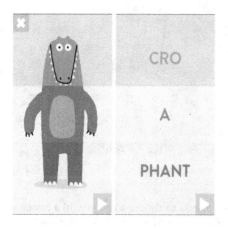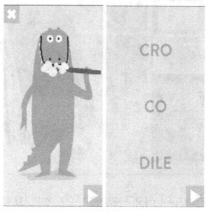

Figure 3.2 App "MIXIMAL" showing (a) pictures and matching syllables of three different animals and (b) a picture of a crocodile and its name divided into three syllables

Source: (Luca Zanotti/*YATATOY*)

2 "I spy with Lola" is a search game for word learning. The user travels
around the world with the protagonist Lola and can choose between different countries, as shown in Figure 3.3a. The task is to find objects based on
auditory and written clues given by Lola (see Figure 3.3b) that are collected

Figure 3.3 App "I spy with Lola" with (a) a world map to choose a country, (b) a camping
site to search for theme-related objects, and (c) the searched object under a
magnifier

Source: (BeiZ Oy)

Figure 3.3 (Continued)

by tapping on the object on the screen. The clues vary depending on the chosen level of difficulty. The easiest level is available free of charge in the Apple and Google Play stores; the premium version with different levels of difficulty can be purchased for 3.49 euro. "I spy with Lola" belongs to the educational category in the app store and is recommended from the age of 4 onward.

Results

Based on the theory of sociocultural learning and the approach developed by Carr (2001), we structure our qualitative analysis of the tablet activities along three categories (A, B, and C):

A   *Occasions for communication and interaction* during the tablet activity. This category corresponds to Carr's (2001) learning disposition of *taking an interest, getting involved,* and *expressing ideas and feelings.*

B   *Practices of participation and contribution* during the tablet activity. This category is used to encompass dispositions of *taking interest* and the *need for belonging* as well as the disposition of *taking responsibility* and the *need for contribution.*

C   *Media-related practices* of ECEC professionals during the tablet activity. This category is linked to Carr's approach (2001) of furthering children's possibility to *explore* their environment and materials, and of encouraging them to show *persistence* during the activity.

Although not all results can be shown here, we shall report some observations in the two kindergartens with the aim of illustrating how both children and educators create situations with digital media that influence communication, interaction, and participation among diverse children. We chose situations that can be interpreted as being important for children's opportunities to extend their learning dispositions and children's needs for *belonging, well-being, exploration, communication,* and *contribution.* The results of this study point to children's unequal chances of participation. In the following interpretation, Carr's (2001) learning dispositions and underlying needs are written in italics in the parentheses.

(A)   Occasions for communication and interaction during the tablet activity

Right from the beginning, children wanted to participate in the activity and paid a lot of attention even when they had to wait for their turn (*taking an interest, getting involved*). Within the first few minutes, only a little communication took place because the focus seemed to be on the apps. The children showed their interest more physically by leaning far over the table to watch the game or by surrounding their peers playing on the tablet (*taking an interest, getting involved*). With the ongoing activity, communication among the children increased. The children helped each other verbally ("Look there, the sunglasses!" "There it is!" "Take this!") (*expressing ideas*). The game brought children into the expert role: They could explain the games' principles to each other ("There, you have to choose Egypt"). They also negotiated verbally over who may play next and which game should be played (*taking responsibility*). In this sense, it can be argued that the tablet activity also activated social skills. Other literacy activities included imitating or answering the sound output of the two apps: In "MIXIMAL," the children repeated the syllables of the animals' names and discussed whether the animal was real (*getting involved*). In some cases, children – especially the older ones – put together wrong animal combinations intentionally and had fun listening to the new word creations (*expressing ideas*). Whereas some children without an observed disability engaged intensively in the tasks exactly as the game had foreseen, other children were much more interested in the tablet itself rather than the specific game and enjoyed the activity of wiping pages, watching changes in the displayed graphics, and not being overly concerned about finding correct answers. But even these "incorrect" activities provoked shared joy in play, as indicated by shared laughter and communication (*getting involved*). For instance, in "I spy with Lola," the children felt addressed by the protagonist praising a child when she or he had found the hidden object and repeated Lola's positive reaction ("I found the sunglasses").

We interpret children's behavior as interest in the tablet activities. They played together or commented on the game and laughed together. This suggests that joint attention was created during the activity, which is an important goal of early education and participation. Furthermore, Carr's (2001) learning dispositions of *taking interest* and *taking responsibility, expressing ideas,* and *getting involved* were observed. Hence, for some children, the activity could have addressed their needs for *belonging* and being appreciated by others, as well as their need for *exploration* of their environment; for verbal, nonverbal, and symbolic *communication*; and for *contribution* and participation within social learning situations. Some children created new fantasy animals and words with the game. Referring to Baacke's (1997) concept of media literacy, this could be viewed as media design competence – that is, the ability to manipulate media (content) for aesthetic purposes.

(B) Practices of participation and contribution during the tablet activity

In Kindergarten A, jointly playing on a tablet was encouraged right from the start. However, when putting together groups, children with obvious disabilities were encouraged by the educators to play together. These children were particularly encouraged to participate in the activity with the tablet *(limiting their need for exploration)*. Professionals helped them to assemble the animals correctly on "MIXIMAL" or to find the objects they were looking for in "I spy with Lola" *(helping and limiting the learning disposition of persisting with challenges and uncertainty)*.

In Kindergarten B, a child with obvious trisomy 21 was not invited by the educator to join the tablet activity *(hindering all learning dispositions and violating need for belonging and contributing)*. The girl sat at the back of the room when the tablet was introduced (this kindergarten had introduced the tablet to the children a week before without our knowledge; we do not know whether this child had also been excluded back then or whether she did not like to play in the first place). The educator invited her to join the activity only after the observer asked the educator why this girl did not join. She then invited the girl into the group with two other girls who were already playing with the tablet. She then happily joined *(taking an interest)*. When joining, this girl was denied independent activity with the tablet by the educator *(limiting her opportunities for persisting with uncertainty and challenges and for taking responsibility)*. The educator took over both holding the device and selecting the game. Nonetheless, the girl had fun wiping the game cards together to create funny animal combinations and listening to the animals' names announced by the tablet *(taking interest, getting involved)*. She did not seem to have difficulties in playing, and it was not obvious why she was not offered the opportunity to hold the tablet by herself. Instead, the educator asked two other girls without an obvious disability to show the girl the animal combinations they had created with "MIXIMAL" and praised them for their sharing *(taking responsibility)*. However, the educator rejected the two girls' suggestion and desire that the child with a disability should be placed between them so that she could see better *(taking responsibility)*, although this could have enabled the girl to participate more fully. The educator refused and kept the girl next to herself while continuing to hold the tablet for her.

In both kindergartens, children with disabilities were treated differently than either children without an obvious disability or children with another mother tongue than German. They were influenced in the way they formed groups with peers and received more help even when it did not seem necessary.

This finding can be interpreted in the sense of the principle that children with special needs should be treated just like children without a disability whenever possible but get help whenever necessary (Wagner, 2013). However, it could also be interpreted as a positive form of discrimination, as it sometimes seemed questionable whether the aid actually was necessary or whether it arose out of habit. This shows how, in some cases, it can be a challenging task for educators to overcome two-group thinking (Heimlich, 2013), to avoid reproducing the handicap, and to allow all children the same possibilities for participation.

In this way, the educator limited the girl's *willingness of exploration* and did not adapt learning situations optimally to match her abilities, thereby limiting her fulfillment of needs such as the *feeling of belonging*, participating and *contributing*. In contrast, the educator's task for the other two girls to share their results addressed their *needs for contributing* and *exploration*.

Hindering the girl's attempts to interact by obstructing her physical and social environment and assuming the task is too difficult for someone with a disability can be interpreted as "doing disability" (Albrecht, Seelman, & Bury, 2001) or as treating digital media as something very special and difficult, while assuming that they are very precious/dangerous/valuable and therefore cannot be used by any child. Both assumptions construct the girl as being "special", as a child who cannot be treated in the same way as other children without disabilities. Thereby, the educator limits her chances for participation and *contribution* in the cases described here and thwarts the idea of tablet gaming as an opportunity for equal participation. This can be interpreted as not always – and maybe specifically not when technology is involved – fully embracing the opportunities for fulfilling children's needs for a *feeling of belonging* to and appreciation by others, limiting their need for the perceived possibility of *exploration* of their environment, limiting opportunities for verbal, nonverbal, and symbolic *communication* and for optimal *contribution*, and hindering their participation within social learning situations.

(C)   Media-related practices by educators during the tablet activity

The professionals in both kindergartens had been given an introduction to the hardware and software by the researchers beforehand. They were asked to let the children play with the two games in groups when the researchers came for the observation.

The professionals agreed to follow rules with the children before the first use of the tablets. These rules concerned the time scale and the group composition (individually or jointly). However, the actual activity was very different in the two kindergartens.

In Kindergarten A, the tablets were introduced to them jointly (*allowing everyone to take interest and participate*). Professionals asked the children about their experience with tablets and showed them the two apps. Then they were allowed to try out the tablet independently and were actively encouraged to do so by the professionals. At first, they asked the children which game they wanted to play (*need for exploration*) and moderated the activity by asking questions about the games. After getting to know the device as well as the content, the children were allowed to use the tablet to play the games either alone or together with other children. However, their participation in the tablet activity was not obligatory; it was just one offer among other activities in the room.

In Kindergarten B, we found out during our observation that educators had used the tablets and played the games with the group the week before we came, and this had already established a routine. Children were not advised, but obviously knew what to do and how to behave with the tablets. When we came, educators asked children to take the tablets and play. We did not hear much explanation to the children over how the activity should take place. Children immediately merged into groups and seemed to know what they were expected to do. During play, educators intervened rapidly when children did not immediately do the "right" thing in the game. They explained to the child what she or he should click or do on the tablet. When something did not work, educators took the tablet and tried to fix it *without letting children explore by themselves*. However, during the course of the tablet activity, professionals started to trust most children when they noticed that they were comfortable with the equipment and understood the games. They even left for another room for a moment and let children play alone, saying that the children no longer needed them.

In the second group in Kindergarten B, the children were instructed on exactly how to use the tablet, even though the professionals had already tried out the tablets with the children before the observation. Furthermore, the professionals decided which child was allowed to play which game and for how long. Each child was allowed to play alone with a tablet for about 10 minutes; children's attempts at cooperative play were initially prevented by the professionals, arguing that the child in charge of the tablet had to concentrate (*hindering of children taking responsibility within the activity*). The researchers' idea of joint interactions within tablet activities was counteracted by designing the activity as a one-on-one session (*hindering the need for contribution*). Furthermore, the professionals led the conversation by giving instructions to the children (*hindering the need for exploration*). This, in turn, did not necessarily require a verbal response from the children, which also counteracted the study's objective of designing a mediated group activity to promote common play and communication (*hindering the need for communication*). Additionally, younger children and children with disabilities were denied playing "I spy with Lola," arguing that it was (still) too difficult for them. Later, the educator told us that she was disappointed with the game because she would use tablets only if they helped to learn colors and forms.

We saw big differences in how educators designed the tablet activities in the different institutions and groups. In Kindergarten A the design of the tablet activity by professionals seemed to be geared toward promoting children's agency, explaining the new game to them, and then letting children *take interest, explore*, and decide what to do.

In Kindergarten B, educators had tried out the tablet activity before the agreed date. We interpret this as either insecurity about the tablet activity or about being observed by the researchers. We do not view this as a sign of being keen on using tablets in ECEC because we did not find other indications of enthusiasm among the educators but rather skepticism. In conclusion, the technology-related activities seem to have raised some insecurities among the professionals. Furthermore, in Kindergarten B's second group, the researchers' intention to design an inclusive, playful activity with digital media was turned into a learning setting by the educators in which they controlled the situation by setting many rules and asking children to concentrate and not help each other. This reminded the observers of a test situation in school. Opportunities for children *to explore their environment or to learn to persist and overcome challenges* were not fully embraced.

These findings could be interpreted in terms of professionals' media educational competencies – an aspect that is all the more challenging in inclusive settings due to the range of children's individual interests and needs.

Limitations

The study has some limitations to its explanatory power because of the small number of cases. In addition, results from the two facilities are not comparable insofar as in one of the kindergartens, the iPads had already been used with the children before the actual observation. Moreover, because our objective was a field exploration, less structured forms of data collection might have been more appropriate. It is also questionable how far simply announcing that the project was on the use of tablets for language learning raised expectations among professionals that were not fulfilled retrospectively. In this respect, an open discussion about how playful communication and interaction – rather than systematic language learning – can contribute to the inclusion of marginalized children might have been helpful.

Discussion

The analysis of the observations indicates that the use of tablet games in kindergarten can promote not only the participation of differently abled children in such activities but also interaction between various children. Children obviously seemed to have fun playing, showed interest, and communicated with each other in the shared activity. Even when the game was played individually, other children wanted to participate, watch, and "help" by talking and explaining game issues.

Translating into Carr's definition of learning dispositions, we can state that playing tablet games may offer children the opportunities to expand their learning dispositions to take an interest, get involved, persist with uncertainty and challenges, express ideas and feelings, and take responsibility. Tablet games hold the potential to get diverse children to choose to play together, to take interest in each other's activities, and to initiate and participate in communication about a shared interest. Findings show ways in which children actively take interest in the activity and interact through both verbal (explaining activities or solutions to each other, repeating the words of the game, negotiating turn taking) and nonverbal (wiping together, laughing together about funny creations and funny or successful solutions) communication with each other. Thus, digital game playing can offer shared interesting activities accessible for children with different abilities or language skills and offer an attractive inclusive communication setting.

Depending on the pedagogical framing of the activity, however, there remain risks of unintended practices of separation or even exclusion when designing didactic settings. This could be attributed not only to the professionals' reservations about the suitability of digital media for inclusive education but also to their lack of experience in using digital media for educational rather than organizational purposes. The tablet games' potential needs to be framed by a valuable didactical setting.

Referring to its educational mission, early education faces the challenge of developing concepts that offer equal opportunities for all children. Kindergartens play a central role in implementing inclusive education right from the start (Federal Ministry of Labor and Social Affairs, 2011). Yet, inclusion alone is already a challenging pedagogical task – regardless of digital media. This exploratory study shows that the use of digital media holds a valuable potential for inclusive communicative play, but that it does not automatically promote inclusion and may promote inequality and exclusion instead. Even in institutions experienced with the care of differently abled children, there seems to be a need to design inclusive settings when digital media are involved. This requires knowledge and training which, in turn, could promote a more positive attitude toward digital media. As media become ubiquitous and play a pivotal role from early childhood onward, education with and about media is becoming an integral element in many education curricula in Germany (Ministry of Family Affairs, Children, Youth, Culture, and Sports [MFKJKS], 2016). The findings of our study show that digital media activities offer meaningful communication opportunities: talking *about* media and interacting *with* media. Therefore, early literacy skills and media-related activities should be given more attention and be seen as complementary areas in both education and opportunities for participation.

Findings show that despite the potential that tablet games offer for inclusive play and for enabling many diverse children to participate in a motivating joint activity, the way such media are introduced into the educational setting may help inclusion and participation but may sometimes also be counterproductive. We saw educators who were not familiar with using new technology in education creating the educational setting with tablets in a way that rather separated children from each other. This finding may be interpreted as indicating new challenges posed by the technology. Thaler and Zorn (2010) called this a form of "doing technology" by educators: Technology could be perceived as something special, complicated, challenging, and expensive. These views may lead educators to subconsciously set unnecessarily high standards on who can play with it and how it should be played – standards that could differ from how they create an educational participatory activity among children playing traditional games such as reading books or drawing on paper. Such standards can then lead to new exclusions and hindrances to participatory play, as documented in our findings on the exclusion of the child with trisomy 21.

The same applies to the professionals when it comes to their inclusive and media-pedagogical competencies. Here, too, synergetic effects seem possible, but up to now they have received only limited attention in education and training. As the results of this study illustrate, every media use – be it either picture books or digital media – requires pedagogical concepts. Otherwise, it can lead to paradoxical interventions such as the control of children's (inter)actions or the separation of children. Well-intentioned aid such as extraverbal communication should be applied carefully to ensure that it does not disable children, as argued within disability studies. Therefore, the implementation of (digital) media in education curricula also requires training professionals about these media so that they can use them in a pedagogically valuable way.

The findings highlight the need for further research on the potential of digital media in inclusive early childhood settings, including a discussion over the comprehensive understanding of learning, the definition of media-pedagogical competence, and the development of inclusive concepts.

Conclusion: training and change of beliefs required

What kind of knowledge and training in early education is required to take full advantage of the potential of digital media for inclusive settings? Findings show that training is needed in both media-related activities and inclusive practices. It seems that a combination of both (planning and guiding media education activities in inclusive contexts) needs to be addressed. Concepts regarding what kind of training ECEC professionals need for inclusive practices have been explored (German Youth Institute [DJI], 2013). Training for media educational activities in early education has also been described (Roboom, 2017; Six & Gimmler, 2007), and the design of media educational activities in inclusive settings and the need to train educators are starting to be sketched out (Nimm – Netzwerk Inklusion mit Medien[3]). However, one continuing blind spot is the potential synergy we have tried to illustrate regarding how to teach the design of meaningful, inclusive media activities with the goals of furthering early literacy and communication or media literacy and participation. Early education is not the only educational field lacking a perspective on inclusive media activities; the blind spot on how to include digital media literacy in inclusive settings can be found in almost all educational fields (Bosse, Schluchter, & Zorn, 2019). In an empirical study with early educators, Marci-Boehncke (2019) found that attitudes toward digital media education play an important role and can best be changed when educators observe the self-efficacy and joy that children demonstrate when interacting with them. Therefore, in-service training should not be granted just to single educators but rather to the whole team. As a framework for such trainings, she suggests an I-TPACK model – that is, to combine elements of inclusion, technology, pedagogy, content and knowledge in a mediatized society. Nonetheless, how exactly inclusive competencies can be trained has yet to be clarified. We suggest that elements of inclusive competencies, such as those described by DJI (2013), should be explored with media: When teaching educators what they need to know, choose, and present suitable gaming materials for all children, they have to be given knowledge about suitable media, criteria for their choices, objectives for using or not using certain media and, last but not least, a means of presenting such media to children.

Three key considerations for parents, educators, and producers

- Professionals in early childhood education require specific training in the use of media so that they can make use of suitable (digital) media in a pedagogically valuable way to meet children's individual interests, needs, and abilities.
- Inclusion needs to become a basic element in the training of professionals in early childhood education and care (ECEC) in Germany. This is the only way to prepare professionals to create inclusive settings for play, communication, and interaction.
- Further research and training focusing on the synergies between inclusion and the use of digital media in ECEC is required to fully exploit the potential of digital media use in inclusive early childhood settings.

Notes

1 In Germany, early childhood education focuses typically on the institutional care of children between the ages of 3 and 6 years in so-called "KiTa" or "kindergarten". Here, the educational approach is based on some structured and many unstructured activities such as playing, singing, drawing, and social interaction. Although English-speaking countries use the term "kindergarten" as well, they have another focus: In the United States, for example, kindergartens are part of elementary school education in which children are taught basic reading and calculating skills. In Germany, such skills are taught only from the first grade of schooling onward.

2 Whereas speech and language therapy focus separately on children with a diagnosed disorder and are not necessarily conducted in kindergarten, the concept of

language learning in everyday life targets all children as a group in early childhood settings (Ministry of Family Affairs, Children, Youth, Culture, and Sports [MFKJKS], 2016). The idea is to monitor children's individual language development and stimulate their communicative skills within everyday conversations and play situations (MFKJKS, 2014).
3 For further information, see www.inklusive-medienarbeit.de/.

References

Albrecht, G. L., Seelman, K. D., & Bury, M. (Eds.). (2001). *Handbook of disability studies*. Thousand Oaks, CA: Sage.

Baacke, D. (1997). *Medienpädagogik. Grundlagen der Medienkommunikation. Band 1*. Tübingen, Germany: de Gruyter.

Biermann, T., Daveri, L., & Eder, S. (2015). *Alltagsintegrierte Medien- und Sprachbildung in Kindertageseinrichtungen: Handreichung mit Aktivitäten für die Praxis*. Düsseldorf, Germany: Landesanstalt für Medien Nordrhein-Westfalen (LfM).

Bosse, I., Schluchter, J.-R., & Zorn, I. (2019). *Handbuch Inklusion und Medienbildung*. Weinheim: Beltz Juventa.

Carr, M. (2001). *Assessment in early childhood settings: Learning stories*. London, England: Paul Chapman Publishing.

Csikszentmihalyi, M. (1997). *Finding flow: The psychology of engagement with everyday life*. New York, NY: Basic Books.

Dahlberg, G. (2004). Kinder und Pädagogen als Co-Konstrukteure von Wissen und Kultur: Frühpädagogik in postmoderner Perspektive. In W. Fthenakis & P. Oberhuemer (Eds.), *Frühpädagogik international. Bildungsqualität im Blickpunkt* (pp. 13–30). Wiesbaden, Germany: Springer.

Diskowski, D. (2008). Bildungspläne für Kindertagesstätten – Ein neues und noch unbegriffenes Steuerungsinstrument. In H.-G. Roßbach & H.-P. Blossfeld (Eds.), *Frühpädagogische Förderung in Institutionen* (pp. 47–61). Zeitschrift für Erziehungswissenschaft, Sonderheft 11. doi:10.1007/978-3-531-91452-7_4

Federal Ministry of Labor and Social Affairs (BMAS). (2011). *Unser Weg in eine inklusive Gesellschaft: Der Nationale Aktionsplan der Bundesregierung zur Umsetzung der UN-Behindertenrechtskonvention*. Retrieved from www.bmas.de/SharedDocs/Downloads/DE/PDF-Publikationen/a740-nationaler-aktionsplan-barrierefrei.pdf?__blob=publicationFile

Feierabend, S., Plankenhorn, T., & Rathgeb, T. (2015). *miniKIM 2014. Kleinkinder und Medien. Basisuntersuchung zum Medienumgang 2- bis 5-Jähriger in Deutschland*. Retrieved from www.mpfs.de/fileadmin/files/Studien/miniKIM/2014/Studie/miniKIM_Studie_2014.pdf

Friedrichs-Liesenkötter, H. (2016). *Medienerziehung in Kindertagesstätten – Habitusformationen angehender ErzieherInnen*. Wiesbaden, Germany: VS Verl. für Sozialwissenschaften.

German Institute for Trust and Security on the Internet (DIVSI) (Series Ed.). (2015). *DIVSI U9-Studie Kinder in der digitalen Welt. Eine Grundlagenstudie des SINUS-Instituts Heidelberg im Auftrag des Deutschen Instituts für Vertrauen und Sicherheit im Internet (DIVSI)*. Retrieved from www.divsi.de/wp-content/uploads/2015/06/U9-Studie-DIVSI-web.pdf

German Youth Institute (DJI). (2005). *Projektzeitung Bildungs- und Lerngeschichten. Wissenschaft – Politik – Praxis. Heft 1.* München, Germany: dp druck und prägung.

German Youth Institute (DJI). (2013). *Inklusion – Kinder mit Behinderung: Grundlagen für die kompetenzorientierte Weiterbildung; ein Wegweiser der Weiterbildungsinitiative Frühpädagogische Fachkräfte (WiFF).* München, Germany: Deutsches Jugendinstitut e.V. (DJI). Retrieved from www.weiterbildungsinitiative.de/uploads/media/WW6_Inlusion_Kinder_mit_Behinderung.pdf

German Youth Institute (DJI). (2016). *Prof. em. Dr. Iris Füssenich über Sprachtherapie-Bedarf und Inklusion in der Kita.* Retrieved from www.youtube.com/watch?v=_TETjEkXRhQ

Haas, S. (2012). *Das Lernen feiern. Lerngeschichten aus Neuseeland.* Weimar, Germany: Verlag Das Netz.

Hallbauer, A. (2014). Literacy bei Rett-Syndrom. In U. Braun & A. Koch-Buchtmann (Eds.), *Augenblicke: Unterstützte Kommunikation und Rett-Syndrom* (pp. 30–51). Karlsruhe: Von-Loeper-Literaturverl.

Heimlich, U. (2013). *Kinder mit Behinderung: Anforderungen an eine inklusive Frühpädagogik; eine Expertise der Weiterbildungsinitiative Frühpädagogische Fachkräfte (WiFF).* In *WIFF-Expertisen Inklusion* (Vol. 33). München: Deutsches Jugendinstitut.

Jones, E. A., & Carr, E. G. (2004). Joint attention in children with autism: Theory and intervention. *Focus on Autism and Other Developmental Disabilities, 19*(1), 13–26. doi:10.1177/10883576040190010301

Lave, J., & Wenger, E. (1991). *Situated learning: Legitimate peripheral participation: Learning in doing.* Cambridge, England: Cambridge University Press.

Leinonen, J., & Sintonen, S. (2014). Productive participation: Children as active media producers in kindergarten. *Nordic Journal of Digital Literacy, 9*(3), 216–236.

Marci-Boehncke, G. (2019). Professionalisierung in der frühkindlichen Bildung. In I. Bosse, J.-R. Schluchter, & I. Zorn (Eds.), *Handbuch Inklusion und Medienbildung* (1. Auflage, pp. 288–296). Weinheim, Germany: Beltz Juventa.

Mayring, P. (2015). *Qualitative Inhaltsanalyse: Grundlagen und Techniken.* Weinheim, Germany: Beltz.

Meister, D. M., Friedrichs-Liesenkötter, H., Keller, K., Pielsticker, A., & Temps, T. T. (2012). *Chancen und Potenziale digitaler Medien zur Umsetzung des Bildungsauftrags in Kindertageseinrichtungen in NRW* [Forschungsbericht der Gesellschaft für Medienpädagogik und Kommunikationskultur (GMK) und der Universität Paderborn]. Paderborn: Gesellschaft für Medienpädagogik und Kommunikationskultur (GMK), Universität Paderborn, Germany.

Ministry of Family Affairs, Children, Youth, Culture, and Sports (MFKJKS). (2014). *Alltagsintegrierte Sprachbildung und Beobachtung im Elementarbereich – Grundlagen für Nordrhein-Westfalen.* Retrieved from www.kita.nrw.de/fachkraefte-fachberatung/sprachliche-bildung

Ministry of Family Affairs, Children, Youth, Culture, and Sports (MFKJKS) (Ed.). (2016). *Bildungsgrundsätze: Mehr Chancen durch Bildung von Anfang an; Grundsätze zur Bildungsförderung für Kinder von 0 bis 10 Jahren in Kindertagesbetreuung und Schulen im Primarbereich in Nordrhein-Westfalen.* Freiburg, Germany: Herder.

Preiser, W. F. E., & Ostroff, E. (2001). *Universal design handbook.* New York, NY: McGraw-Hill.

Renninger, K. A., Hidi, S., & Krapp, A. (Eds.). (1992). *The role of interest in learning and development*. Hillsdale, NJ: Erlbaum.

Rice, M. L. (1993). Social consequences of specific language impairment. In H. Grimm & H. Skowronek (Eds.), *Language acquisition problems and reading disorders: Aspects of diagnosis and intervention* (pp. 111–128). Berlin, Germany: de Gruyter.

Ritchhart, R. (2002). *Intellectual character: What it is, why it matters, and how to get it*. San Francisco, CA: Jossey-Bass.

Roboom, S. (2017). *Mit Medien kompetent und kreativ umgehen: Basiswissen & Praxisideen. Kita kompakt*. Weinheim, Germany: Beltz Nikolo.

Rogoff, B. (2003). *The cultural nature of human development*. New York, NY: Oxford University Press.

Sandvik, M., Smørdal, O., & Østerud, S. (2012). Exploring iPads in practitioners' repertoires for language learning and literacy practices in kindergarten. *Nordic Journal of Digital Literacy, 7*(3), 204–221.

Schluchter, J.-R. (Ed.). (2015). *Medienbildung als Perspektive für Inklusion: Modelle und Reflexionen für die pädagogische Praxis*. München, Germany: kopaed.

Shanahan, T., & Lonigan, C. J. (2010). The national early literacy panel: A summary of the process and the report. *Educational Researcher, 39*(4), 279–285. doi:10.3102/0013189X10369172

Six, U., & Gimmler, R. (2007). Die Förderung von Medienkompetenz im Kindergarten: Eine empirische Studie zu Bedingungen und Handlungsformen der Medienerziehung. In *Schriftenreihe Medienforschung der Landesanstalt für Medien Nordrhein-Westfalen* (Vol. 57). Berlin, Germany: Vistas.

Stephenson, J., & Limbrick, L. (2015). A review of the use of touch-screen mobile devices by people with developmental disabilities. *Journal of Autism and Developmental Disorders, 45*(12), 3777–3791. doi:10.1007/s10803-013-1878-8.

Thaler, A., & Zorn, I. (2010). Issues of doing gender and doing technology: Music as an innovative theme for technology education. *European Journal of Engineering Education, 35*(4), 445–454. Retrieved from www.informaworld.com/10.1080/0 3043797.2010.490578

Vandenbroeck, M., & Bouverne-De Bie, M. (2006). Children's agency and educational norms: A tensed negotiation. *Childhood, 13*(1), 127–143. doi:10.1177/ 0907568206059977

Wagner, P. (Ed.). (2013). *Handbuch Inklusion: Grundlagen vorurteilsbewusster Bildung und Erziehung* (rev. 3rd ed). Freiburg im Breisgau, Germany: Herder.

Wirts, C., Egert, F., & Reber, K. (2017). Early Literacy in deutschen Kindertageseinrichtungen. Eine Analyse der Häufigkeit von Literacy-Aktivitäten im Kita-Alltag. *Forschung Sprache* (2), 96–106.

Zorn, I. (2019). Berufsfeld Frühkindliche Bildung. In I. Bosse, J.-R. Schluchter, & I. Zorn (Eds.), *Handbuch Inklusion und Medienbildung* (1. Auflage, pp. 104–112). Weinheim, Germany: Beltz Juventa.

Zorn, I., Justino, J., Schneider, A., & Schönenberg, J. (2016). Potentials of digital technology for participation of special needs children in kindergarten. In K. Miesenberger, C. Bühler, & P. Penaz (Eds.), *Computers helping people with special needs: 15th international conference, ICCHP 2016, Linz, Austria, July 13–15, 2016, proceedings, part I: Series: Lecture notes in computer science* (9758, pp. 301–304). Cham, Germany: Springer International Publishing. doi:10.1007/978-3-319-41267-2_41

Chapter 4

The caregiver's role in keeping a child–robot interaction going

Katharina J. Rohlfing, Angela Grimminger, and Britta Wrede

Introduction

Looking at young children, they seem to be masters of exploration in their curiosity about the world. However, when we zoom out from the individual child, we see that children's exploration is almost always embedded in a social environment. Social relations are, accordingly, one of the crucial forces driving children's learning. They offer not only an environment for learning but also guidance and interpretation—crucial advantages of learning that is social (Feinman, 1985).

This guidance is important, especially in situations that appear unfamiliar to children. When, for example, novel objects are introduced to them or they are addressed by an unfamiliar interaction partner, children depend on their caregivers' interpretation to make sense of the new situation and act appropriately. In developmental psychology, this phenomenon has been called "social referencing" (Feinman, 1982, p. 445). We are referring to this phenomenon because we want to point to several aspects that emerge in a situation in which a child interacts with a robot. Social robots have proven educational potential for children (Belpaeme et al., 2013; Kory-Westlund, Jeong, & Breazeal, 2013). Through having a body, robots can interact with children multimodally—an advantage that clearly differentiates these from other technical devices (see also Chapters 5 and 7). In addition, studies on child–robot interaction have demonstrated improvements in children's language skills when robots are applied systematically; they have reported progress not only in vocabulary and learning new words (Kory-Westlund & Breazeal, 2019; Movellan, Eckhardt, Virnes, & Rodriguez, 2009; Vogt, de Haas, de Jong, Baxter, & Krahmer, 2017) but also in the narrative skills of 3- to 4-year-olds (Fridin, 2014) and in an increased emotional vocabulary of 6-year-olds (Leite et al., 2017). However, in their critical review of the educational effects of robots on children's language learning, Kanero and colleagues (2018; see also Chapter 7) concluded that more research is needed to confirm that the current evidence cannot be attributed solely to the novelty of the robot as a teaching device, and the curiosity and thus learning motivation this fosters.

In contrast to studies on child – robot interaction, research on social robotics focuses on integrating artificial intelligence to enable a robot to learn how to adapt its behavior toward a human interaction partner (e.g., Hemminghaus & Kopp, 2018). Such approaches assume implicitly that the human interaction partner has a complete model of how this interaction should proceed. Hence, they expect the human interaction partner to shape the interaction.

Whereas for older children – who have been at the focus of research – a social robot might increase motivation, this may not be the case for younger children. They may well perceive a robot as an unknown interaction partner, thereby finding themselves in a situation in which they need guidance from their caregivers. Recognizing that social referencing might be an important phenomenon in child–robot interaction, in this chapter, we analyze whether guidance provided by parents is necessary in this particular setting, and how such guidance might help to resolve communicative breakdowns in child–robot interactions. In the first part of this chapter, we give an overview of the phenomenon of social referencing before summarizing research on how caregivers support children's use of media such as watching TV. Studies on media such as TV are relevant because they reveal how caregivers scaffold children in understanding and dealing with technical devices. In contrast to such existing research, child–robot interaction is a new field that has only just begun to be investigated from an interdisciplinary perspective (Belpaeme et al., 2013). Currently, this field is focusing on how children can learn from and within this setting, and research hardly ever takes a broader view on caregivers or educators as a part of the social learning environment (Siebert, Tolksdorf, Rohlfing, & Zorn, 2019).

Social referencing

In 1987, Hornik, Risenhoover, and Gunnar investigated how infants' responses to a new toy depend on the mother's affective communication. The study confirmed the social referencing hypothesis, suggesting that children's emotions in response to the physical world are influenced by social partners (Feinman, 1982). According to their hypothesis, the term *social referencing* captures the phenomenon that children's perception of objects, events, or people seems to be biased by an emotional attitude that the children adopt from caregivers who communicate their own emotions. For example, when seeing their caregivers being enthusiastic about a new toy, children were more likely to approach and explore it than when seeing a caregiver being averse to it. Moreover, this phenomenon seems to be more pronounced when conditions are highly ambiguous or uncertain. Feinman (1982, p. 446) proposes that social referencing takes place when reality is "socially constructed," and a child acts on the basis of an interpretation provided by another person. This construction is achieved by a social interaction consisting of nonverbal and verbal exchanges. Kauschke and Klann-Delius (2010) analyzed rich verbal input offered by caregivers in a situation in which social referencing took place. They found that caregivers unfold a specific, regulatory discourse to convey properties of the referent as well as their emotional attitude toward it. This discourse seems relevant for the child's feelings toward the referent. As a result, infants respond to the novel circumstance in accordance with their parents' affective display (Hornik, Risenhoover, & Gunnar, 1987). Interestingly, a negative parental affect seems to regulate the child more immediately than a positive display. Feinman (1982) proposed that this is not just restricted to infants, but that people in general use other persons' interpretations to form a better understanding of a given situation.

Caregivers' support of children's use of media

Research on children's use of media has also studied the parents' involvement (e.g., Barr & Nichols Linebarger, 2017, for an extensive overview). We summarize this research by proposing that infants and children benefit from adults introducing a practice. By practice, we mean a way to consume a medium, beginning with what to attend to and proceeding to the construction of meaning. For example, the practice of watching TV contains how to make the medium available (switching on the device), how to select the content, how to pick up the important information and, finally, how to understand the storyline. Whereas how to make a medium available is easy to achieve, children's understanding and learning of the content presented benefit significantly from adults introducing them to not only a storyline but also the nature of the information available via this medium (Moses, 2008). For watching TV, the terms *coviewing* and *mediation* have been introduced to capture the involvement of an adult as "an interpreter of what a medium transfers and how to use it" (Moses, 2008, p. 35; see also, e.g., Lerner, 2017) who also limits the time for its consumption and provides explanations (Pempek & Lauricella, 2017). Whereas mediation refers to an active intervention, coviewing captures the presence of a caregiver who does not necessarily have to intervene (Pempek & Lauricella, 2017). The explanation for why children benefit from a sensitive adult coviewing with them is that caregivers are tuned to their children's cognitive and linguistic competencies (e.g., Snow, 1977) and are experienced in interpreting the world for their children (Hornik et al., 1987). Therefore, they succeed in directing children toward content that becomes "attention-worthy" (Troseth, Strouse, & Johnson, 2017, p. 45) by drawing connections to the child's prior experience, 'translating' the content presented via this medium to the child's needs, interests, and past events, thereby individualizing her or his viewing experience (Pempek & Lauricella, 2017, p. 59). Although research suggests that individualizing the viewing experience can foster learning (see Pempek & Lauricella, 2017, for a summary), there are some important limits: Until 30 months of age, children do not transfer the learning content from the viewing experience to the real world. Moreover, there has been hardly any research on how far caregivers can support such a transfer intuitively, and how this support changes with age. Despite these gaps in research, studies generally recommend and support the active involvement of caregivers in the context of media (Pempek & Lauricella, 2017, p. 69). In addition to tailoring an interaction to a child's interests and possibilities, this translation process offers a welcome opportunity for a verbal exchange in which children receive comments and feedback and use these to process the storyline, to generate a form of understanding for it, and to learn new vocabulary (Diergarten & Nieding, 2012; Lemish & Rice, 1986). It appears that especially young children have a strong desire to share their emotions and thus the need to have their experience interpreted by their caregivers.

Social robots in interaction with children

Intrinsically, young children prioritize social interactions (Walter-Laager et al., 2016), and they find them more attractive than interactions with technical devices. Interaction with a robot, however, can be considered as both media consumption and a social interaction. It should be noted here that currently, robots are applied only in school education (see Anwar, Bascou, Menekse, & Kardgar, 2019, for a recent review), and only a few pilot studies have been conducted in early education (e.g., Fridin, 2014; Kory-Westlund & Breazeal, 2019; Tanaka, Cicourel, & Movellan, 2007). Overall, however, we lack insights into how kindergarten teachers could manage to apply robotic technology to promote early literacy. Taken as a technology, the robot can be viewed as a medium that is capable of a behavior that is programmed. Thus, children can consume the behavior by, for example, playing a game with a robot. However, in contrast to a vacuum cleaner, a robot that is capable of interaction behavior is also social. Belpaeme et al. (2013) report that children "typically do not see a robot as a mechatronic device running a computer program, but attribute characteristics to the robot which are typically expected to be attributed to living systems" (p. 452; see also Breazeal et al., 2016). The observation that children might consider the robot as a living system is relevant when it comes to raising further questions about whether a child–robot interaction might be ethically problematic. This is not just because of deceiving children by creating the illusion of a social partner (Sharkey, 2016); but more concretely, because such an illusion of a robot being a social partner comes hand in hand with the illusion of a particular (interactive) competence. A robot that is too good at emulating an interactive behavior of a human can evoke too high expectations about an interaction as well as emotional attachment in children. However, because robotic technology and the design of the interaction still lack some crucial developments such as children's speech recognition (see Chapter 5; Kennedy, Baxter, & Belpaeme, 2017), there is a risk that children will experience some flaws in the interaction, and that this will result in either learning about social skills being impeded (Sharkey, 2016, p. 290) or negative experience with artificial intelligence (AI) technology.

Interestingly, only Kauschke and Klann-Delius (2010) have looked at how children react to a robot as a novel object and how caregivers help them to process this experience. In social robotic studies, in contrast, the focus of investigation has been on children without taking the role of caregivers into account. This approach is problematic with respect to the research ethics of child–robot interaction studies because the following concern arises: If children regulate their emotions within an interaction with the caregiver, then a situation in which they are left without a caregiver might discomfort them. Clearly, we need more insights into how important the role of a caregiver is when children interact with a robot, and what kind of support children expect when the interaction breaks down. This was our motivation for the following study.

Hypotheses

For our investigation and with respect to the question regarding the importance of the role of the caregiver, we formulated two alternative hypotheses: Current studies on child–robot interaction strongly suggest that children consider the robot as a social partner who can provide them with new information (Breazeal et al., 2016). For this reason, it may well be that children will experience a smooth interaction (Vulchanova, Baggio, Cangelosi, & Smith, 2017) and not require any assistance from their caregiver (Hypothesis 1). Alternatively, following Kennedy and colleagues' (2017) finding that current robotic technology is still not adapted to the child's way of communication (see also Chapter 5), children might be timid and anxious (Vogt et al., 2017) and thus require a lot of support from their caregivers, not only for their emotional regulation (social referencing) but also to keep the interaction ongoing (Hypothesis 2). In fact, in a recent study, the presence of an adult person sitting next to the child during a warm-up phase was reported to positively motivate children in their responses to a robot (Vogt et al., 2017). Further, in their pilot study of a child–robot interaction in a book-reading situation, Grimminger and Rohlfing (2017) observed that in cases of communicative breakdown, the child requested assistance from an adult who then mediated the interaction.

Concerning the question of what kind of support children expect when an interaction breaks down, we anticipated behavior similar to that observed in coviewing. More specifically, it seems reasonable to 'translate' some of the actions of the robot in order to make them more relevant for the child. In addition, because the study is about a joint task that the robot performs with the child, we expected parents to scaffold the child's behavior. Scaffolding behavior has been observed in task-oriented adult–child interactions in which an adult provides contingent support based on both the child's performance and her or his cognitive and linguistic abilities. In other words, the adult increases or reduces assistance (Wood, Bruner, & Ross, 1976). The goal of scaffolding behavior is to allow a child to participate in an interaction, and to contribute to a task, first with the support of an adult but, in the end, independently and in a self-regulated way (Mermelshtine, 2017; Scharlach, 2008). Thus, scaffolds are temporary. The notion of scaffolding is special in that it emphasizes that it is not just support or assistance given by a more competent partner, but learning that is co-constructed by both the learner, who signals her or his individual level of readiness, and the more competent partner, who adapts accordingly and provides support just above the learner's cognitive or linguistic abilities (Amerian & Mehri, 2014).

Method

In our study, we analyze the data from a child–robot interaction reported by Lücking, Rohlfing, Wrede, and Schilling (2016).

Participants

From the original sample of 12 children, we excluded 2 children; the first because of fuzziness (i.e., not willing to interact), and the second because of repeated technical failure. The mean age of the remaining 10 children was 59 months (range: 51–65 months, SD = 4.9 months). The children and their parents were recruited from the Bielefeld region (North Rhine-Westphalia, Germany) and invited to come to the laboratory at Bielefeld University. Participants were reimbursed with a book for their child.

Procedure

The setting is depicted in Figure 4.1. The caregiver sat next to or behind the child, who interacted with the robot in the middle of the room. A session in this study lasted around 10 minutes for each child and consisted of several parts: (1) the introduction, in which the robot asked for the participant's name and announced that it would like to play with the child; (2) an elicitation of bodily contact with the robot to start the game, in which the robot invited the child to touch its head, saying "If you are ready to start, you can touch the blue light on my head"; (3) a guessing game in which the robot introduced the child to the game, in which the robot then started to play some animals' sounds and the child

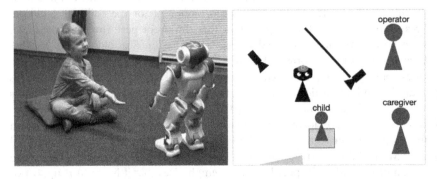

Figure 4.1 The setting: The child's place was marked by a cushion. The caregiver sat next to the child. The operator was partially visible to the child

had to recognize and label the animals; and (4) a joint attention game in which the robot pointed to some pictures in the room, and the child was expected to follow the robot's pointing gesture.

Robot

In the study, we used the NAO platform. NAO is a humanoid robot with a height of 58 cm and 25 degrees of freedom in 25 joints in its arms, fingers, legs, feet, neck, and head. These joints allow it to walk, sit, stand up, and move its arms and fingers to produce pointing or iconic gestures as well as head movements for gaze behavior. This enables NAO to support smooth, human-like movements. The sensors consist of two cameras (one for face detection and one for obstacle avoidance during walking), touch sensors on its head and torso, and microphones. Based on these sensors, the robot was programmed to react to the child's speech and some of its movements. Whereas in many child–robot studies, the robot is controlled by an operator (this kind of research is called a "Wizard-of-Oz study") as summarized in Riek (2012), the present study used a fully autonomous robot that recognized the child's verbal behavior, tracked the child's face, and guided the child through the interactive game sequence via a state-based interaction model (see Lücking et al., 2016, for more technical details).

Coding

The focus of the present analysis is on the guessing game in which the child was already familiarized with the robot and had a clear role to play within the interaction. Altogether, the robot offered 10 sounds, so the child could participate in 10 trials. For an exact analysis of the success of the interaction, we defined a three-step unit of analysis (see Figure 4.2): The robot presents the sound, the child responds verbally, and the robot evaluates the trial.

This unit reflects the verbal turn-taking found in studies on child–robot interaction. Turn-taking refers to a rapid exchange that takes place within verbal communication by using short turns (Levinson, 2016). Verbal behavior was studied as the core of the coding unit because the robot was programmed only to perceive and react to the child's verbal behavior.

With this unit, we could evaluate whether children responded to the robot asking for the animal's name during exactly that timeslot in the interaction for

Figure 4.2 Unit of analysis in the guessing game

which the robot was programmed to perceive any verbal answer. In contrast, during other timeslots (e.g., while the robot was asking the child), the robot was unable to perceive the child's verbal behavior (the robot's microphones were turned off when its speakers were switched on). Because the robot was operated semiautomatically and perceived only whether the child provided an answer but was unable to evaluate its correctness, it generated positive feedback each time. For a trial to be rated a success, the child had to respond to the robot's question with a verbal and temporal alignment, and the robot had to perceive this response correctly. Hence, in this scenario, the interaction can break down for two reasons: (1) because the child does not respond to the robot (no direct response or addressing the parent to request help) and (2) because the robot's speech recognition failed. In both situations, a caregiver can provide support to repair the interaction and maintain the flow.

Results

This section is divided into two parts. In the first (*cooperation*), we report on whether and to what extent children cooperated verbally with the robot. In the second (*support*), we report on whether and how caregivers provided support when communication broke down.

Cooperation

First, we focus on a successful unit, i.e., those cases in which children's responses were aligned to the robot both verbally and temporally after it had asked for the animal's name, and in which the robot perceived the children's answers without any repair behavior being needed. Figure 4.3 depicts the numbers of successful

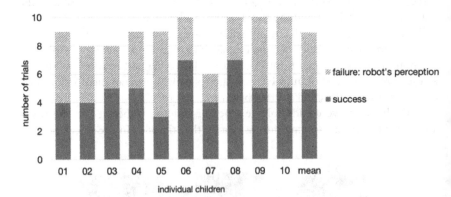

Figure 4.3 Number of units in which children cooperated with the robot: The dark gray bars show the number of successful trials; the hatched bars, trials in which the robot failed to perceive the child's answer

trials as dark gray bars. On average, the children and the robot were able to accomplish 5 (out of 10) trials successfully (range: 3–7 trials). Altogether, 49% of trials were successful.

Next, we focus on when the robot failed to perceive the child's answer. These were cases in which the children were willing to cooperate and answered the robot's question (see Figure 4.2). Results are presented in Figure 4.3 (hatched bars).

On average, 4 trials (out of 10; i.e., 40%; range: 2–5 trials) did not succeed initially because the robot failed to perceive the child's answer. Accordingly, in 40% of trials, children answered the robot's question without any help, but the robot failed to perceive their answer. Combining this with the results on successful trials presented earlier, we can report that in 89% of all trials, children provided a verbal answer to the robot's question and thus cooperated to a great extent.

Because the robot was programmed to perceive and react to the children's verbal answers, our quantitative results focus on verbal turn-taking within an interaction. However, qualitative observations revealed that children managed some turns multimodally (see Rohlfing, Leonardi, Nomikou, Rączaszek-Leonardi, & Hüllermeier, 2019, for the scientific background to this multimodal phenomenon). For example, in one case, the robot asked a question, and the girl started to produce an "ahm" as well as a 'thinking gesture'—that is, she moved her hand toward her chin and mouth, clearly indicating that she was thinking about the answer and therefore had to prolong her turn. Unfortunately, the technology being used was unable to perceive a nonverbally performed turn.

Support

Looking at all trials (10 trials by each of 10 children, resulting in 100 trials), there were 40 in which the robot did not perceive the child's very first answer. However, in 28 of these trials, children were able to repair the interaction by themselves without any intervention by the caregiver. More specifically, it seems that there was a problem with timing the child's turn to the robot's perception: Children answered before the robot finished the question. Repair behavior was either done spontaneously by the children, that is, after the robot finished, some children repeated their answers; or it was initiated by the robot, that is, it repeated the question, leading to a better timing of the children's answers. We will return to this timing problem in the discussion. When repair behavior was taken into account, 79% of all trials were successful (M = 8 trials).

We will now turn to the cases in which children did not respond verbally to the robot and neither the child nor the robot was able to repair the interaction. In 21% of trials, the verbal child–robot communication broke down (see Figure 4.4; hatched and black units on top of the bars), thus giving caregivers the opportunity to provide support.

As Figure 4.4 shows, seven children in our sample (indicated by hatched and black units) experienced a minimum of one or a maximum of three trials (as is

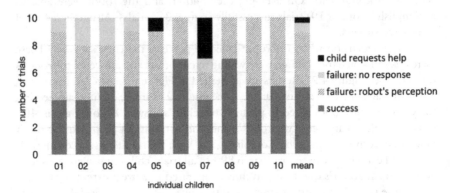

Figure 4.4 Number of unsuccessful units because interaction broke down (indicated in light gray and black units on top of the bars)

the case for Child 07) that were not successful. Whereas four of the children did not respond verbally, three of them turned explicitly to the caregiver and requested help. Some caregivers provided support even though the child did not request help explicitly.

Next, we turn to the question regarding what kind of support the caregivers offered. Table 4.1 presents an overview of the different types of support provided.

Looking at the different types of support, we propose that they fit into two main categories. The first category refers to different forms of instructions. It comprises suggestions about how to cope with the robot's perception (e.g., *You have to speak louder!* or *Say it again!*). An explanation for this type of instruction can be twofold; on the one hand, caregivers could be aware of some of the problems that the technology might have when perceiving a human voice, and on the other hand, caregivers might simply use the repair strategies they usually apply in human–human communication (e.g., with elderly people) and advise their children accordingly. Another type of suggestion concerning the robot's perception is about how to improve the timing of the child's response (e.g., *You have to wait a little longer!*). As stated previously, the appropriate timing of the child's answer to the robot was problematic because children often answered while the robot was still asking the question. Obviously then, some caregivers were able to identify exactly this problem in the dialogue and provide concrete metacommunicative instructions to the child on how to cope with it.

The second category of caregiver support comprises a way of scaffolding a child's correct answer. As already mentioned in the introduction, scaffolding behavior refers to the caregiver's way of engaging the child's active role in an interaction by considering her or his linguistic and cognitive abilities. We noted three different forms of such scaffolding. First, caregivers just repeated the robot's question, thereby facilitating the child's perception of it by framing it

Table 4.1 Type of support provided by caregivers

Type of support provided by caregivers	Examples
Instructing on specific behavior	
How to cope with robot's perception	*You have to speak louder!*
How to improve the timing of child's response	*You have to wait a little longer!*
Scaffolding the correct answer	
By repeating the robot's question	
By providing a hint	*Sounds like a big cat!*
By negotiating the correct answer in caregiver–child interaction	

within a familiar voice or prosodic marking. This gave the child a further chance to respond to the question and succeed in the task. Second, caregivers provided some hints about the correct answer (e.g., *Sounds like a big cat!* or *Maybe a pig?*). Note that the hint, *Maybe a pig?* gives the answer in the frame of a question, leaving it up to the child to reuse it within her or his own interaction with the robot. Third, we could observe some kind of negotiating of the correct answer to the robot's question in a preliminary caregiver–child interaction. This indicates that a child would prefer to turn to the parent rather than to the robot to check her or his answer. What caregivers did in such a situation was to confirm the answer and motivate their child to give the correct answer to the robotic partner. Clearly, the familiar mother–child interaction was taken as a resource with which to encourage the child to go back to the interaction with the robot and accomplish the task with new ideas about the correct answer.

Summing up the results on support provided to children in the child–robot interaction, we wish to highlight the fact that our observations contradict the first hypothesis claiming that caregivers' strategies will be similar to coviewing – a form of translating the actions in response to the robot and making them more relevant. Instead, we found support for differentiated scaffolding behavior. Caregivers instructed their children in terms of how to coordinate their behavior better with what the robot was perceiving (as a basis for smooth interaction), or they suggested the correct answer in order to maintain the child's contact with the robotic partner. In this way, they were helpful for the children who were then able to fulfill the task.

Discussion

Cooperation with the robot

Caregivers' behavior is crucial when children face new situations and have to cope with new tasks (Feinman, 1985). Social referencing has been proposed as a phenomenon that captures young children's need to regulate their emotions toward the physical world (entities, events) by contacting their caregivers (Feinman, 1982). Research on social referencing has confirmed that children's perception of the physical world seems to be biased by an emotional attitude that children adopt from the emotions communicated to them by their caregivers. This effect seems to be more pronounced under conditions with high uncertainty. A robotic partner constitutes a novel situation for a child. Indeed, some effects of child–robot interaction are attributed to the robot being novel and thus interesting to them (e.g., Kanero et al., 2018). A study by Kauschke and Klann-Delius (2010) with children aged 15 to 21 months used a robot to establish a novel situation and elicit a particular form of linguistic input. As characteristics of this rich input, the authors found that positive and negative attitudes and feelings (in both the child and the mother) toward the robot were a prevalent form of 'evaluation' in the interaction (see also Chapter 2 for a consideration of emotional evaluation). Interestingly, in this situation, pure labeling of the novel object (*this is a robot*) was rare. Instead, descriptions of the object's characteristics and functions were produced. Similar to coviewing (Pempek & Lauricella, 2017; Troseth et al., 2017), caregivers also commented on actions to be performed to a great degree. However, we should bear in mind that the robot in Kauschke and Klann-Delius' study was not capable of interactive behavior.

In our study with an interactive robot, we found that caregivers' input was not required, and that 4-year-old children are well able to interact with a robot on their own. In addition, they repaired the interaction when it broke down, revealing their competence in overcoming communication difficulties and applying coping strategies. Hence, our results on cooperation lead us to conclude that children engage in child–robot interaction and apply their interactive abilities in competent ways. Our Hypothesis 2 – that children would require extensive assistance from their caregiver – can thus be rejected, even though there is clear support for the finding that current robotic technology is still not adapted to the child's way of communicating and that interactions break down because of robotic failure. In this respect, technological advances are necessary to adapt to particular ways of communication that seem to be more multimodal in children than in adults. More specifically, the robot in this study was able to react only to a child's verbal behavior. However, turns can also be accomplished nonverbally (e.g., Rohlfing et al., 2019). Referring to our observations earlier, when a child performs a 'thinking gesture,' a robot could acknowledge this by waiting longer or encouraging the child nonverbally. Hence, robotic partners not only have to apply gestures (Kennedy, Baxter et al., 2017) but also have to make use of children's manual and head gestures and process these as crucial communicative signals. This might improve the smoothness of child–robot interaction.

Concerning the necessary developments to improve child–robot interaction, we can also postulate other crucial aspects when designing child-oriented social robots: (1) a better perception of the child to enable the robot to acknowledge a child's intent to communicate. At a minimum, this requires a multimodal component such as lip monitoring (Richter et al., 2016) or lipreading (Freiwald et al.,

2018) that informs the robot that the child is speaking or attempting to speak. However, because children demonstrate a significantly higher variability than adults in their articulation, pronunciation, and prosody, this calls for child-specific speech recognition (Kennedy, Lemaignan et al., 2017). In addition, (2) a better model of the interaction sequence is needed that will allow a robot to anticipate characteristics in interactions with children, such as an initial increase in shy behavior. Accordingly, a robot could use adaptive strategies such as providing greater contingency through multimodal interactive behavior (e.g., Pitsch et al., 2009) and tolerating longer pauses. Finally, (3) child–robot interaction requires highly reactive behavior such as incremental processing that would make it possible for the child to interrupt the robot (e.g., Carlmeyer, Schlangen, & Wrede, 2014).

Support from caregivers

Looking at the support provided by caregivers during our study, we found that only a few children turned to their caregivers and requested help explicitly. When analyzing the way caregivers support their children, we found some differences compared to Kauschke and Klann-Delius' (2010) study. First, the strategies caregivers apply seem to differ from coviewing. Instead of 'translating' the robot's actions to make them relevant to the child, we found more scaffolding in the input. This scaffolding behavior aimed to promote the active participation of the child to improve persistence in the task with a robotic partner. The strategies comprised concrete metacommunicative instructions on how to repair the interaction (repeat question, speak louder) as well as assuring the child that the answer is correct (see also Chapter 2). They all served to maintain the child's contact with the robotic partner. We speculate that assuring the child that her or his answer is correct is one way of lightening the effort of negotiating the contribution. Given this assurance, a child can then return to the interaction: Being now more aware that the task is to provide only one answer, the child may well be able to focus better on the way to deliver it (speak clearly, look at the robot directly).

Taken together, our findings on cooperating with the robot and the support of caregivers strongly suggest that caregivers do not have to adopt an active role when 4-year-olds engage in child–robot interaction. However, and we need to highlight this, caregivers were present in the room throughout the interaction. This places some clear limitations on our analysis, as it is likely that either the mere presence or some nonverbal checking in the form of looking at each other served already as powerful signals indicating that support resources were available to the child and could be drawn upon when necessary. Further studies clearly need to investigate the nonverbal exchanges that take place between children and their caregivers in order to uncover further details on the role of caregivers within child–robot interaction.

Before further investigations can deliver more information on this topic, we strongly suggest that the presence of caregivers is beneficial when children interact with a robot because they can help a child to act within this unusual situation and cope with this particular partner. As with other media, children can and should benefit from jointly focusing attention on and interpreting this technological device (Lerner, 2017; Troseth et al., 2017). Because a robotic partner is new to the caregivers as well, a topic for further investigations should be their role in how to support their children's use of a robotic partner.

In this vein, our study reveals that a robotic partner that is able to interact affords a different behavior in caregivers. It is less about 'translating' the perceived actions into the child's individual world in order to make them relevant (Pempek & Lauricella, 2017; Troseth et al., 2017), and more about providing concrete support with respect to the specifics of the interaction and how to cope with them. This finding offers important educational possibilities for children to experience not only more about interaction and its components but also more about a particular AI technology. Having experienced a child–robot interaction once, opportunities and limitations of AI technology could be discussed with adults. Both opportunities (AI technology in general and interaction with it in particular) have barely been recognized in research so far. However, they might lead to a new role for adults (caregivers, parents, and teachers) in not only assisting their children in a task but also in metacommunicatively reflecting with them on what elements the interaction consists of (e.g., by pointing out that perception of voice is crucial for receiving an answer) and considering possible technological improvements (e.g., by pointing to the fact that the robot could be programmed in a different way). After recently conducting an extensive child–robot study on word learning, we have now just started to explore caregivers as a new resource in children's technological thinking (Tolksdorf, Siebert, & Rohlfing, 2019). By contributing to knowledge about interaction (metacommunicative knowledge) as well as critical technical thinking, such reflections about AI technology might provide not only interesting and enjoyable but also educationally important opportunities to advance children's awareness of digital entities in their world.

Three key considerations for parents, educators, and producers

- Social robots have proved to have educational potential for children. Because they have a body, they can interact with children multimodally—an advantage that clearly differentiates these from other technical devices.
- With any kind of new technology, children need to be introduced to it by sensitive caregivers who are aware that children adopt an emotional attitude toward an interaction partner and need to be shown some strategies regarding how to cope with breakdowns in interaction.
- In our study in which caregivers were present in the same room, most 4-year-olds interacted with the robot on their own. However, the breakdowns – mostly caused by the robot (in 40% of exchanges) – could be addressed by programming a robot to perceive children's multimodal responses.

Acknowledgment

We thank all the parents and children who participated in this study. We also thank our colleagues, Isabel Zorn, Dorothea Kolossa, and Ilona Horwath, for extensive discussions about different roles that a robot can take within an interaction. In addition, we are grateful to Paul Höchter for his work on the coding system applied in this study.

References

Amerian, M., & Mehri, E. (2014). Scaffolding in sociocultural theory: Definition, steps, features, conditions, tools, and effective consideration. *Scientific Journal of Review, 3*, 756–765.

Anwar, S., Bascou, N. A., Menekse, M., & Kardgar, A. (2019). A systematic review of studies on educational robotics. *Journal of Pre-College Engineering Education Research (J-PEER), 9*(2), 1–15. doi:10.7771/2157-9288.1223

Barr, R., & Nichols Linebarger, D. (Eds.). (2017). *Media exposure during infancy and early childhood: The effects of content and context on learning and development.* New York, NY: Springer.

Belpaeme, T., Baxter, P., Greeff, J. de, Kennedy, J., Read, R., Looije, R., . . . Zelati, M. C. (2013). Child-robot interaction: Perspectives and challenges. In G. Herrmann, M. Pearson, A. Lenz, P. Bremner, A. Spiers, & U. Leonards (Eds.), *Social robotics* (pp. 452–459). Chem, Switzerland: Springer.

Breazeal, C., Harris, P. L., DeSteno, D., Kory-Westlund, J. M., Dickens, L., & Jeong, S. (2016). Young children treat robots as informants. *Topics in Cognitive Science, 8*, 481–491.

Carlmeyer, B., Schlangen, D., & Wrede, B. (2014). Towards closed feedback loops in HRI: Integrating InproTK and PaMini. *Proceedings of the 2014 workshop on multimodal, multi-party, real-world human-robot interaction* (pp. 1–6). New York, NY: ACM Press.

Diergarten, A. K., & Nieding, G. (2012). Einfluss des Fernsehens auf die Entwicklung der Sprachfähigkeit. *Sprache Stimme Gehör, 36*, 25–29.

Feinman, S. (1982). Social referencing in infancy. *Merrill-Palmer Quarterly, 28*, 445–470.

Feinman, S. (1985). Emotional expression, social referencing and preparedness for learning in infancy. In G. Zivin (Ed.), *The development of expressive behavior: Biology-environment interactions* (pp. 291–318). Orlando, FL: Academic Press.

Freiwald, J., Karbasi, M., Zeiler, S., Melchior, J., Kompella, V., Wiskott, L., & Kolossa, D. (2018). Utilizing slow feature analysis for lipreading. *Speech Communication; 13th ITG-Symposium* (pp. 1–5). Oldenburg, Germany: VDE.

Fridin, M. (2014). Storytelling by a kindergarten social assistive robot: A tool for constructive learning in preschool education. *Computers & Education, 70*, 53–64.

Grimminger, A., & Rohlfing, K. J. (2017). "Can you teach me?": Children teaching new words to a robot in a book reading scenario. *Proceedings of the 6th International Workshop on Child Computer Interaction* (pp. 28–33). Glasgow, UK.

Hemminghaus, J., & Kopp, S. (2018). Adaptive behavior generation for child-robot-interaction. *HRI Pioneers Workshop at ACM/IEEE Human-Robot Interaction (HRI 2018).* Chicago, IL, USA. doi:10.1145/3173386.3176916

Hornik, R., Risenhoover, N., & Gunnar, M. (1987). The effects of maternal positive, neutral, and negative affective communications on infant responses to new toys. *Child Development, 58,* 937–944.

Kanero, J., Geçkin, V., Oranç, C., Mamus, E., Küntay, A. C., & Göksun, T. (2018). Social robots for early language learning: Current evidence and future directions. *Child Development Perspectives, 12*(3), 146–151.

Kauschke, C., & Klann-Delius, G. (2010). How mothers introduce a new, surprising object: A study on early word learning in discourse. *Proceedings of the XIV European Conference on Developmental Psychology–ECDP* (pp. 117–122). Vilnius, Lithuania.

Kennedy, J., Baxter, P., & Belpaeme, T. (2017). The impact of robot tutor nonverbal social behavior on child learning. *Frontiers in ICT, 4,* 6.

Kennedy, J., Lemaignan, S., Montassier, C., Lavalade, P., Irfan, B., Papadopoulos, F., Senft, E., & Belpaeme, T. (2017). Child speech recognition in human-robot interaction: Evaluations and recommendations. In *Proceedings of the 2017 ACM/ IEEE international conference on human-robot interaction* (pp. 82–90). New York, NY: ACM Press.

Kory-Westlund, J. M., & Breazeal, C. L. (2019). A long-term study of young children's rapport, social emulation, and language learning with a peer-like robot playmate in preschool. *Frontiers in Robotics and AI, 6,* 81.

Kory-Westlund, J. M., Jeong, S., & Breazeal, C. L. (2013). Robotic learning companions for early language development. In *Proceedings of the 15th ACM on international conference on multimodal interaction* (pp. 71–72). New York: ACM Press.

Leite, I., McCoy, M., Lohani, M., Ullman, D., Salomons, N., Stokes, C., Rivers, S., & Scassellati, B. (2017). Narratives with robots: The impact of interaction context and individual differences on story recall and emotional understanding. *Frontiers in Robotics and AI, 4,* 29.

Lemish, D., & Rice, M. L. (1986). Television as a talking picture book: A prop for language acquisition. *Journal of Child Language, 13,* 251–274.

Lerner, C. (2017). Context matters: How co-using screen media impacts young children: Commentary on chapter 11. In R. Barr & D. Nichols Linebarger (Eds.), *Media exposure during infancy and early childhood: The effects of content and context on learning and development* (pp. 195–203). Cham, Switzerland: Springer.

Levinson, S. C. (2016). Turn-taking in human communication: Origins and implications for language processing. *Trends in Cognitive Sciences, 20,* 6–14.

Lücking, P., Rohlfing, K., Wrede, B., & Schilling, M. (2016). Preschoolers' engagement in social interaction with an autonomous robotic system. *Proceedings of the IEEE Joint Conference on Development and Learning and Epigenetic Robotics* (pp. 210–216). Cergy-Pontoise/Paris.

Mermelshtine, R. (2017). Parent-child learning interactions: A review of the literature on scaffolding. *British Journal of Educational Psychology, 87,* 241–254.

Moses, A. M. (2008). Impacts of television viewing on young children's literacy development in the USA: A review of the literature. *Journal of Early Childhood Literacy, 8,* 67–102.

Movellan, J., Eckhardt, M., Virnes, M., & Rodriguez, A. (2009). Sociable robot improves toddler vocabulary skills. In *Proceedings of the 4th ACM/IEEE international conference on human robot interaction* (pp. 307–308). La Jolla, CA: ACM Press.

Pempek, T. A., & Lauricella, A. R. (2017). The effects of parent-child interaction and media use on cognitive development in infants, toddlers, and preschoolers. In F. C. Blumberg & P. J. Brooks (Eds.), *Cognitive development in digital contexts* (pp. 53–74). London, England: Academic Press.

Pitsch, K., Kuzuoka, H., Suzuki, Y., Sussenbach, L., Luff, P., & Heath, C. (2009). "The first five seconds": Contingent stepwise entry into an interaction as a means to secure sustained engagement in HRI. *RO-MAN 2009: The 18th IEEE International Symposium on Robot and Human Interactive Communication* (pp. 985–991). Toyama, Japan.

Richter, V., Carlmeyer, B., Lier, F., Meyer zu Borgsen, S., Schlangen, D., Kummert, F., Wachsmuth, S., & Wrede, B. (2016). Are you talking to me?: Improving the robustness of dialogue systems in a multi party HRI scenario by incorporating gaze direction and lip movement of attendees. In *Proceedings of the fourth international conference on human agent interaction* (pp. 43–50). New York, NY: ACM Press.

Riek, L. D. (2012). Wizard of Oz studies in HRI: A systematic review and new reporting guidelines. *Journal of Human-Robot Interaction, 1*(1), 119–136.

Rohlfing, K. J., Leonardi, G., Nomikou, I., Rączaszek-Leonardi, J., & Hüllermeier, E. (2019). Multimodal turn-taking: Motivations, methodological challenges, and novel approaches. *IEEE Transactions on Cognitive and Developmental Systems, 12*, 260–271.

Scharlach, T. D. (2008). START comprehending: Students and teachers actively reading text. *The Reading Teacher, 62*, 20–31.

Sharkey, A. J. C. (2016). Should we welcome robot teachers? *Ethics and Information Technology, 18*, 283–297.

Siebert, S., Tolksdorf, N., Rohlfing, K. J., & Zorn, I. (2019). Raising robotic natives? Persuasive potentials of social robots in early education. *Journal of Communication and Media Studies, 4*(4), 21–35.

Snow, C. E. (1977). The development of conversation between mothers and babies. *Journal of Child Language, 4*, 1–22.

Tanaka, F., Cicourel, A., & Movellan, J. R. (2007). Socialization between toddlers and robots at an early childhood education center. *Proceedings of the National Academy of Sciences, 104*(46), 17954–17958.

Tolksdorf, N. F., Siebert, S., & Rohlfing, K. J. (2019, August). *Parents' view on social robots for language learning.* Poster presented at the International Conference for Development and Learning (ICDL). Oslo, Norway.

Troseth, G. L., Strouse, G. A., & Johnson, C. E. R. (2017). Early digital literacy: Learning to watch, watching to learn. In F. C. Blumberg & P. J. Brooks (Eds.), *Cognitive development in digital contexts* (pp. 29–51). London, England: Academic Press.

Vogt, P., de Haas, M., de Jong, C., Baxter, P., & Krahmer, E. (2017). Child-robot interactions for second language tutoring to preschool children. *Frontiers in Human Neuroscience, 11*, 73.

Vulchanova, M., Baggio, G., Cangelosi, A., & Smith, L. (2017). Editorial: Language development in the digital age. *Frontiers in Human Neuroscience, 11*, 447.

Walter-Laager, C., Brandenberg, K., Tinguely, L., Moschner, B., Schwarz, J., & Pfiffner, M. R. (2016). Interesse von Kleinkindern an unterschiedlichen Sprachlernmedien. *Frühe Bildung, 5*, 40–49.

Wood, D., Bruner, J. S., & Ross, G. (1976). The role of tutoring in problem solving. *Journal of Child Psychology and Psychiatry, 17*, 89–100.

Chapter 5

Beyond words

Children's multimodal responses during word learning with a social robot

Nils F. Tolksdorf and Ulrich J. Mertens

Introduction

Today's children are growing up in a world in which they increasingly encounter digital technologies, and this is happening not only earlier in their development but also more frequently than ever before. Nowadays, young children can handle digital devices such as tablet computers with a high degree of sophistication, and they experience educational apps that offer rich possibilities for collaborative interaction, independent learning, or the fostering of literacy competencies (Flewitt, Messer, & Kucirkova, 2015). In the digital age, technology may offer an opportunity to improve the quality of education and to develop new approaches in the field of pedagogy (Ladel, Knopf, & Weinberger, 2018). One digital technology of growing importance is social robots that are increasingly occupying a place in our society and being integrated progressively into educational practices (Belpaeme, Kennedy, Ramachandran, Scassellati, & Tanaka, 2018).

Social robots offer versatile possibilities to engage children in social interaction. Compared to other digital devices, social robots provide features of social signals that can enrich an interaction (e.g., eye gaze, gestures, or body posture) – features that are crucial for robust and comprehensive learning (Konishi, Kanero, Freeman, Golinkoff, & Hirsh-Pasek, 2014). Therefore, social robots differ from other digital technologies that can be used for language learning, and they allow a transition from physical to social interaction (Mubin, Stevens, Shahid, Mahmud, & Dong, 2013). In light of the benefits of an embodied social agent, research in child–robot interaction (cHRI) has begun to investigate how robots can be used to facilitate learning gains in fields ranging from first- and second-language education (Kory Westlund et al., 2017; Vogt et al., 2019, see also Oranç et al. in Chapter 7) to the promotion of children's growth mindset (Park, Rosenberg-Kima, Rosenberg, Gordon, & Breazeal, 2017) or the support of computational thinking skills (Ioannou & Makridou, 2018). However, in the field of child–robot interaction, especially when the goal is to expand children's vocabulary, current dialogue design – that is, the way in which the interaction between a child and a robot unfolds – is often derived from interaction with adults. In particular, it relies on a turn-taking behavior that is characterized by verbal exchanges

(Levinson, 2016). More specifically, in the sequential organization of interaction, in which children usually expect a behavior contingent to their verbal and non-verbal utterances from their interaction partner, the only response modality that the robot considers is verbal lexical utterances. This unimodal design approach, however, runs counter to research highlighting that turn-taking is a multimodal phenomenon, and that interaction partners use not only verbal utterances but also a host of visual signals to communicate (Holler & Levinson, 2019; Rohlfing, Leonardi, Nomikou, Rączaszek-Leonardi, & Hüllermeier, 2019). In this vein, this study aims to address the question of how children interact multimodally with an artificial interaction partner such as a social robot during a language learning task, which is of particular interest if social robots are intended to be used in educational settings.

Past research has shown that children interact across different modalities and make use of multimodal signals to a high degree, especially when exposed to a complex communicative task – for example, retelling an event or retrieving an unfamiliar word from memory. More specifically, the authors propose that "relative to linguistic expressions, gestures and other visual signals may be easier for children" (Doherty-Sneddon & Kent, 1996, p. 957). Indeed, early verbal children use their pointing gestures to indicate things and events in an interaction (e.g., Rohlfing, Grimminger, & Lüke, 2017), and word learning studies take this nonverbal behavior into account when assessing children's word knowledge. For example, Csibra (2010) tested understanding of newly learned words by asking children to point to a picture of the referent. This approach reflects findings indicating that children are able to represent knowledge nonverbally before they can verbalize it (Doherty-Sneddon & Kent, 1996).

Child–robot interaction research is currently exploring the effects of nonverbal signals. Baxter, Ashurst, Read, Kennedy, and Belpaeme (2017) have shown that the more responsive the nonverbal behavior provided by a robot, the more positive the children's impression of this interaction. This suggests that children are not just responding with nonverbal behavior but are also sensitive to it. In fact, it has been shown that within an interaction in which a robot taught new words to the children, the way that preschool children used the nonverbal resources of this social robot was similar to the way they would use those of a human interlocutor (Kory Westlund et al., 2017). However, so far, the focus has been primarily on investigating which aspects of the robot's multimodal behavior provide advantages within an interaction, rather than on how the children interact and respond multimodally to the robot. In addition, there is hardly any insight into how children's behavior develops over a longer period of time in complex communicative tasks with a robot (Tolksdorf, Mertens, & Rohlfing, 2019). This lack of a long-term perspective is particularly critical because research shows that familiarization with a situation leads children to adapt and change their means of communication – both verbally and nonverbally (Grimminger, Lüke, Ritterfeld, Liszkowski, & Rohlfing, 2016; Marcos, 1991). Nonetheless, current dialogue design is still not adjusted to either the phenomenon of children's multimodal turn-taking or their developmental needs. More specifically, Rohlfing et al. (see Chapter 4) have demonstrated that in a simple game played with a robot, it was the robot rather than the children that caused a breakdown in the interaction, and this was precisely because the robot was programmed in such a way that it could address only children's verbal utterances.

An additional element in the context of multimodal turn-taking is children's verbal nonlexical utterances such as delay markers. These play an important role in interaction with an interlocutor (Van der Wege & Ragatz, 2004). Children use delay markers (e.g., *um* and *uh*) when they are as young as 2 years of age; and 6-year-olds are well aware of the basic use of these signals and apply them in a similar way to adults (Hudson Kam & Edwards, 2008; Van der Wege & Ragatz, 2004). Thus, children's use of delay markers can shed light on their comprehension or their uncertainty within an interaction, and they indicate that a child is either still planning the content of a turn (Hudson Kam & Edwards, 2008) or still searching for a word in memory (Goodwin & Goodwin, 1986).

In the field of child–robot interaction, we know very little about the role of children's use of delay markers when interacting with a social robot, despite being aware of their important functions in human–human interactions. In fact, the picture that emerges hitherto is that research has concentrated on studying the effects when a robot uses a certain multimodal behavior such as delay markers and less on the behavior of the children themselves, or on how the child's behavior develops over multiple interactions with a robot (Kanda, Shiomi, Miyashita, Ishiguro, & Hagita, 2009; Shiwa, Kanda, Imai, Ishiguro, & Hagita, 2008). For example, Wigdor, de Greeff, Looije, and Neerincx (2016) implemented delay markers on NAO robots and let children play a quiz game over two sessions with two different robots. In one session, the children interacted with a robot that used delay markers within the dialogue; in the other session, with a robot that did not use delay markers. In a post-session questionnaire, the authors assessed children's views on the different robots and found that they perceived the robot that used delay markers to be more responsive, human-like, alive, and likable, leading the authors to conclude that delay markers might be a way to "mitigate the negative effects caused by unwanted robot response delays" (Wigdor et al., 2016, p. 224).

Whereas these studies on the effect of different multimodal signals (i.e., the use of delay markers) employed by a social robot are highly valuable because they broaden our understanding of the effects of certain communicative signals in interaction, they often describe only one causal link between the effects of these signals and, for example, the learning gains of the children or the perceived abilities of the robot. In addition, a common key element in this existing work is that these studies aim to improve the interaction and the adaptability of the robot. What is missing, however, is research on the child's communicative behavior within a child–robot interaction. Analyzing such behavior provides the opportunity to design future child–robot dialogue in such a way that the robotic system will be adapted and responsive to the child's multimodal signals, rather than the child needing to adapt to the robot's behavior. So far, little is known about how children respond multimodally in an interaction with a robot and how their behavior develops over a longer period of time.

In sum, when an interaction is designed for children, it needs to consider both verbal and nonverbal ways of turn-taking. Only then will a child–robot interaction allow us to fully assess the children's understanding and the conversational context (Okita, Ng-Thow-Hing, & Sarvadevabhatla, 2011). Thus, our argument is that because current robot dialogue design is unable to monitor the multi-modal behavior of the children sufficiently, the interaction flow suffers from it. Following up on children's turn-taking as a multimodal phenomenon (Levinson, 2016; Rohlfing et al., 2019), our slow-mapping study asked whether a robot needs to consider various multimodal behaviors as responses to its verbal turn. Based on the aforementioned findings that children communicate across differ-ent modalities (Doherty-Sneddon & Kent, 1996) and also change their com-municative behavior with increasing familiarization (Grimminger et al., 2016; Marcos, 1991), we hypothesized that children's reactions would be manifold, and that the means of communication would change in a long-term interaction with a social robot.

Method

Participants

Thirty-one preschool children participated in the study. Data from six children were excluded because they did not attend all sessions or discontinued the inter-action with the robot. Hence, 25 children (13 males and 12 females with a mean age of 5.7 years, $SD = 0.2$, range: 5.3 to 6.0) were included in the final analysis. Collected data were stored securely and not presented in a way that might dis-close individual identities. Children were visited in the familiar environment of their kindergartens. In total, we selected four different kindergarten classes in the state of North Rhine-Westphalia, Germany. In accordance with university ethics procedures for research with children, parents provided written consent prior to their children's participation. Children also provided verbal assent prior to taking part in the interaction with the robot, and they could discontinue the interaction at any time at no disadvantage to themselves. Furthermore, familiar educators were present during the interaction but not actively involved in it.

Experimental procedure

We explored children's multimodal behavior over a long-term period in order to account for the fact that language learning requires repetition and time (Axels-son & Horst, 2014; Rohlfing, Wrede, Vollmer, & Oudeyer, 2016). Additionally, long-term studies are essential to investigate effects of familiarization, especially because many studies have shown that the novelty effect of a robot wears off rapidly (Leite, Martinho, & Paiva, 2013). Thus, children participated in four sessions, each lasting around 15 minutes. Moreover, prior to the first session, an additional introductory session was organized with the whole kindergarten group in order to successfully introduce the robot to the children (Tolksdorf, Siebert, Zorn, Horwath, & Rohlfing, 2020; Vogt, de Haas, de Jong, Baxter, & Krahmer, 2017). The four sessions took place over a period of two weeks, with two to three days between each session. After the introductory session, each child interacted with the robot (NAO) alone and was exposed to four new words (two nouns, two verbs) that were accentuated by iconic gestures and embedded within a story that the robot told to the children. The referent of the novel word was illustrated on the tablet placed next to the robot (see Figure 5.1 for the setup) while it was interacting with the child. Except for the fourth session, the robot told the story in each session. In addition, in each session, both the understanding and the production of the target words were tested by the robot asking the child to point to the correct referent of the word and also to produce the target word.

Whereas the original purpose of the study was to tap into children's long-term language learning, and these results will be reported elsewhere (Mertens &

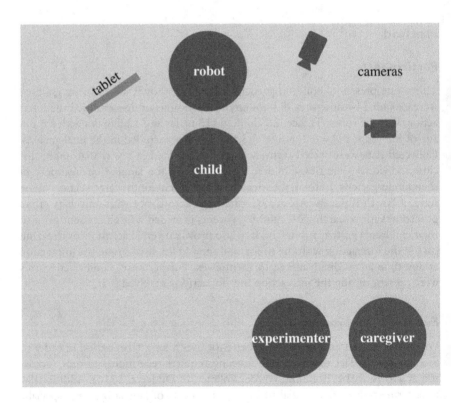

Figure 5.1 Setup of the study

Rohlfing, 2020), our aim here was to investigate children's multimodal behavior in reaction to a challenging communicative task with a robot – namely, to respond to the robot's request to produce the learned words.

Stimuli

The robot used was the NAO from Softbank Robotics. This is a small, toy-like, humanoid robot that is used widely in child–robot interaction studies (Belpaeme et al., 2018; Conti, Cirasa, Di Nuovo, & Di Nuovo, 2019). NAO is 58 cm high with 25 degrees of freedom. None of the children had ever seen the robot before the experiment. The robot was teleoperated by the experimenter, who was also present during the interaction but sat in the background behind the child. Teleoperation was employed to enable the robot to act contingently and to avoid unreliable automatic speech recognition for children's speech (Kennedy et al., 2017). The story told by the robot was developed by Vogt and Kauschke (2017) and has already been applied successfully in a word learning study with preschool children. The story included four target words: two nouns representing rare animal species ("the rail" and "the fennec") and two verbs representing unfamiliar types of movement ("to stalk" and "to creep"). The robot named the target words over the course of the story; and during each naming, the robot performed an iconic gesture that picked up attributes of either the animal or the movement.

Coding

In our analysis, we were interested in children's multimodal response behavior during the pauses that arose immediately after the robot asked the child to produce the learned words. This pause was a signal for the child not only to take the turn but also to answer the request. We chose to analyze this sequence because, in contrast to other parts of the interaction during which the child only listened to the robot, the child was confronted here with the challenge of retrieving the word from memory and responding to the robot. Examining this sequence is particularly relevant because it provides an opportunity to understand how children respond multimodally when the goal is to foster language learning with a social robot. During the production task, the children saw a picture of the referent on a tablet screen. As illustrated in Figure 5.2, we annotated children's multimodal behavior and focused on the verbal utterances and gestural behavior within this sequence of the child–robot interaction.

Therefore, the coding of children's gestural behavior included all communicative gestures such as pointing, head shaking, shoulder shrugging, or deliberation gestures. Coding of children's verbal utterances included the use of delay markers (i.e., vocal nonlexical utterances such as *uh* and *um*). Two coders independently coded 15% of the data. We used Cohen's kappa coefficient to measure intercoder

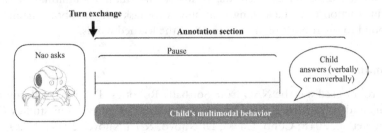

Figure 5.2 Annotation section considered in the analysis

agreement separately for verbal utterances and gestural behavior. The mean value for gestural behavior was κ = 1.0; for verbal utterances, κ = .887.

Results

We present our results in two parts: (1) a description of children's gestural behavior and how that gestural behavior developed over the course of the sessions and (2) a description of children's use of delay markers and their use over sessions. Finally, we report the results on the children's total accumulated multimodal signals.

Analysis of children's gestural behavior

We found that the children used gestures to shape the pauses during which they were expected to take their turn. Observations revealed that they shaped their responses in diverse ways and produced and expressed most gestures during the first session (Session 1) (M = 1.04, SD = 1.56). In Session 2, children used fewer gestures (M = 0.44, SD = 0.70), and continued on this level during Session 3 (M = 0.48, SD = 0.97) and Session 4 (M = 0.33, SD = 1.07). To further explore differences over the course of sessions, we conducted a Friedman two-way ANOVA (Howell, 2017) with the number of gestures as the dependent variable. The ANOVA revealed a significant effect ($p < .01$) and a significant change ($p < .05$) between Session 1 and Session 2, with an effect size of Z = -2.29, r = .46. The data showed a significant decrease in the children's gestural behavior after the first session, possibly indicating that the children initially responded with more modalities, but then become familiar with the situation that the robot considered only verbal turn-taking behavior.

Analysis of children's verbal behavior

Taking a closer look at children's use of verbal nonlexical utterances (i.e., delay markers), we also found a significant change in their production ($p < .05$). According to the Friedman two-way ANOVA, a significant change ($p < .05$) took place between the first and second session with an effect size of $Z = -2.49$, $r = .50$, but there was no significant decrease thereafter. Children reacted most frequently in Session 1 and produced a mean of 1.20 ($SD = 1.52$) delay markers. In Session 2, they expressed a mean of 0.48 ($SD = 0.64$) delay markers, and continued again on this level during Session 3 ($M = 0.52$, $SD = 0.77$) and Session 4 ($M = .46$, $SD = .82$). Table 5.1 presents the descriptive statistics from the analysis of the verbal and gestural behavior of the children.

Analysis of children's multimodal behavior in total

As Figure 5.3 shows, in a second step, we aggregated children's multimodal signals in order to address both verbal (use of delay markers) and nonverbal (use of gestures) behavior in total. To once again explore differences over the course of sessions, we conducted an ANOVA for the dependent variable number of

Table 5.1 Results of the analysis of children's gestural and verbal behavior: means (M) and standard deviation (SD)

	Session 1		Session 2		Session 3		Session 4	
	M	SD	M	SD	M	SD	M	SD
Children's gestural behavior	1.04	1.56	0.44	0.70	0.48	0.97	0.33	1.07
Children's verbal behavior	1.20	1.52	0.48	0.64	0.52	0.77	0.46	0.82

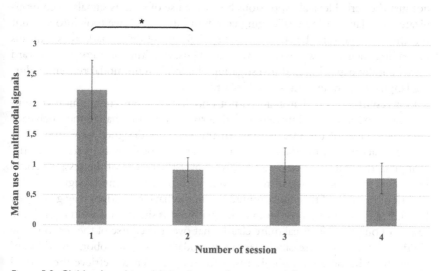

Figure 5.3 Children's multimodal signals over the course of the sessions

Note: *$p < .05$

multimodal signals. The overall ANOVA revealed a significant effect ($p = .001$) with a significant change ($p < .01$) between the first ($M = 2.24$, $SD = 2.39$) and the second session ($M = 0.92$, $SD = 0.98$) with an effect size of $Z = -3.07$, $r = .61$. The number of multimodal signals did not decrease between Sessions 2 and 3 ($M = 1.00$, $SD = 1.35$), but decreased again between Sessions 3 and 4 ($M = 0.79$, $SD = 1.22$).

In summary, by analyzing children's multimodal behavior such as gestures or delay markers, we demonstrated that children used various signals to shape the pauses during which they were expected to take their turn. That might suggest that they know that the turn is theirs, but do not necessarily respond verbally with a lexical utterance. Moreover, the children seemed to adapt to the behavior of the robot and become familiar with the situational demands – that is, the production of the learned word asked for by the robot. More specifically, the children adapted to the situation that the robot considered only turn-taking behavior characterized by verbal utterances. This could be observed in the decrease in gestural behavior and the use of delay markers.

Discussion and conclusions

In this child–robot study, we took a long-term perspective over four sessions in order to explore how preschoolers interacted with a robot peer. More specifically, we analyzed how children responded multimodally to the robot's verbal turn and how their responses changed over the course of the four sessions. Our analysis focused on the sequence in which the robot in the interaction requested the children to produce the learned words. Following the findings that children do not just use verbal lexical expressions but make use of various signals to communicate, especially during challenging communicative tasks, we took into account the children's gestural behavior as well as their use of delay markers as a means of shaping their turn within the dialogue. Thus, our study is a first step toward systematically exploring and investigating children's multimodal responses during language learning with a social robot.

Our results suggest that children not only use different communicative multimodal strategies when interacting with a robot, but also change their behavior over the course of the interactions. In the dialogue designed here, the robot did not react to multimodal signals such as gestures or delay markers. Thus, the change in the children's response behavior over the course of the sessions could be due to the robot's lack of responsiveness to their multimodal signals in this situation. Because of this noncontingent robot behavior, children may give up or become frustrated when communicating within this situation. In this regard, the results of our analysis reveal quite clearly that over the course of the sessions, the children interacted increasingly less multimodally with the robot. In addition, it may have become increasingly easier for the children to retrieve the learned word and respond verbally with a lexical element. Consequently, they were less dependent on alternative modalities such as gestures or delay markers. However, our data show that especially at the beginning of the interactions, it is essential to consider children's multimodal signals in a child–robot dialogue because this is the stage at which they fall back most frequently on various multimodal signals.

Our findings have implications for the future design of child–robot interactions because they demonstrate the importance of addressing children's response behavior beyond verbal lexical utterances, especially in an initial session in which the children first encounter a robot and experience how to interact with it. In this vein, children may use gestures or mark speech difficulties by using delay markers to indicate that they need more time or support within a situation (Van der Wege & Ragatz, 2004). To this end, Ramachandran, Huang, and Scassellati (2017) recently introduced a child–robot dialogue in which the robot provided personalized timing strategies by considering children's individual behavior, and the robot offered more time for the learning activity when needed – which also led to enhanced learning gains. Such approaches, which address the child's behavior within the interaction, could be promising feature that would provide a way to design child–robot interactions in a more child-oriented way. In addition, particularly if social robots are to be used for language learning, it is crucial to consider that children are able to display knowledge nonverbally before they are able to verbalize it (Doherty-Sneddon & Kent, 1996). This emphasizes the particular importance of considering gestural information within an interaction, especially when it comes to recalling a learned word. Thus, a dialogue design needs to consider children's multimodal answers if it is to become responsive and helpful in interaction with a child.

Although more studies need to be conducted on the multimodal behavior of children in longitudinal sessions, this study has taken a first step and delivered results not only on how children react multimodally to a challenging task given by a robot but also on how the signals they give evolve over the long term. In line with the introduction of social robots as new digital tools that could support and expand early childhood education, our findings suggest that in order to develop a multimodal dialogue design, current child–robot dialogues need to go beyond focusing primarily on the verbal modality.

Three key considerations for parents, educators, and producers

- Social robots have the potential to be promising interaction partners due to their embodiment and their ability to use social signals in an interaction. However, current child–robot dialogues are often derived from interaction with adults and rely on turn-taking behavior that is characterized by verbal exchanges.

- This study shows that children interact highly multimodally with a robot and respond to its turn exchange with gestures or nonlexical utterances, especially in first encounters. Over the further course of the sessions, they communicate increasingly less multimodally.

- To become helpful and responsive, digital technologies such as social robots should pay sufficient consideration to both verbal and nonverbal ways of communicating. Only then can they adapt to the nature of multimodal turn taking and be oriented toward children's communicative needs within an interaction.

Acknowledgment

We gratefully thank all the educators and children who participated in this study. The preparation of the chapter was made possible by the Digital Society research program (merits-project to Nils Tolksdorf) funded by the Ministry of Culture and Science of the German State of North Rhine-Westphalia.

References

Axelsson, E. L., & Horst, J. S. (2014). Contextual repetition facilitates word learning via fast mapping. *Acta Psychologica, 152*, 95–99. doi:10.1016/j.actpsy.2014.08.002

Baxter, P., Ashurst, E., Read, R., Kennedy, J., & Belpaeme, T. (2017). Robot education peers in a situated primary school study: Personalisation promotes child learning. *PLoS One, 12*(5), e0178126. doi:10.1371/journal.pone.0178126

Belpaeme, T., Kennedy, J., Ramachandran, A., Scassellati, B., & Tanaka, F. (2018). Social robots for education: A review. *Science Robotics, 3*(21), eaat5954. doi:10.1126/scirobotics.aat5954

Conti, D., Cirasa, C., Di Nuovo, S., & Di Nuovo, A. (2019). "Robot, tell me a tale!": A social robot as tool for teachers in kindergarten. *Interaction Studies, 20*(2), 1–16.

Csibra, G. (2010). Recognizing communicative intentions in infancy. *Mind & Language, 25*(2), 141–168. doi:10.1111/j.1468-0017.2009.01384.x

Doherty-Sneddon, G., & Kent, G. (1996). Visual signals and the communication abilities of children. *Journal of Child Psychology and Psychiatry, 37*(8), 949–959.

Flewitt, R., Messer, D., & Kucirkova, N. (2015). New directions for early literacy in a digital age: The iPad. *Journal of Early Childhood Literacy, 15*(3), 289–310. doi:10.1177/1468798414533560

Goodwin, M., & Goodwin, C. (1986). Gesture and coparticipation in the activity of searching for a word. *Semiotica, 62*, 51–76. doi:10.1515/semi.1986.62.1-2.51

Grimminger, A., Lüke, C., Ritterfeld, U., Liszkowski, U., & Rohlfing, K. J. (2016). Effekte von Objekt-Familiarisierung auf die frühe gestische Kommunikation: Individuelle Unterschiede in Hinblick auf den späteren Wortschatz. *Frühe Bildung, 5*(2), 91–98. doi:10.1026/2191-9186/a000257

Holler, J., & Levinson, S. C. (2019). Multimodal language processing in human communication. *Trends in Cognitive Sciences, 23*(8), 639–652. doi:10.1016/j.tics.2019.05.006

Howell, D. C. (2017). *Fundamental statistics for the behavioral sciences* (9th ed.). Boston, MA: Cengage Learning.

Hudson Kam, C. L., & Edwards, N. A. (2008). The use of uh and um by 3-and 4-year-old native English-speaking children: Not quite right but not completely wrong. *First Language, 28*(3), 313–327.

Ioannou, A., & Makridou, E. (2018). Exploring the potentials of educational robotics in the development of computational thinking: A summary of current research and practical proposal for future work. *Education and Information Technologies, 23*(6), 2531–2544. doi:10.1007/s10639-018-9729-z

Kanda, T., Shiomi, M., Miyashita, Z., Ishiguro, H., & Hagita, N. (2009). An affective guide robot in a shopping mall. *Proceedings of the 4th ACM/IEEE International Conference on Human Robot Interaction–HRI '09* (pp. 173–180). doi:10.1145/1514095.1514127

Kennedy, J., Lemaignan, S., Montassier, C., Lavalade, P., Irfan, B., Papadopoulos, F., Senft, E., & Belpaeme, T. (2017). Child speech recognition in human-robot interaction: Evaluations and recommendations. *Proceedings of the 2017 ACM/IEEE International Conference on Human-Robot Interaction–HRI '17* (pp. 82–90). doi:10.1145/2909824.3020229

Konishi, H., Kanero, J., Freeman, M. R., Golinkoff, R. M., & Hirsh-Pasek, K. (2014). Six principles of language development: Implications for second language learners. *Developmental Neuropsychology, 39*(5), 404–420. doi:10.1080/8756564 1.2014.931961

Kory Westlund, J. M., Jeong, S., Park, H. W., Ronfard, S., Adhikari, A., Harris, P. L., . . . Breazeal, C. L. (2017). Flat vs. expressive storytelling: Young children's learning and retention of a social robot's narrative. *Frontiers in Human Neuroscience, 11*(295), 1–20. doi:10.3389/fnhum.2017.00295

Ladel, S., Knopf, J., & Weinberger, A. (Eds.). (2018). *Digitalisierung und Bildung.* Wiesbaden, Germany: Springer VS.

Leite, I., Martinho, C., & Paiva, A. (2013). Social robots for long-term interaction: A survey. *International Journal of Social Robotics, 5*(2), 291–308. doi:10.1007/ s12369-013-0178-y

Levinson, S. C. (2016). Turn-taking in human communication: Origins and implications for language processing. *Trends in Cognitive Sciences, 20*(1), 6–14. doi:10.1016/j.tics.2015.10.010

Marcos, H. (1991). How adults contribute to the development of early referential communication? *European Journal of Psychology of Education, 6*(3), 271–282. doi:10.1007/BF03173150

Mertens, U. J., & Rohlfing, K. J. (2020). Progressive reduction of iconic co-speech gesture contributes to children's increased word production in child-robot interaction. Manuscript in preparation.

Mubin, O., Stevens, C. J., Shahid, S., Mahmud, A. A., & Dong, J.-J. (2013). A review of the applicability of robots in education. *Technology for Education and Learning, 1*(1), 1–7. doi:10.2316/Journal.209.2013.1.209-0015

Okita, S. Y., Ng-Thow-Hing, V., & Sarvadevabhatla, R. K. (2011). Multimodal approach to affective human-robot interaction design with children. *ACM Transactions on Interactive Intelligent Systems, 1*(1), 1–29. doi:10.1145/2030365.2030370

Park, H. W., Rosenberg-Kima, R., Rosenberg, M., Gordon, G., & Breazeal, C. (2017). Growing growth mindset with a social robot peer. *12th ACM/IEEE International Conference on Human-Robot Interaction (HRI)* (pp. 137–145). Vienna, Austria.

Ramachandran, A., Huang, C.-M., & Scassellati, B. (2017). Give me a break! Personalized timing strategies to promote learning in robot-child tutoring. *Proceedings of the 2017 ACM/IEEE International Conference on Human-Robot Interaction–HRI '17* (pp. 146–155). doi:10.1145/2909824.3020209

Rohlfing, K. J., Grimminger, A., & Lüke, C. (2017). An interactive view on the development of deictic pointing in infancy. *Frontiers in Psychology, 8*(1319), 1–6. doi:10.3389/fpsyg.2017.01319

Rohlfing, K. J., Leonardi, G., Nomikou, I., Rączaszek-Leonardi, J., & Hüllermeier, E. (2019). Multimodal turn-taking: Motivations, methodological challenges, and novel approaches. *IEEE Transactions on Cognitive and Developmental Systems*, 1–12. doi:10.1109/TCDS.2019.2892991

Rohlfing, K. J., Wrede, B., Vollmer, A.-L., & Oudeyer, P.-Y. (2016). An alternative to mapping a word onto a concept in language acquisition: Pragmatic frames. *Frontiers in Psychology, 7*, 470. doi:10.3389/fpsyg.2016.00470

Shiwa, T., Kanda, T., Imai, M., Ishiguro, H., & Hagita, N. (2008). How quickly should communication robots respond? *Proceedings of the 3rd International Conference on Human Robot Interaction–HRI '08* (pp. 153–160). doi:10.1145/1349822.1349843

Tolksdorf, N. F., Mertens, U., & Rohlfing, K. (2019, July). *When learning words with robots, children's answers are multimodal: A challenge for a dialogue design.* Paper presented at the International Conference on Human-Computer Interaction. Orlando, USA.

Tolksdorf, N. F., Siebert, S., Zorn, I., Horwath, I., & Rohlfing, K. J. (2020). Ethical considerations of applying robots in kindergarten settings: Towards an approach from a macro-perspective. *Journal of Social Robotics.* https://doi.org/10.1007/s12369-020-00622-3

Van der Wege, M. M., & Ragatz, E. C. (2004, August). *Learning to be fluently disfluent.* Paper presented at the Annual Meeting of the Cognitive Science Society. Chicago, USA.

Vogt, P., de Haas, M., de Jong, C., Baxter, P., & Krahmer, E. (2017). Child-robot interactions for second language tutoring to preschool children. *Frontiers in Human Neuroscience, 11*(73), 1–6. doi:10.3389/fnhum.2017.00073

Vogt, P., van den Berghe, R., de Haas, M., Hoffman, L., Kanero, J., Mamus, E., . . . Pandey, A. K. (2019). Second language tutoring using social robots: A large-scale study. *14th ACM/IEEE International Conference on Human-Robot Interaction (HRI)* (pp. 497–505). doi:10.1109/HRI.2019.8673077

Vogt, S., & Kauschke, C. (2017). Observing iconic gestures enhances word learning in typically developing children and children with specific language impairment. *Journal of Child Language, 44*(6), 1458–1484. doi:10.1017/S0305000916000647

Wigdor, N., de Greeff, J., Looije, R., & Neerincx, M. A. (2016). How to improve human-robot interaction with conversational fillers. *25th IEEE International Symposium on Robot and Human Interactive Communication (RO-MAN)*, 219–224. doi:10.1109/ROMAN.2016.7745134

Part 2

(Early) literacy learning with digital media

Chapter 6

Promising interactive functions in digital storybooks for young children

Astrid Wirth, Simone C. Ehmig, Lukas Heymann, and Frank Niklas

Nowadays, smartphones and tablet computers are very common in European families. Consequently, such devices are frequently available for young children from a very early age. Engaging with these new technologies at home or at a childcare center offers a range of opportunities to promote children's literacy competencies using e-books and storybook apps.

In this chapter, we aim to outline how the use of digital media can address and motivate children and, in particular, children in need of literacy support. To this end, we review the current literature and results of relevant studies. First, we try to identify reasons why children differ consistently in their reading comprehension skills, how such differences develop in early childhood, and which groups are in additional need of support. Then, we discuss children's digital home learning environments and the possibilities of reading with digital media in early childhood. Finally, we conclude by discussing practical implications for the use of digital media with children in educational contexts.

Children's reading skills and the need for early literacy support

The linguistic input young children receive at home and their linguistic experiences in early childhood lay the foundation for the development of literacy skills (Rodriguez & Tamis-LeMonda, 2011). Hence, the basis for differences in children's reading comprehension skills is established long before children start school. This includes the ability to retrieve information from written texts, to make inferences, to interpret information, and to evaluate content.

The Home Learning Environment (HLE; Burgess, Hecht, & Lonigan, 2002; Niklas & Schneider, 2013) is a multifaceted construct that comprises, in regard to literacy activities, aspects such as reading to children, parental reading, library visits, and the number of books in a household (Niklas, 2015). The HLE significantly influences the development of a child's reading comprehension and its precursors such as vocabulary and phonological awareness (De Jong & Leseman, 2001; Frijters, Barron, & Brunello, 2000; Sénéchal & LeFevre, 2014). As can be seen in Figure 6.1, the HLE acts as a mediator

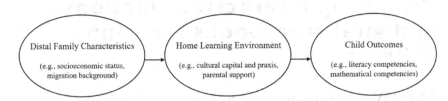

Figure 6.1 Association of family characteristics, the Home Learning Environment, and child outcomes

Source: (cf. Niklas, 2017)

between family background variables such as socioeconomic status (SES) and migration background and child outcomes such as literacy competencies (Aikens & Barbarin, 2008).

According to international large-scale assessment studies such as the Progress in International Reading Literacy Study (PIRLS) (Mullis, Martin, Foy, & Hooper, 2017a), poor reading skills in elementary school children are a widespread and persistent problem. Support for children's linguistic and literacy learning should thus start early within the family context and in the context of early childhood education and care (e.g., daycare centers, nursery schools, and afternoon childcare). Since the start of PIRLS in 2001, data suggest that children's gender, children's migration background, and their parents' SES are the **three key factors associated with performance differences in reading skills** in almost every participating country (Mullis, Martin, Gonzalez, & Kennedy, 2001). In order to understand their association with reading skills, it is necessary to address each in turn:

1   In international studies, girls already outperform boys in reading and spelling at the beginning of elementary school (Niklas & Schneider, 2017). Indeed, the gender gap has even increased in recent years (Brozo et al., 2014). The origins of gender differences are noteworthy (see Logan & Johnston, 2010, for a review); they are often traced back to early gender role models and stereotypes (Wolter, Braun, & Hannover, 2015). Boys often consider reading to be a feminine activity (McGeown, Goodwin, Henderson, & Wright, 2012) – a perception that results in less engagement in linguistic activities such as reading for pleasure at home (Lynn & Mikk, 2009).

2   Children with a migration background often show poorer reading skills in elementary school. According to the PIRLS results, if both parents are born abroad, these performance disadvantages may equate up to six months' or even up to one year's learning (Mullis et al., 2017a). However, in a few countries (e.g., Australia), children with a migration background do not differ from their peers in this respect and may even outperform them (OECD, 2016). Such findings indicate that it may not be simply the migration

background that is linked causally with children's outcomes. Instead, such contradictory findings may be due to the close association of migration status with SES in some countries; and it is this association that, in turn, leads to an interaction between both characteristics (Hillmert & Weßling, 2014; Lüdemann & Schwerdt, 2010). Learning a new language adds an additional challenge to achieving academic success in school, and for migrant children, reading difficulties may be explained by cultural differences (Ma, 2003). These cultural differences may manifest as fewer opportunities for learning in the home environment. For these reasons, the educational achievement of children whose parents have a migration and/or low socioeconomic background are often associated with a lower-quality HLE (Ebert et al., 2013; Schmitt, Simpson, & Friend, 2011).

3   The association between differences in children's reading skills and their parents' SES is well documented in international studies such as PIRLS and the Programme for International Student Assessment (PISA) (Mullis et al., 2017a; OECD, 2016). By 18 months of age, the vocabulary and linguistic abilities of children from higher and lower SES families differ significantly (Fernald, Marchman, & Weisleder, 2013). From the beginning of kindergarten until the end of elementary school, SES differences are associated with differences in the growth of decoding and reading comprehension skills (Hecht, Burgess, Torgesen, Wagner, & Rashotte, 2000). Most kindergarten predictors of elementary school reading skills such as phonological awareness, letter sound knowledge, and naming speed are associated with parental SES (Noble, Farah, & McCandliss, 2006; Schatschneider, Fletcher, Francis, Carlson, & Foorman, 2004).

We now turn our attention to the application of digital media to consolidate and extend literacy competencies in early childhood. Further, we discuss the ways in which digital media may provide access to the previously mentioned target groups and enhance the quality of their HLE.

Supporting early reading with digital media

As more and more of our daily reading happens online (Stiftung Lesen, 2008), the ability to interact with digital devices and the ability to read become closely intertwined. Consequently, the traditional definition of literacy is being scrutinized, and the understanding of reading in our daily life is changing rapidly (Burnett, 2017; Jones-Kavalier, & Flannigan, 2006). The definition of literacy has expanded from traditional notions of reading and writing and now includes the ability to learn, comprehend, and interact with technology (de Jong & Bus, 2002). The term *multiliteracy* takes this development into account by defining literacy as a complex construct that includes literacy practices such as reading and writing texts on multimodal or multimedia devices (Rowsell, 2013).

Reading with digital media

Reading with digital media includes screen-based reading on computers, tablets, e-book readers, and smartphones. In comparison with traditional print reading, it is characterized by different reading patterns such as nonlinear, selective reading and keyword spotting (Liu, 2005). Different and new skills are required when interacting with digital media, and these are particularly skills related to information communication technology (ICT), including basic computer skills such as navigation and self-directed selection of text (Hahnel, Goldhammer, Naumann, & Kröhne, 2016). In addition, knowledge about norms and practices can be understood as being concerning the usage of digital media is required (Meyers, Erickson, & Small, 2013).

In this light, being illiterate today can be understood as being to mean being unable to learn from and use digital technologies. Consequently, common definitions of illiteracy that refer to persons who cannot read or write may be substituted with broader definitions (Palaiologou, 2016). Taking the changes in literacy definitions and, subsequently, the changes in required skills into account, we must also change our perspective on children's early literacy learning and the support they experience in home learning environments. Additionally, the potential digital media holds for supporting reading means that we have to reevaluate our understanding of reading as being focused strictly on print media.

Children's digital home learning environment

Given that digital media are commonplace nowadays and that European children grow up in media-rich homes (Chaudron, 2015), digital media have become indispensable in the everyday lives of today's children. Due to the latest technical developments and new habits of children's immediate caregivers who now deal with media frequently, children also experience media daily and consider digital devices as very important (miniKIM, 2014). Toddlers and preschoolers learn by observing and interacting with their parents and siblings, and they imitate their handling of digital media from an early age onward (So-Har Wong, 2015). The majority of 3- to 5-year-old children use computer-based and internet-based digital technologies at home on a regular basis and they spend, on average, more than 30 minutes using digital technologies on weekdays and even more time during weekends (Palaiologou, 2016). The number of storybook and early language education apps available for children has increased in the last couple of years, and the majority of top-selling paid apps in 2011 were targeted at young children (Judge, Floyd, & Jeffs, 2015). Mullis et al. (2017a) showed that in many countries, a higher number of digital devices in households coincides with better reading skills in children. Consequently, the number of digital devices at home may be an important variable contributing to the quality of children's digital home learning environments. In turn, a greater number of digital devices may support children's literacy learning, similar to other environmental variables such as the number of books and children's books in a household.

The ePIRLS study (Mullis, Martin, Foy, & Hooper, 2017b) assessed digital reading skills of elementary school children from 17 countries. Children were asked to answer questions in a simulated online environment. Their reading comprehension was also assessed online. Nearly all participating children reported a high degree of self-efficacy in computer use and were able to navigate and locate information across webpages. When comparing achievements in informational reading, many elementary school children performed better when reading digitally than when using print media (Mullis et al., 2017b). Consequently, it is inappropriate to separate the development of children's traditional literacy skills from digital literacy skills (Neumann, Finger, & Neumann, 2017), and it stands to reason that supporting the development of children's literacy competencies with digital media combines learning benefits in both areas.

Digital media links reading with children's lived experience

Reading support needs to consider the world a child experiences and lives in today. This includes digital reading and reading media in the environments in which children grow up. According to such an ecocultural approach, digital media can facilitate and shape reading support when the important role of the immediate environment in young children's learning is acknowledged (Plowman, 2015). Further, the availability of various digital devices may multiply the opportunities for shared reading and learning due to their mobility and the various usage possibilities (Turner et al., 2017). In particular, digital devices such as tablets, with their convenient screen size and easy-to-handle touchscreens, can be valuable tools to support the development of child competencies (Kankaanranta, Koivula, Laakso, & Mustola, 2017). Consequently, a perceived advantage of storybook apps and children's e-books is that children can use them on the go, when no printed book is at hand (Ehmig & Seelmann, 2014).

Children have multiple possibilities to use digital media for reading. In addition to e-books, storybook apps, and educational apps for children, new devices combine printed and digital media – such as tiptoi electronic pens, or interactive books that can be read in a print version but are accompanied by apps with supplementary content. Many e-books or storybook apps for children are based on picture book series from the respective publisher or use famous children's book characters, thereby complementing the possibilities offered by printed media.

With these integrated approaches, digital media can contribute to enhanced enjoyment of content that promotes reading – for example, by adding audio elements that may intensify the emotional impact of an already familiar text passage or establish a fitting background atmosphere (Stichnothe, 2014). Storybook apps even provide the opportunity to expand linear stories to reader-defined narratives by giving readers the opportunity to change and develop the story themselves (Wooten & McCuiston, 2015), and thus may anchor the importance of stories and reading in children's everyday lives.

Moreover, some applications and e-books emphasize interactive aspects, thereby providing opportunities for children to foster their emerging understanding of literacy (Beschorner & Hutchison, 2013). For instance, such additional features may include narrator voices or digitized speech, sometimes providing word pronunciations, definitions, dictionaries, or multimedia aspects such as animations, videos, sound and music elements, and embedded minigames (Conrad Barnyak & McNelly, 2015). These features serve different purposes and can create tension, add humor, or provide extra information and thus support the reading experience in a positive manner (Stichnothe, 2014).

The interaction with digital devices creates opportunities for children to explore the content of a book or an application independently, and this may well motivate them to acquire early literacy competencies (So-Har Wong, 2015). From 3 years of age, children's media use encourages them to develop understandings about texts and the skills needed to read these texts – that is, their media use encourages phonological awareness and a general confidence in handling print (Levy, 2009). Indeed, young children's use of touchscreen tablets is associated positively with emergent literacy, print awareness, print knowledge, and sound knowledge (Neumann, 2016).

In a study by Korat and Shamir (2012), e-books that included words with a definition option facilitated learning in preschool-age children. In addition, e-books seem to provoke more complex utterances by parents than those evoked by print media (Kim & Anderson, 2008). Further, digital media allow more flexibility in content selection and text layout, and thus can be adapted more easily to match children's needs and interests (Biancarosa & Griffiths, 2012). According to these findings, a digital home learning environment offers new possibilities to support children's literacy development and reflects the current convergence of literacy and multimedia skills.

Digital media addresses and motivates target groups in particular need of support

Using digital media to promote reading in early childhood turns out to be particularly expedient for families that are more difficult to reach with print media. Using digital media may be an appropriate approach to improve the reading skills of boys who are in need of special support. In international studies, boys consistently demonstrate lower reading abilities and motivation compared to girls of the same age, and this gender gap has even increased in recent years (e.g., Brozo et al., 2014). Although there is some classroom evidence that screen-based reading diminishes the gender gap in reading achievement and that boys show better reading performances on computer-based tests than on paper-based tests (Horne, 2007), girls still perform substantially better than boys in reading achievement tasks (Huang, Liang, & Chiu, 2013; Sokal & Katz, 2008). In addition, girls profit more from the use of e-books that support emergent literacy in preschool-age children in the form of print awareness and vocabulary (Ihmeideh, 2014).

However, evoking literacy interest and reading motivation is the essential first step to get boys engaged in the reading process, and the special interest boys often have in digital media can be used effectively to support such interest and motivation from an early age (Newkirk, 2006). For instance, digital storybook reading can be used as an incentive to foster reading motivation and enjoyment. Whereas girls read more often for pleasure and report that they enjoy reading more often than boys (Clark, 2012), there is no gender difference for children's frequency of e-book reading (Kucirkova & Littleton, 2016). Indeed, there are indicators that reading digitally is perceived to be more pleasurable by boys than by girls (Liu & Huang, 2008). Ciampa (2012) showed that a digital children's literature program with multimedia and digital storybook reading had positive motivational effects, particularly for children who had not experienced success in reading before. Further, reading preferences of boys include books with short text passages supported by photographs, drawings, and hypertext elements (Farris, Werderich, Nelson, & Fuhler, 2009). These are demands that can be served readily by storybook apps and e-books.

Because research on role models suggests that gender-matched role models are most productive and promising for children in terms of reaching academic achievement goals (Zirkel, 2002), and because boys continue to regard reading as a feminine activity (Dutro, 2002), motivating fathers to read to their children using digital media may help to create a more supportive reading environment. A study conducted by the German Reading Foundation (Stiftung Lesen, 2012) showed that fathers, who typically read less often to their children than mothers (Logan & Johnston, 2010), like to use storybook apps with their children because of the additional features such as animations and sounds. Hence, they are more likely to be reading role models for their children when they use digital media.

In summary, shared digital reading (especially with male attachment figures) and the provision of appealing e-books and storybook apps may be a successful approach to enhance boys' reading motivation and to create a favorable digital home literacy environment. This might be easy to achieve as digital media such as tablets, personal computers (PCs), and smartphones are now present in almost all European households (Chaudron, 2015). When it comes to the possession of digital devices, there is little difference between parents with lower or higher levels of education (Kutscher, 2010). In a study comparing families across seven countries, the lower-income and less-educated families tended to have a relatively high ratio of technical device ownership at home (Livingstone, Mascheroni, Dreier, Chaudron, & Lagae, 2015). Consequently, all parents seem to have access to storybook apps and may use them with their children, independent of the number of books in a household or the parental education level (Constantino, 2005).

As children with low compared with high socioeconomic backgrounds have been shown to enjoy reading less, to read less frequently, and to read for shorter periods of time (Clark, 2012), the equal distribution of digital devices independent of family background provides an important opportunity to address literacy competencies of children with a low SES background. These children often spend more time using digital devices and online search functions compared with children who have higher socioeconomic backgrounds – a finding attributable partly to insufficient access to printed books at home (McGeown, Osborne, Warhurst, Norgate, & Duncan, 2016).

In fact, e-book reading interventions with low SES children have shown positive effects on children's word comprehension, receptive and expressive vocabulary, and phonological awareness (Korat, Shamir, & Heibal, 2013; Korat & Shneor, 2019). Further, low SES children rate themselves more often as poor readers (Clark, 2012), and they may benefit from the additional information available in multimedia learning environments (Bus, Takacs, & Kegel, 2015; Karemaker, Pitchford, & O'Malley, 2010; Korat & Shamir, 2008). This also applies to children with a migration background. Short videos in storybook apps were found to be particularly effective for expressive vocabulary acquisition of children learning a second language (Verhallen & Bus, 2010). Storybook apps and e-books for children usually comprise narrator voices or digitized speech in different languages. This offers great advantages for parents and educators who work with bilingual children: Parents who do not speak the society's main language and educators who do not speak the family language of migrant children may still be able to provide reading experiences in both languages using digital devices together with bilingual children.

In order to support second-language learning, children should be read to as much as possible – not only in a second language but also in the child's first language (Gagarina, Posse, Gey, Golcher, & Topaj, 2017; Klassert & Gagarina, 2010). A study with children in Austria who have a Turkish background showed the potential advantages of such approaches. Reading to children in Turkish encouraged not only their first language development but also their German language skills (Eisenwort, Aslan, Yesilyurt, Till, & Klier, 2018). Additionally, bilingual shared reading in nurseries and childcare centers can directly enhance migrant children's literacy self-concept by showing them that their first language is valued in an education context (Verhoeven, 2007).

Practical implications

Using digital devices with young children for educational purposes

Children experience early literacy not only in the home environment, but also in nurseries or childcare facilities. Findings suggest that parents' shared storybook reading behavior, the home literacy environment, and the childcare literacy environment each contribute to preschoolers' vocabulary learning (Grolig, Cohrdes, Tiffin-Richards, & Schroeder, 2018). Studies with both German and English samples have shown that parents and educators often have concerns about reading to their children with digital devices (Kucirkova & Littleton, 2016; Stiftung Lesen, 2012). Such concerns include children's increased screen time, potential exposure to inappropriate content, and an anticipated loss of interest in printed books. When selecting e-books and storybook apps for shared reading at home or in kindergarten classrooms, parents and educators are required to make a choice between a wide range of different products or modalities, many of which are not ideal for supporting children's emergent literacy. Consequently, advice and guidance for parents and educators is urgently needed to allay fears. Parents need information, examples, and specific recommendations.

In the following section, bringing together scientific findings on the benefits of storybook apps and children's e-books for children's literacy learning, we provide some concrete recommendations in which digital devices may be well-applied to support reading interest and differing abilities.

Choice of storybook apps and children's e-books: features to look out for

Educational quality of storybook apps and e-books varies a lot, and several apps and e-books targeted at children of preschool age are not well designed to support the development of emergent literacy (De Jong & Bus, 2003; Roskos, Brueck, & Widman, 2009). Therefore, educators and parents need to check the content and educational approach of such books before using digital media with children.

According to Hirsh-Pasek et al. (2015), educational apps for children need to be designed to promote (a) active, (b) engaged, (c) meaningful, and (d) socially interactive learning. Further, they conclude that children learn best when learning is also guided by a specific goal (i.e., the educational context of apps). Apps that include these four pillars encourage deep learning and are thus more likely to support children's learning. Consequently, all interactive and multimodal elements need to match the text and underline its central message.

In particular, interactive media that include practicing letters, syllables, and word recognition can improve early reading skills (Radesky, Schumacher, & Zuckerman, 2015). Moving images that match the content of the presented text may help children to integrate nonverbal information and language, and to keep them in mind (Bus et al., 2015). This also applies to e-books with hotspots (embedded animations in the illustration) that match the story content and thus foster understanding of the storyline and encourage the child's ability to recall a narrative (Labbo & Kuhn, 2000).

Using recorded narrator voices and highlighted text during e-book reading may increase children's literacy skills. In a Japanese study, the presentation of a recorded narrator voice while corresponding words were highlighted simultaneously in red in a digital children's book supported 4-year-old children's word acquisition to a greater extent than shared reading of the same printed book by their mother (Masataka, 2014). Moreover, the stability of changes in children's performance was confirmed by retests four weeks later. In particular, literacy learning of children with reading difficulties may be supported by multimodal e-books that include highlighted texts and combine these with sounds and animation (Morgan, 2013). However, a close congruency and temporal proximity between narration and nonverbal information is needed to create positive effects for children's literacy learning (Bus et al., 2015).

Parents who use e-books with their children consider narrative voice, visual highlighting of a word when tapped on, and the reading aloud of a word by the narrative voice upon tapping to be very helpful features (Vaala & Takeuchi, 2012). In contrast, features such as interactive hotspots and minigames are deemed to be distracting in the parents' view (see also Chapter 2). This has also been supported by research results reporting that hypermedia interactive elements such as minigames and hotspots can reduce performance in tests on text understanding and vocabulary knowledge. This is because switching between various elements may lead to cognitive overload (Dalla Longa & Mich, 2013). Consequently, parents and educators should avoid children's apps and e-books that require many (unnecessary) interactions from children because such distractions may reduce children's concentration (Wang, Lee, & Ju, 2018).

In summary, using digital media with integrated elements such as animated images, music, and sound effects may be of significant benefit for children when it comes to understanding the text and using vocabulary actively (Takacs, Swart, & Bus, 2015), but only if the digital media is designed appropriately (cf. Hirsh-Pasek et al., 2015).

Appropriate use of digital reading devices

The social context of learning is important, and this is equally applicable to interactions with digital media (Buckingham, 2007). Studies suggest that joint mother–child e-book reading is more effective for children's receptive and expressive word learning than independent e-book reading (Korat & Shneor, 2019). Consequently, it is important to note that it is preferable for young children not to use digital media alone or passively. Moreover, parents should not use digital devices as a substitute for human interaction. However, research suggests that it is only every second household in which parents supervise their (preschool-aged) children's use of digital media (Marci-Boehncke, Müller, & Rath, 2012).

The American Academy of Pediatrics (2016) generally discourages media use by children younger than 2 years, due to the lack of evidence supporting its educational or developmental benefits for children in this age group. Between the ages of 2 and 5, children should use digital media for a maximum of one hour daily. Digital media should not be used directly before bedtime and should be turned off during mealtimes. These maximum screen time recommendations are supported by the World Health Organization's guidelines (WHO, 2019), with the additional encouragement to read and talk while being engaged in screen-based activities.

In addition to these restrictions, the International Reading Association (2009) points out the importance of integrating digital media into current literacy programs. Developmentally appropriate and well-developed digital media offer an array of new learning opportunities and activities, particularly for children in need of additional support. Consequently, digital media also present opportunities for the inclusion of all children regardless of their literacy skills. Here, educators and parents have an important role in supporting the safe, meaningful, and transformative use of digital technologies and media with children (Kumpulainen & Gillen, 2017). To facilitate this, educators and parents require well-designed storybook apps and e-books in which they have confidence – as Müller-Brauers and colleagues point out in Chapter 9 of this book.

Once the appropriate and targeted use of digital media as a support for literacy learning is established in families and education curricula, digital media may lead to the reduction of performance differences between boys and girls and between children from different family backgrounds, thereby maximizing synergies by combining literacy and media literacy learning.

Three key considerations for parents, educators, and producers

- Reading with digital media offers new opportunities to support children's literacy development – particularly for children who are difficult to reach with common print media.
- Because the quality of available storybook apps and e-books for children varies, parents and educators need to check the content and educational approach of such media thoroughly before using it with children.
- Digital media should not replace child interactions with parents or educators but create opportunities for shared experiences with supporting features and interactive elements, and that can be used to encourage conversations.

References

Aikens, N. L., & Barbarin, O. (2008). Socioeconomic differences in reading trajectories: The contribution of family, neighborhood, and school contexts. *Journal of Educational Psychology*, *100*(2), 235–251.

American Academy of Pediatrics. (2016). Media and young minds: Council on communications and media. *Pediatrics*, *138*.

Beschorner, B., & Hutchison, A. C. (2013). iPads as a literacy teaching tool in early childhood. *International Journal of Education in Mathematics Science and Technology*, *1*(1), 16–24.

Biancarosa, G., & Griffiths, G. G. (2012). Technology tools to support reading in the digital age. *The Future of Children*, *22*(2), 139–160.

Brozo, W. G., Sulkunen, S., Shiel, G., Garbe, C., Pandian, A., & Valtin, R. (2014). Reading, gender, and engagement: Lessons from five PISA countries. *Journal of Adolescent & Adult Literacy*, *57*(1), 584–593.

Buckingham, D. (2007). Digital media literacies: Rethinking media education in the age of the internet. *Research in Comparative and International Education*, *2*(1), 43–55.

Burgess, S. R., Hecht, S. A., & Lonigan, C. J. (2002). Relations of the home literacy environment (HLE) to the development of reading-related abilities: A one-year longitudinal study. *Reading Research Quarterly, 37*(4), 408–426.

Burnett, C. (2017). Reading the future: The contribution of literacy studies to debates on reading and reading engagement for primary-aged children. In C. Ng & B. Bartlett (Eds.), *Improving reading and reading engagement in the 21st century* (pp. 119–140). Singapore: Springer.

Bus, A. G., Takacs, Z. K., & Kegel, C. A. (2015). Affordances and limitations of electronic storybooks for young children's emergent literacy. *Developmental Review, 35*, 79–97.

Chaudron, S. (Ed.). (2015). *Young children (0–8) and digital technology: A qualitative exploratory study across seven countries.* Luxembourg: Publications Office of the European Union.

Ciampa, K. (2012). Reading in the digital age: Using electronic books as a teaching tool for beginning readers. *Canadian Journal of Learning and Technology, 38*(2), 1–26.

Clark, C. (Ed.). (2012). *Children's and young people's reading today: Findings from the 2011 National Literacy Trust's annual survey.* London, England: National Literacy Trust.

Conrad Barnyak, N., & McNelly, T. A. (2015). Supporting young children's visual literacy through the use of e-books. In K. L. Heider & M. Renck Jalongo (Eds.), *Young children and families in the information age: Applications of technology in early childhood* (pp. 15–41). Dordrecht, Netherlands: Springer.

Constantino, R. (2005). Print environments between high and low socioeconomic status communities. *Teacher Librarian, 32*(3), 22–25.

Dalla Longa, N., & Mich, O. (2013). Do animations in enhanced ebooks for children favour the reading comprehension process? A pilot study. In N. Mana, O. Mich, A. De Angeli, & A. Druin (Eds.), *Workshop at Interaction Design and Children (IDC)* (pp. 24–27). New York, NY: ACM Press.

De Jong, M. T., & Bus, A. (2002). Quality of book-reading matters for emergent readers: An experiment with the same book in a regular or electronic format. *Journal of Educational Psychology, 94*(1), 145–155.

De Jong, M. T., & Bus, A. (2003). How well suited are electronic books to supporting literacy? *Journal of Early Childhood Literacy, 3*(2), 147–164.

De Jong, P. F., & Leseman, P. P. M. (2001). Lasting effects of home literacy on reading achievement in school. *Journal of School Psychology, 39*(5), 389–414.

Dutro, E. (2002). Us boys like to read football and boy stuff: Reading masculinities, performing boyhood. *Journal of Literacy Research, 34*(4), 465–500.

Ebert, S., Lockl, K., Weinert, S., Anders, Y., Kluczniok, K., & Rossbach, H. (2013). Internal and external influences on vocabulary development in preschool children. *School Effectiveness and School Improvement: An International Journal of Research, Policy, and Practice, 24*, 138–154.

Ehmig, S., & Seelmann, C. (2014). Das Potenzial digitaler Medien in der frühkindlichen Lesesozialisation [Potential of digital media in early childhood reading socialization]. *Frühe Bildung, 3*(4), 196–202.

Eisenwort, B., Aslan, H., Yesilyurt, S. L., Till, B., & Klier, C. M. (2018). Sprachentwicklung bei Kindern mit Migrationshintergrund und elterliches Vorlesen

[Language development in children with migration background and parental reading to children]. *Zeitschrift für Kinder- und Jugendpsychiatrie und Psychotherapie*, *46*, 99–106.

Farris, P. J., Werderich, D. E., Nelson, P. A., & Fuhler, C. J. (2009). Male call: Fifth-grade boys' reading preferences. *The Reading Teacher*, *63*(3), 180–188.

Fernald, A., Marchman, V. A., & Weisleder, A. (2013). SES differences in language processing skill and vocabulary are evident at 18 months. *Developmental Science*, *16*(2), 234–248.

Frijters, J. C., Barron, R. W., & Brunello, M. (2000). Direct and mediated influences of home literacy and literacy interest on prereaders' oral vocabulary and early written language skill. *Journal of Educational Psychology*, *92*(3), 466–477.

Gagarina, N., Posse, D., Gey, S., Golcher, F., & Topaj, N. (2017). Bilingual lexicon development in German in preschool children with the home languages Russian and Turkish. In H. Peukert & I. Gogolin (Eds.), *Dynamics of linguistic diversity* (pp. 125–142). Amsterdam, Netherlands: John Benjamins.

Grolig, L., Cohrdes, C., Tiffin-Richards, S. P., & Schroeder, S. (2018). Effects of preschoolers' storybook exposure and literacy environments on lower level and higher level language skills. *Reading and Writing*, *32*(4), 1061–1084.

Hahnel, C., Goldhammer, F., Naumann, J., & Kröhne, U. (2016). Effects of linear reading, basic computer skills, evaluating online information, and navigation on reading digital text. *Computers in Human Behavior*, *55*, 486–500.

Hecht, S. A., Burgess, S. R., Torgesen, J. K., Wagner, R. K., & Rashotte, C. A. (2000). Explaining social class differences in growth of reading skills from beginning kindergarten through fourth-grade: The role of phonological awareness, rate of access, and print knowledge. *Reading and Writing*, *12*, 99–128.

Hillmert, S., & Weßling, K. (2014). Soziale Ungleichheit beim Zugang zu berufsqualifizierender Ausbildung – Das Zusammenspiel von sozioökonomischem Hintergrund, Migrationsstatus und schulischer Vorbildung [Social inequality in the transition to vocational education and training: The interplay of socioeconomic background, immigrant status and general schooling]. *Sozialer Fortschritt*, *63*, 72–82.

Hirsh-Pasek, K., Zosh, J. M., Michnick Golinkoff, R., Gray, J. H., Robb, M. B., & Kaufman, J. (2015). Putting education in "educational" apps: Lessons from the science of learning. *Psychological Science in the Public Interest*, *16*(1), 3–34.

Horne, J. (2007). Gender differences in computerised and conventional educational tests. *Journal of Computer Assisted Learning*, *23*(1), 47–55.

Huang, Y., Liang, T., & Chiu, C. (2013). Gender differences in the reading of e-books: Investigating children's attitudes, reading behaviors, and outcomes. *Educational Technology and Society*, *16*(4), 97–110.

Ihmeideh, F. M. (2014). The effect of electronic books on enhancing emergent literacy skills of pre-school children. *Computers & Education*, *79*, 40–48.

International Reading Association. (2009). *New literacies and 21st century technologies: A position statement of the International Reading Association.* Newark, DE: Author.

Jones-Kavalier, B., & Flannigan, S. L. (2006). Connecting the digital dots: Literacy of the 21st century. *Educause Quarterly*, *2*, 8–10.

Judge, S., Floyd, K., & Jeffs, T. (2015). Using mobile media devices and apps to promote young children's learning. In K. L. Heider & M. Renck Jalongo (Eds.),

Young children and families in the information age: Applications of technology in early childhood (pp. 117–131). Dordrecht, Netherlands: Springer.

Kankaanranta, M., Koivula, M., Laakso, M.-L., & Mustola, M. (2017). Digital games in early childhood: Broadening definitions of learning, literacy, and play. In M. Ma & A. Oikonomou (Eds.), *Serious games and edutainment applications* (Vol. II, pp. 349–367). Cham, Germany: Springer International Publishing.

Karemaker, A., Pitchford, N. J., & O'Malley, C. (2010). Enhanced recognition of written words and enjoyment of reading in struggling beginner readers through whole-word multimedia software. *Computers & Education, 54*(1), 199–208.

Kim, J. E., & Anderson, J. (2008). Mother-child shared reading with print and digital texts. *Journal of Early Childhood Literacy, 8,* 213–245.

Klassert, A., & Gagarina, N. (2010). Der Einfluss des elterlichen Inputs auf die Sprachentwicklung bilingualer Kinder: Evidenz aus russischsprachigen Migranten-familien in Berlin [Parental influence on bilingual children's language development: Evidence from Russian speaking migrant families in Berlin]. *Diskurs Kindheits- und Jugendforschung, 4,* 413–425.

Korat, O., & Shamir, A. (2008). The educational electronic book as a tool for supporting children's emergent literacy in low versus middle SES groups. *Computers & Education, 50,* 110–124.

Korat, O., & Shamir, A. (2012). Direct and indirect teaching: Using e-books for supporting vocabulary, word reading, and story comprehension for young children. *Journal of Educational Computing Research, 46*(2), 135–152.

Korat, O., Shamir, A., & Heibal, S. (2013). Expanding the boundaries of shared book reading: E-books and printed books in parent-child reading as support for children's language. *First Language, 33*(5), 504–523.

Korat, O., & Shneor, D. (2019). Can e-books support low SES parental mediation to enrich children's vocabulary? *First Language, 39*(3), 344–364.

Kucirkova, N., & Littleton, K. (2016). *The digital reading habits of children: A national survey of parents' perceptions of and practices in relation to children's reading for pleasure with print and digital books, book trust.* Retrieved from www.book-trust.org.uk/news-andblogs/news/1371

Kumpulainen, K., & Gillen, J. (2017). Young children's digital literacy practices in the home: A review of the literature. *COST ACTION ISI1410 DigiLitEY* (pp. 1–34). Sheffield, England: University of Sheffield.

Kutscher, N. (2010). Digitale Ungleichheit: Soziale Unterschiede in der Mediennut-zung [Social inequality: Social differences in media usage]. In G. Cleppien & U. Lerche (Eds.), *Soziale Arbeit und Medien* (pp. 153–163). Wiesbaden, Germany: VS Verlag für Sozialwissenschaften.

Labbo, L. D., & Kuhn, M. R. (2000). Weaving chains of affect and cognition: A young child's understanding of CD-ROM talking books. *Journal of Literacy Research, 32*(2), 187–210.

Levy, M. (2009). Technologies in use for second language learning. *The Modern Language Journal, 93,* 769–782.

Livingstone, S., Mascheroni, G., Dreier, M., Chaudron, S., & Lagae, K. (2015). *How parents of young children manage digital devices at home: The role of income, education and parental style.* London, England: EU Kids Online, LSE.

Liu, Z. (2005). Reading behavior in the digital environment: Changes in reading behavior over the past ten years. *Journal of Documentation, 61*(6), 700–712.

Liu, Z., & Huang, X. (2008). Gender differences in the online reading environment. *Journal of Documentation*, 64(4), 616–626.

Logan, S., & Johnston, R. (2010). Investigating gender differences in reading. *Educational Review*, 62(2), 175–187.

Lüdemann, E., & Schwerdt, G. (2010). Migration background and educational tracking: Is there a double disadvantage for second-generation immigrants? *CESifo Working Paper No. 3256*, Center for Economic Studies and Ifo Institute (CESifo), Munich, Germany.

Lynn, R., & Mikk, J. (2009). Sex differences in reading achievement. *Trames Journal of the Humanities and Social Sciences (TRAMES)*, 13, 3–13.

Ma, X. (2003). Measuring up: Academic performance of Canadian immigrant children in reading, mathematics, and science. *Journal of International Migration and Integration*, 4(4), 541–576.

Marci-Boehncke, G., Müller, A., & Rath, M. (2012). Medienkompetent zum Schulübergang. Erste Ergebnisse einer Forschungs- und Interventionsstudie zum Medienumgang in der frühen Bildung [Being media-literate for school transition: First results of a research and intervention study on media usage in early education]. *Medienpädagogik. Zeitschrift für Theorie und Praxis der Medienbildung*, 22, 1–22.

Masataka, N. (2014). Development of reading ability is facilitated by intensive exposure to a digital children's picture book. *Frontiers in Psychology*, 5, 1–4.

McGeown, S. P., Goodwin, H., Henderson, N., & Wright, P. (2012). Gender differences in reading motivation: Does sex or gender identity provide a better account? *Journal of Research in Reading*, 35(3), 328–336.

McGeown, S. P., Osborne, C., Warhurst, A., Norgate, R., & Duncan, L. G. (2016). Understanding children's reading activities: Reading motivation, skill, and child characteristics as predictors. *Journal of Research in Reading*, 39, 109–125.

Meyers, E. M., Erickson, I., & Small, R. V. (2013). Digital literacy and informal learning environments: An introduction. *Learning, Media and Technology*, 38(4), 355–367.

miniKIM. (2014). *Kleinkinder und Medien. Basisuntersuchung zum Medienumgang 2- bis 5-Jähriger in Deutschland* [Infants and media: A basic study on the media usage of 2- to 5-year-olds in Germany]. Stuttgart, Germany: Medienpädagogischer Forschungsverbund Südwest.

Morgan, H. (2013). Multimodal children's e-books help young learners in reading. *Early Childhood Education Journal*, 41(6), 477–483.

Mullis, I. V. S., Martin, M. O., Foy, P., & Hooper, M. (2017a). *PIRLS 2016 international results in reading*. Retrieved from http://timssandpirls.bc.edu/pirls2016/international-results/

Mullis, I. V. S., Martin, M. O., Foy, P., & Hooper, M. (2017b). *ePIRLS 2016 international results in online informational reading*. Chestnut Hill, MA: TIMSS & PIRLS International Study Center, Boston College. Retrieved from http://timssandpirls.bc.edu/pirls2016/international-results/

Mullis, I. V. S., Martin, M. O., Gonzalez, E. J., & Kennedy, A. M. (2001). *PIRLS 2001 international report: IEA's study on reading achievement in primary schools*. Chestnut Hill, MA: Boston College.

Neumann, M. M. (2016). Young children's use of touch screen tablets for writing and reading at home: Relationships with emergent literacy. *Computers & Education*, 97, 61–68.

Neumann, M. M., Finger, G., & Neumann, D. L. (2017). A conceptual framework for emergent digital literacy. *Early Childhood Education Journal, 45*(4), 471–479.

Newkirk, T. (2006). With boys in mind: Media and literacy, what's good? *Educational Leadership, 64,* 62–66.

Niklas, F. (2015). Die familiäre Lernumwelt und ihre Bedeutung für die kindliche Kompetenzentwicklung [The learning environment provided by the family and its impact on the development of child competencies]. *Psychologie in Erziehung und Unterricht, 62*(2), 106–120.

Niklas, F. (2017). *Frühe Förderung innerhalb der Familie. Das kindliche Lernen in der familiären Lernumwelt: Ein Überblick* [Early promotion within the family context: Children's learning in the family learning environment: An overview]. Wiesbaden, Germany: Springer essentials.

Niklas, F., & Schneider, W. (2013). Home literacy environment and the beginning of reading and spelling. *Contemporary Educational Psychology, 38,* 40–50.

Niklas, F., & Schneider, W. (2017). Home learning environment and development of child competencies from kindergarten until the end of elementary school. *Contemporary Educational Psychology, 49,* 263–274.

Noble, K. G., Farah, M. J., & McCandliss, B. D. (2006). Socioeconomic background modulates cognition-achievement relationships in reading. *Cognitive Development, 21*(3), 349–368.

OECD. (2016). *PISA 2015: Excellence and equity in education* (Vol. 1). Paris, France: OECD Publishing.

Palaiologou, I. (2016). Children under five and digital technologies: Implications for early years pedagogy. *European Early Childhood Education Research Journal, 24,* 5–24.

Plowman, L. (2015). Researching young children's everyday uses of technology in the family home. *Interacting with Computers, 27,* 36–46.

Radesky, J. S., Schumacher, J., & Zuckerman, B. (2015). Mobile and interactive media use by young children: The good, the bad, and the unknown. *Pediatrics, 135,* 1–3.

Rodriguez, E. T., & Tamis-LeMonda, C. S. (2011). Trajectories of the home learning environment across the first 5 years: Associations with children's vocabulary and literacy skills at prekindergarten. *Child Development, 82*(4), 1058–1075.

Roskos, K., Brueck, J., & Widman, S. (2009). Investigating analytic tools for e-book design in early literacy learning. *Journal of Interactive Online Learning, 8*(3), 218–240.

Rowsell, J. (Ed.). (2013). *Working with multimodality: Rethinking literacy in a digital age.* New York, NY: Routledge.

Schatschneider, C., Fletcher, J. M., Francis, D. J., Carlson, C. D., & Foorman, B. R. (2004). Kindergarten prediction of reading skills: A longitudinal comparative analysis. *Journal of Educational Psychology, 96*(2), 265–282.

Schmitt, S. A., Simpson, A. M., & Friend, M. (2011). A longitudinal assessment of the home literacy environment and early language. *Infant Child Development, 20*(6), 409–431.

Sénéchal, M., & LeFevre, J. A. (2014). Continuity and change in the home literacy environment as predictors of growth in vocabulary and reading. *Child Development, 85*(4), 1552–1568.

So-Har Wong, S. (2015). Mobile digital devices and preschooler's home multiliteracy practices. *Language and Literacy*, *17*(2), 75–90.

Sokal, L., & Katz, H. (2008). Effects of technology and male teachers on boys' reading. *Australian Journal of Education*, *52*, 81–94.

Stichnothe, H. (2014). Engineering stories? A narratological approach to children's book apps. *Barnelitterært Forskningstidsskrift*, *5*.

Stiftung Lesen. (2008). *Lesen in Deutschland 2008. Eine Studie der Stiftung Lesen* [Reading in Germany 2008: A study by the German Reading Foundation]. Mainz, Germany: Stiftung Lesen.

Stiftung Lesen. (2012). *Vorlesestudie 2012. Vorlesen mit Bilder- und Kinderbuch-Apps. Repräsentative Befragung von 250 Vätern und 250 Müttern* [Reading aloud study 2012: Reading aloud with picture and children's book apps: Representative survey of 250 fathers and 250 mothers]. Mainz, Germany: Stiftung Lesen.

Takacs, Z. K., Swart, E. K., & Bus, A. G. (2015). Benefits and pitfalls of multimedia and interactive features in technology-enhanced storybooks: A meta-analysis. *Review of Educational Research*, *85*(4), 698–739.

Turner, K. H., Jolls, T., Hagerman, M. S., O'Byrne, W., Hicks, T., Eisenstock, B., & Pytash, K. E. (2017). Developing digital and media literacies in children and adolescents. *Pediatrics*, *140*, 122–126.

Vaala, S., & Takeuchi, L. (2012). *Parent co-reading survey*. The Joan Ganz Cooney Center. Retrieved from www.joanganzcooneycenter.org/wp-content/uploads/2012/11/jgcc_ereader_parentsurvey_quickreport.pdf

Verhallen, M. J. A. J., & Bus, A. G. (2010). Low-income immigrant pupils learning vocabulary through digital picture storybooks. *Journal of Educational Psychology*, *102*, 54–61.

Verhoeven, L. (2007). Early bilingualism, language transfer, and phonological awareness. *Applied Psycholinguistics*, *28*(3), 425–439.

Wang, L., Lee, H., & Ju, D. Y. (2018). Impact of digital content on young children's reading interest and concentration for books. *Behaviour and Information Technology*, *38*, 1–8.

WHO (2019). *WHO guidelines on physical activity, sedentary behavior, and sleep for children under 5 years of age*. Geneva, Switzerland: World Health Organization.

Wolter, I., Braun, E., & Hannover, B. (2015). Reading is for girls!? The negative impact of preschool teachers' traditional gender role attitudes on boys' reading related motivation and skills. *Frontiers of Psychology*, *6*, 1267.

Wooten, D. A., & McCuiston, K. F. (2015). Children's literature book apps: Exploring new paths for books and literacy development. *Journal of Children's Literature*, *41*(2), 26–30.

Zirkel, S. (2002). Is there a place for me? Role models and academic identity among white students and students of color. *Teachers College Record*, *104*(2), 357–376.

Chapter 7

A look into the future

How digital tools may advance language development

*Cansu Oranç, Gökçe Elif Baykal, Junko Kanero,
Aylin C. Küntay, and Tilbe Göksun*

Children's interaction with their social and physical environments is essential for their language development. Their language skills benefit from the models they are exposed to and the communicative partners with whom they interact (Hoff, 2006). Embodied and situated cognition theories suggest that children's interaction with their environments is an important contributor to their language development, and that digital tools with educational goals capitalize on this role of interaction (Vulchanova, Baggio, Cangelosi, & Smith, 2017). Science of learning studies also show that children's language skills benefit from interactive and responsive contexts, and this includes interacting with digital media (Dore, Zosh, Hirsh-Pasek, & Golinkoff, 2017). Building on this role of interaction in language development, technological tools are already in use to foster children's language skills. Other chapters in this book discuss digital storybooks (Chapter 1) and mobile applications (Chapter 8) in the context of literacy and language development. Meanwhile, technological advances are making new interactive tools available that allow for unique forms of learning experience. This chapter focuses on such emerging technologies carrying that potential to understand how technology can foster children's language skills.

The first section of this chapter focuses on *social robots*, robots that follow the behavioral norms to be expected in human interactions. As an agent with a physical body, a robot can use communicative skills such as gestures and eye gaze to simulate human interaction in the real world. The second section features applications using computer-generated images: *virtual reality (VR)*, *augmented reality (AR)*, and *virtual agents*. VR brings social interaction from the physical world into a virtual world by immersing the user in a computer-generated environment. In contrast, AR refers to applications that superimpose virtual information on the user's immediate physical environment through a platform such as a screen or a head-mounted display. Virtual agents are general terms for embodied computer-generated actors and are similar to social robots in their function. The third section concerns *tangible user interfaces* (TUIs), in which physical objects are coupled seamlessly with embedded, discrete, or collocated computation.

We address each of these digital tools by first giving an overview of their strengths and then discussing research findings on vocabulary and narrative development in first language (L1) and second language (L2) as precursors of literacy development. Vocabulary is an important index of sentence knowledge and reading comprehension (Whitehurst & Lonigan, 1998), and narrative skills help children's transition from oral language to literacy (Snow, Tabors, & Dickinson, 2001). Because digital media differ with respect to the appropriate age range, we include studies with children from preschool to elementary school. As discussed in Chapter 3 of this book, technology can help create inclusive classrooms by promoting social participation among children with disabilities and children from migrant backgrounds. At the end of the chapter, we address how the tools we review can also contribute to the language development of both children with special needs and classrooms in general. Hence, this chapter will inform parents, educators, and developers who interact with and work for children with different educational needs.

Social robots

Although social robots differ vastly in their appearance, they are all designed to simulate vocal, gestural, emotional, and facial expressions found in human–human interaction. For example, unlike other devices such as smartphones, robots with arms can perform movements and gestures, which are known to facilitate language learning in children (Tellier, 2008). Robots can point at objects to name them. Robots can also perform iconic gestures – gestures that represent the meaning of words, as in opening their arms to represent the word "big." As such, the advantage of the physical presence of a robot has been discussed in different learning contexts (e.g., Kennedy, Baxter, & Belpaeme, 2015; Köse et al., 2015). Another strength of robots is that they are adaptive: through various sensors, they can detect humans' motivational and educational needs and change their behavior accordingly. In addition, unlike human teachers who may well be perceived as authoritative figures, robots can be friendly peers that children play with or even care receivers that the children themselves have to look after. In one study, Japanese-speaking 3- to 6-year-olds successfully learned English verbs by teaching the words to an incompetent robot that made mistakes (Tanaka & Matsuzoe, 2012). It is important to note that most tutor robots are not designed to replace human teachers but to provide additional, uniquely tailored support to learners.

Kanero et al. (2018) surveyed experimental studies on child–robot interaction to evaluate whether social robots can scaffold vocabulary learning and language production in young children. The authors suggest that (a) there is no evidence of robots being more effective at teaching vocabulary than other digital devices or human teachers, (b) social robots may be more effective in scaffolding children's abilities to produce language than other digital devices, and (c) not enough controlled research has been conducted to draw a definitive conclusion (see van den Berghe, Verhagen, Oudgenoeg-Paz, van der Ven, & Leseman, 2019, for a review on other skills such as reading and grammar; see Belpaeme,

Kennedy, Ramachandran, Scassellati, & Tanaka, 2018, for a review on the use of social robots for education in general). Regardless of these suggestions, some promising trials have been carried out.

Vocabulary learning

Many programs using social robots have successfully taught new L1 words to young children. For example, in a four-week reading program, Korean-speaking 4-year-olds learned stories either from an e-book or by interacting with *iRobiQ*, a robot with a moving head and arms. Although children in both groups improved their vocabulary knowledge, the ability to read written words improved only in the robot group, suggesting that social robots bring additional educational benefits (Hyun, Kim, Jang, & Park, 2008). In another study, English-speaking 4- to 6-year-olds learned new words from a stuffed-animal–like robot, *DragonBot* (Kory Westlund et al., 2015). This study compared DragonBot, a human teacher, and a tablet, and found that children learned equally well in all conditions. However, when Japanese-speaking 4- and 5-year-olds learned made-up words from *Robovie*, a social robot with arms, the robot tutor was less effective than the human tutor (Moriguchi, Kanda, Ishiguro, Shimada, & Itakura, 2011).

Another interesting case is teaching sign language. Uluer, Akalın, and Köse (2015) modified the arms of the robot Robovie so that it could sign in Turkish Sign Language (*Türk İşaret Dili* or TİD). Typically developing children and children with hearing impairments (6–16 years of age) as well as adults were equally successful in understanding and remembering the TİD words signed by the robot. Another study by the same research group demonstrated that language proficiency may influence whether hearing-impaired children benefit from a robot tutor (Köse et al., 2015). Children with beginner-level TİD skills and limited sign language experience (7–11 years of age) learned more words when they interacted physically with the robot than when they watched the robot on a screen. On the other hand, children with advanced TİD skills (9–16 years of age) learned equally well in both cases. The fact that children with no or little knowledge of TİD benefited from the lessons invites the idea that social robots may be useful for beginner-level language learners in general.

How have social robots been used for L2 vocabulary learning? In a study by Gordon et al. (2016), English-speaking 3- to 5-year-olds successfully learned Spanish words over eight sessions in a tablet-based learning activity with the robot *Tega* that adjusted its verbal and nonverbal behaviors to the children's facial expressions. There has also been particular interest in supporting L2 of children with autism spectrum disorder (ASD) because these children may feel less stress in interacting with a robot than with a human teacher. For example, researchers in Iran developed a robot-assisted intervention to teach English words to Farsi-speaking 7- to 9-year-olds with ASD. Children's English test scores improved and were maintained after two weeks (Alemi, Meghdari, Basiri, & Taheri, 2015).

Studies mentioned thus far tested a small number of participants, and many did not have a proper control group. Hence, one should be cautious about drawing any general conclusions from them. However, some studies recognized these issues and attempted to show more generalizable results. For example, in the project L2TOR, or *Second Language Tutoring using Social Robots*, Vogt et al. (2019) tested 194 Dutch-speaking 5- and 6-year-olds in tablet-based English lessons. Children learned English vocabulary across seven lessons either with the *NAO* robot and a tablet or just with a tablet. To additionally evaluate the possible benefits of gestures, for half of the children in the robot condition, the robot performed iconic gestures in the lessons that represented the actions or objects (pointing gestures were performed in both cases). In concert with the smaller-scale studies on teaching L1, this study found no difference in children's learning outcomes between the robot and tablet-only conditions. Moreover, the results were the same regardless of whether the robot performed iconic gestures or not. Further research is needed to identify the reasons why the benefits of gestures observed in human studies were not found in this robot study.

Narrative development

Some studies also aimed to improve children's narrative skills by using social robots. In the aforementioned four-week reading program in South Korea, 4-year-olds in the robot condition, but not their peers who only had an e-book, improved their abilities to tell original stories and retell the stories they had learned (Hyun et al., 2008). Other studies focused on testing the expressiveness of the robot. In a study by Conti, Di Nuovo, Cirasa, and Di Nuovo (2017), Italian-speaking 5- to 6-year-olds recalled stories more accurately when the tales were narrated by an expressive social robot that used gestures, eye gaze, and voice tone than when they were told by an inexpressive human teacher. In another study, English-speaking 4- to 6-year-olds participated in eight storytelling sessions with the aforementioned *DragonBot* (Kory Westlund & Breazeal, 2015). When the complexity of the robot's stories (e.g., syntactic complexity of sentences) matched the children's language level, the children's own stories became longer and included more diverse words. The same research group also reported data from a mix of native and nonnative English-speaking children at 4 to 7 years of age. The robot narrated a story from a picture book, and children were asked to retell the story. Compared to children in the flat (i.e., nonexpressive) condition, children in the expressive robot condition emulated the robot's story more in their story retellings and told longer stories 4–6 weeks after the initial reading (Kory Westlund et al., 2017).

Narrative skills of children with special needs have also received considerable attention. In a study by Boccanfuso et al. (2017), English-speaking preschoolers with ASD and speech problems improved their receptive and expressive communication skills. In another study by Kim et al. (2013), English-speaking 4- to 12-year-olds with high-functioning ASD interacted in various combinations with adults, a touchscreen computer game, and a dinosaur robot. When interacting with the robot and an adult, children produced more utterances (toward the robot and the adult) than when they interacted with two adults or with the computer and one adult.

L2 narrative development has also been studied. In a study by Hong, Huang, Hsu, and Shen (2016), fifth graders in Taiwan practiced English skills in a group lesson led by a human teacher with or without a social robot. Children who studied with the robot reported being more motivated and satisfied with the learning materials, being less anxious, and possessing greater self-esteem than their counterparts who studied without the robot. Their activities included storytelling. Nonetheless, children in the robot-assisted lessons scored higher only on a paper test for listening and reading and not for speaking or writing.

In summary, under the status quo, there is not much evidence suggesting unique benefits in using social robots to teach language to children. However, children generally find learning language with social robots engaging (Kanero et al., 2018), and the quality of human–robot interaction is developing rapidly thanks to advances in both software (e.g., improved speech recognition) and hardware (e.g., smoother gestures). As such, especially in terms of helping children with special needs and meeting the individual needs of children, research on the use of robots in language education should be continued.

Augmented reality, virtual reality, and virtual agents

Augmented reality (AR), virtual reality (VR), and virtual agents also offer a contingent interaction. Technology can be used to combine real and virtual worlds in different ways on a *virtuality continuum* ranging from completely real to fully computer-generated environments (Milgram & Kishino, 1994). Unlike AR and VR, virtual agents were not originally placed on this continuum. However, following technological advances, it has been suggested that they should be included because they allow multimodal interactions that can take place anywhere on the continuum (Nijholt, 2006).

VR applications and virtual agents have been proposed as helpful tools for adult language learning (Macedonia, Groher, & Roithmayr, 2014; Repetto, 2014). These tools may also contribute to children's language development due to their unique strengths. AR can support learning by aligning digital content with the physical world, drawing attention to the learning material, and stimulating collaboration among children in both real and virtual spaces (Radu, 2014). By presenting information on the screen complementing the real world around the child, AR can also reduce the dissimilarity between the encoding (i.e., the screen) and the retrieval (i.e., the real world) spaces (Oranç & Küntay, 2019), thereby helping children to make a connection between what they see on the screen (e.g., a dog) and their physical environment (e.g., their dog; Oranç & Küntay, 2019). This in turn reduces the memory load necessary to transfer from one context to another, and thus facilitates learning in general (Barr, 2013) as well as language learning from screens in particular (Linebarger & Vaala, 2010). Capitalizing on these opportunities, AR has been used to support children's alphabet and word learning as well as their story comprehension (Oranç & Küntay, 2019). VR, on the other hand, can mimic the feeling of real social interaction and further create its own realm of communication through *transformed social interactions* (i.e., it can present a different reality tailored to match the specific user's learning needs; see Bailey & Bailenson, 2017). For instance, in a virtual classroom, the system may warn the instructor when they do not make enough eye contact with one of the students, and the seating arrangement can be changed virtually to optimize the learning gains of each student (Bailenson et al., 2008). Finally, virtual agents can – similar to social robots – use verbal and nonverbal communication to facilitate children's language learning (Macedonia, Bergmann, & Roithmayr, 2014). They can also develop parasocial relationships with children through building attachment, their person-like characteristics, and their ability to interact with children's immediate physical environment. All these features in turn facilitate learning (Brunick, Putnam, McGarry, Richards, & Calvert, 2016).

Vocabulary learning

Studies exploring vocabulary learning have focused largely on L2. Among the few that have examined L1 vocabulary learning, Yilmaz (2016) taught new words (e.g., fruits, shapes) to Turkish-speaking 5- and 6-year-olds using AR-based flashcards, puzzles, and match cards. Although teachers found the application useful, when asked to describe what they had seen on the application, children provided only superficial descriptions and did not reflect on what they saw. The authors interpreted this as indicating that the children invested low levels of cognitive effort when using the AR application. Seven- to 12-year-olds with ASD living in the United States also learned new English words through a six-month training with a computer-animated virtual tutor (Bosseler & Massaro, 2003). This tutor was able to give feedback, and the curriculum was designed uniquely for each child based on her or his specific abilities.

In terms of vocabulary learning in L2, AR has been used widely in classrooms. For instance, when the curriculum for Spanish-reared 5-year-olds included AR-based activities, videos, and stories, their English grades improved (measured by vocabulary comprehension and self-expression) compared to the previous year in which they were taught with the regular curriculum (Martínez, Benito, González, & Ajuria, 2017). In two experimental studies conducted in China, 3- to 6-year-olds who used a mobile AR application – which allowed them to scan cards to see the images associated with the words and hear their pronunciations – learned more English words than their peers who learned the same words with traditional methods (Chen, Zhou, Wang, & Yu, 2017; He, Ren, Zhu, Cai, & Chen, 2014). Nine-year-olds from Taiwan also successfully learned English words with an AR game on a tablet, regardless of their learning style and the teaching approach administered by the application (Hsu, 2017). Other studies, however, did not find a superiority of AR over other methods. For example, 3- to 6-year-olds in Malaysia learned English words equally well when studying them on a computer either with or without AR (Dalim, Dey, Piumsomboon, Billinghurst, & Sunar, 2016). Similarly, 4- to 8-year-olds in Taiwan did not differ in the number of English words they learned with either an AR game or physical cards (Pu & Zhong, 2018).

Some studies employed virtual agents to teach children words in L2. In one study, German-speaking children around 11 years of age learned words in an artificial language for four days either (a) with the static image of a virtual agent, (b) by watching a virtual agent's word-related gestures, or (c) by imitating the virtual agent's word-related gestures and repeating the words aloud (Macedonia et al., 2014). Although their overall performance was not high, children recalled more words when they imitated the virtual agent.

Although VR has been used to teach new words to adults (e.g., Ebert, Gupta, & Makedon, 2016), its effects on children's vocabulary have not been empirically tested. This reflects the overall low numbers of immersive VR studies with children (Bailey & Bailenson, 2017).

Narrative development

Unlike the case of vocabulary learning, research on narrative development with AR, VR, and virtual agents has focused mostly on L1. For instance, Israeli 4- to 7-year-olds with deafness or hearing impairments were trained to improve their temporal sequencing abilities in stories with either physical cards or a VR game in which they became a virtual part of the story. Children in the latter group outperformed their peers in storytelling skills following the three-month training (Eden, 2014). Another study by Yilmaz, Kucuk, and Goktas (2017) animated the pages of a picture book using AR. Descriptive statistics showed that the Turkish 5- and 6-year-olds remembered the consequence, place, and time of the story, although they struggled to remember its main theme. The authors speculated that the visual AR elements might have drawn children's attention more to the local details (e.g., place and time of the story) rather than the story's overarching theme. This is indeed one of the pitfalls of using AR in educational settings: Attractive visuals may draw disproportionate attention to certain aspects, often at the expense of essential plot elements. Nonetheless, precautionary design choices can be implemented to counter this (Oranç & Küntay, 2019). One factor preventing the disruptive effects of AR may be social interaction. For example, one study found that Taiwanese parents adopt different communication styles when reading AR picture books with their 5- to 10-year-olds (Cheng & Tsai, 2014). The difference in parental communication styles influenced children's story descriptions. Children who led the reading activity themselves and who interacted over the book with their parents provided extensive descriptions and comments on the story. In contrast, children gave simple descriptions when their parents had dominated the reading activity or when they worked in dyads who did not communicate much.

Virtual peers take technology-based social interaction to a different level. Ryokai, Vaucelle, and Cassell (2003) created a virtual peer who had more advanced language skills than 5-year-olds (i.e., in using quoted speech, and temporal and spatial expressions). The virtual peer was projected on a screen for children to narrate their own stories while playing together by taking turns in telling stories about a figurine. Children who played with the virtual peer used significantly more advanced language in their stories compared to those who played without her. Tartaro and Cassell (2008) conducted a similar study showing that a virtual peer can also help children with ASD improve their narrative skills. In cocreating a narrative, 7- to 11-year-olds with ASD took turns with either a virtual peer or a typically developing human peer. Children with ASD were more likely to give contingent responses and were better in maintaining an ongoing topic when they interacted with the virtual peer compared to the human peer.

In short, studies on vocabulary learning have predominantly used AR and focused on L2, whereas studies on narrative development have used a wider range of technologies and focused on L1. Currently, results on AR's effectiveness on L2 word learning are mixed; studies reporting positive results have compared AR to so-called traditional methods, yet they have failed to describe what that entails. Meanwhile, other studies have found that children may learn L2 words equally well from AR and other means such as computers and physical cards. Together, these findings indicate that AR may help vocabulary development at least to the same extent as other means, but that it may or may not provide additional benefits. In terms of narrative production, studies so far present mostly positive findings. In both domains, virtual agents seem to be helpful, potentially because their inherently social nature aids children's language development.

Tangible user interfaces

Whereas AR, VR, and virtual agents allow children to interact with the digital content (e.g., on the screen), tangible user interfaces (TUIs) allow children to interact with physical, tangible materials that are digitally enhanced. An example is a touchscreen device that is activated by and can interact with physical building blocks. TUIs have great potential as a language learning tool due to their interactive nature across modalities, yet they are still in the early stages of development and evaluation.

The concrete nature of objects enables graspable, embodied, and multimodal interaction. TUIs blend physical objects with digital content, and offer children the opportunity to manipulate interactive objects through a range of possible combinations between physical and digital representations (Marshall, 2007). Research in psychology and education suggests that TUIs can help children build abstract symbolic relations with the physical activity and materials they provide (O'Malley & Fraser, 2004). In the case of language learning, experimenting with objects helps children to learn new words by guiding them to make connections between the objects and their labels (Iverson, 2010), and TUIs can facilitate the process by providing contingent feedback. Moreover, TUIs offer multimodal and collaborative interactions to support the literacy skills of children with special needs (e.g., Farr, Yuill, Harris, & Hinske, 2010; Hengeveld et al., 2009).

Most TUI studies have focused on the usability or design aspects rather than on evaluating learning outcomes. Although usability is a prerequisite for designing learning technologies (Bruckman, Bandlow, & Forte, 2009), the benefits of TUIs in language learning have yet to be explored. In this section, while acknowledging this gap, we summarize related work on how TUIs might foster children's language development.

Vocabulary learning

Some TUI prototypes have been developed to support children's acquisition of new words. *Make a Riddle* by Sifteo Inc. (Hunter, Kalanithi, & Merrill, 2010) is a hybrid tangible–graphic interface. 4- to 7-year-olds manipulate digital cubes to form sentences, and the interface provides narrative feedback to help the children learn spatial prepositions. Although learning gains have not been tested, *Make a Riddle* presents the possibility that TUIs may support word learning in specific domains such as learning spatial concepts. *RoyoBlocks* (Kleiman, Pope, & Blikstein, 2013) is another example, in which children can create their own sentences with 60 digitally enhanced wooden word blocks and listen to the sentences with a talking stuffed toy reading companion. 2- to 7-year-olds successfully formed sentences with these blocks and shared them with the companion.

TUIs have also been used to support vocabulary development in children with special needs. Jadan-Guerrero, Jaen, Carpio, and Guerrero (2015) developed *Kiteracy*, an educational kit designed to improve the recognition and learning of words and syllables by Spanish-speaking children with Down syndrome. The study compared three types of interactions for the tool: cardboard (only physical), multitouch (only digital), and tangible (digital and physical). In contrast to other types of interaction, the tangible version elicited more spontaneous speech from children and teachers. *LinguaBytes* (Hengeveld et al., 2009) is another prototype developed for word learning (e.g., animals, vehicles) that specifically targets toddlers with cerebral palsy. *LinguaBytes* combines wooden pieces with illustrations representing words and an interactive console. Children between 1 and 4 years of age interacted with the prototype during six-week speech therapy sessions. Observations and surveys of therapists revealed that children found more opportunities to express themselves verbally and nonverbally when interacting with the prototype in contrast to using their regular materials (Hengeveld et al., 2009).

Narrative development

TUIs can also be designed to support children's narrative development (Baykal, Veryeri Alaca, Yantaç, & Göksun, 2018). They can make storytelling more playful through tangible characters (e.g., *KidStory* by Stanton et al., 2004; *TellTale* by Ananny, 2002), room-sized ambient storytelling environments (e.g., *Storyroom* by Alborzi et al., 2000; *Pogo World* by Rizzo, Marti, Decortis, Rutgers, & Thursfield, 2018), interactive surfaces (e.g., *StoryMat* by Ryokai & Cassell, 1999; *KidPad* by Hourcade, Bederson, Druin, & Taxén, 2002), tangible word blocks (e.g., *RoyoBlocks* by Kleiman et al., 2013), and books that can become interactive with RFID tags (e.g., *LinguaBytes* by Hengeveld et al., 2009). By creating multimodal, collaborative, and interactive contexts supporting both physical and digital story elements, TUIs create new forms of storytelling.

Given that physical and digital collaborative play facilitates L1 (Newland, Roggman, & Boyce, 2001) and L2 learning (Piirainen-Marsh & Tainio, 2009), TUIs have the potential to support narrative development by stimulating conversation and storytelling, especially for atypically developing children. One empirical study showed that a group of children with ASD engaged in more social activities (i.e., cooperative play, parallel play, and on-looking) while playing with *Topobo* (a tangible construction kit with a kinetic memory by Raffle, Parkes, & Ishii, 2004) than when playing with Lego bricks (Farr, Yuill, & Raffle, 2010). Another study found that a configurable narrative set (*The Augmented Knights Castle*), which enables users to hear the sounds of characters when placed in different locations, led children with ASD to play more collaboratively (i.e., discussing the outcome with the peer) and to engage in less solitary play (i.e., acting on an object alone) than did a nonconfigurable version of the same set (Farr et al., 2010). These findings suggest that embedding toys with programmable digital technology may provide more forms of social interaction compared to physical toys without digital enhancements.

These examples illustrate the promise of tangible technologies as a novel interface design for children's language development, predominantly in L1. Although TUIs have received considerable attention from child–computer interaction designers, their educational value has yet to be tested experimentally.

Conclusion and future directions

Technological advances introduce new tools that may contribute to children's language and literacy skills. However, as also pointed out by Starke, Leinweber, and Ritterfeld in Chapter 8 of this book, the educational impact of new digital tools has not always been tested. We have reviewed empirical research to assess the effectiveness of several interactive technologies and addressed how they can support children's language learning as a correlate of their literacy skills.

The studies we reviewed indicate that different tools may support children's language development in different ways. First, social robots are just as effective as other devices for teaching children new words, although they currently may not provide unique benefits for vocabulary learning over other options. In terms of narrative development, however, social robots support the development of preschoolers' storytelling skills in their native language, especially when the robots are verbally and nonverbally expressive and when they are customized to match the children's specific needs. Embodied expressiveness and adaptivity are indeed among the strengths of robots that help simulate the role of social interaction in developing narrative skills. Second, AR contributes to preschool and elementary school children's learning of L2 words. Whereas some studies show that AR-based curricula may contribute to word learning more than traditional methods, other studies indicate that both may work equally well. Third, virtual agents are helpful for both vocabulary and narrative development in preschool- and elementary school-aged children. Similar to social robots, virtual agents can also mimic human-human interaction, suggesting that children benefit most from technologies that are able to do this. Finally, TUIs have the potential to teach young children new words by enabling them to interact with both physical and digital representations of those words, and they have the potential to support their narrative skills through multimodal interactions. As can be seen, each of these interactive technologies has the potential to foster a specific aspect of children's language development.

One prominent theme across these tools is their contribution to the language and communication development of children with special needs. Our review indicates that elementary school-aged children with ASD may benefit from social robots, virtual agents, and TUIs because these may enhance their word knowledge and narrative skills in their native language. Among children with hearing impairments, preschoolers can improve their storytelling skills in VR environments, whereas older children can learn and practice words in sign language. TUIs have been used mostly with younger children such as toddlers and preschoolers with Down syndrome and cerebral palsy to support their vocabulary and narrative development in their native language. Hence, these tools may assist professionals working with children who have special needs. Existing technologies such as computers are already helping children with special needs to improve their language and communication skills (e.g., Ploog, Scharf, Nelson, & Brooks, 2013; Schery & O'Connor, 1997). The technologies reviewed here can also be incorporated into the practitioner's toolbox because they offer a more interactive and comprehensive learning experience than computers do. Furthermore, actively working and soon-to-be practitioners specializing in children with developmental disabilities have mostly positive attitudes toward the use of robots in these children's education, although they do voice concern about their costliness (Conti, Di Nuovo, Buono, & Di Nuovo, 2017). According to researchers, when the benefits of robots prevail over their financial costs, practitioners' attitudes will be even more positive. This confirms the importance of continuing research on the effectiveness of these technologies.

A second commonality is that these technologies can be implemented in schools to help children learn and practice language skills. Many of the studies reviewed here were conducted in classroom settings, especially those with social robots and AR. These tools may be used to assist teachers, and that may be where their unique advantage lies. Technology-based support is needed in schools for various reasons, such as the increasing number of students and the need to adaptively respond to children's different needs (Belpaeme et al., 2018). For instance, robots may provide assistance in classrooms with the second language skills of not only children who speak the official minority language of their country but also immigrant children (Belpaeme et al., 2015). Given that preschool and elementary school teachers have positive attitudes toward both robots (Fridin & Belokopytov, 2014) and AR (Yilmaz, 2016), these technologies can be implemented in classrooms to support children's language skills and to create inclusive learning environments.

Despite the potential of these devices, high-quality experimental work is still needed before firm conclusions can be drawn about their effectiveness. Studies with powerful sample sizes, good control conditions, and statistically evaluated objective measures of learning gains must be conducted, as well as follow-up studies investigating whether learning gains are maintained over time. More interdisciplinary collaboration is needed because when designers develop novel language learning tools for children with educational goals in mind, their effectiveness is not always assessed as is the case with TUIs. As follows, we provide some directions for future work.

Among the digital tools reviewed in this chapter, social robots have been studied most frequently in the domain of language learning. This creates a solid basis for future research. For example, the programmability of robots enables them to be customized for children with different levels of cognitive, social, and linguistic competence. To accomplish successful personal learning experiences with robots, the effects of such differences on children's language learning must be investigated.

More systematic research is needed to differentiate the unique contribution of AR, VR, and virtual agents to language development in contrast to other digital tools. For instance, AR may be used to teach new words where it is helpful to show the referents in a 3D space rather than 2D, as is the case with spatial relations such as *behind*. On the other hand, VR and virtual agents can provide the gestural input children need when learning language because they can fully imitate a person who is capable of gesturing. Sign language may be one particular field of application. These tools may be especially helpful for children with special needs because they provide lifelike training in a controlled environment with the possibility of infinite repetitions.

Finally, advances in 3D printing and smart materials will make TUIs more prevalent in the near future by reducing costs and simplifying production (Holmquist et al., 2019). Inevitably, this will be reflected in children's daily lives and learning environments. To inform developers, it is important to investigate which factors influence their effectiveness in language learning before they become more widespread in the market. For instance, how TUIs transform verbal and nonverbal adult–child interaction remains an open question. Another direction may be to study children's singular use of TUIs, and to investigate the ways in which the devices can provide sufficient scaffolding without the help of an adult (i.e., through visual, auditory, and/or haptic feedback). Furthermore, the domains in which TUIs may provide a particular benefit must be studied. For instance, because TUIs allow a direct manipulation of physical objects such as shapes, word blocks, and concrete representations of abstract concepts, they may facilitate children's spatial language development (Baykal et al., 2018).

In conclusion, our review shows that by recognizing and utilizing the important role of interactivity in language development, emerging technologies create novel and exciting ways of learning language, and they do this specifically for children with special needs and in formal education settings. Future studies will endorse the capacity of these devices as a language development tool.

Three key considerations for parents, educators, and producers

* Technology can offer multimodal interactions and different sensory experiences for children to support their language development – especially for those with special needs.
* Because technology allows for personalized experience, the unique ways in which technology may scaffold each child's language development must be considered and implemented when possible.
* The interactivity of technology does not and should not replace children's interaction with adults and peers, and it should be integrated within their social environment. To support language development, technology must be used to promote additional social interaction between children and others.

References

Alborzi, H., Druin, A., Montemayor, J., Platner, M., Porteous, J., Sherman, L., . . . Hendler, J. (2000). Designing story rooms: Interactive storytelling spaces for children. In D. Boyarski & W. A. Kellogg (Eds.), *Proceedings of the 3rd conference on designing interactive systems: Processes, practices, methods, and techniques* (pp. 95–104). New York, NY: ACM Press. doi:10.1145/347642.347673

Alemi, M., Meghdari, A., Basiri, N. M., & Taheri, A. (2015). The effect of applying humanoid robots as teacher assistants to help Iranian autistic pupils learn English as a foreign language. In A. Tapus, E. André, J.-C. Martin, F. Ferland, & M. Ammi (Eds.), *Social robotics, ICSR 2015, lecture notes in computer science*, (Vol. 9388, pp. 1–10). Cham, Germany: Springer. doi:10.1007/978-3-319-25554-5_1

Ananny, M. (2002). Supporting children's collaborative authoring: Practicing written literacy while composing oral texts. *Proceedings of the Conference on Computer Support for Collaborative Learning: Foundations for a CSCL Community* (pp. 595–596). Boulder, CO: International Society of the Learning Sciences.

Bailenson, J. N., Yee, N., Blascovich, J., Beall, A. C., Lundblad, N., & Jin, M. (2008). The use of immersive virtual reality in the learning sciences: Digital transformations of teachers, students, and social context. *Journal of the Learning Sciences, 17*(1), 102–141. doi:10.1080/10508400701793141

Bailey, J. O., & Bailenson, J. N. (2017). Immersive virtual reality and the developing child. In F. C. Blumberg & P. J. Brooks (Eds.), *Cognitive development in digital contexts* (pp. 181–200). San Diego, CA: Academic Press. doi:10.1016/B978-0-12-809481-5.00009-2

Barr, R. (2013). Memory constraints on infant learning from picture books, television, and touchscreens. *Child Development Perspectives, 7*(4), 205–210. doi:10.1111 / cdep.12041

Baykal, G. E., Veryeri Alaca, I. V., Yantaç, A. E., & Göksun, T. (2018). A review on complementary natures of tangible user interfaces (TUIs) and early spatial learning. *International Journal of Child-Computer Interaction, 16*, 104–113. doi:10.1016/j. ijcci.2018.01.003

Belpaeme, T., Kennedy, J., Baxter, P., Vogt, P., Krahmer, E. E. J., Kopp, S., . . . Deblieck, T. (2015). L2TOR-second language tutoring using social robots. In *First workshop on educational robots* (WONDER). Berlin, Germany: Springer.

Belpaeme, T., Kennedy, J., Ramachandran, A., Scassellati, B., & Tanaka, F. (2018). Social robots for education: A review. *Science Robotics, 3*(21), 1–9. doi:10.1126/scirobotics.aat5954

Boccanfuso, L., Scarborough, S., Abramson, R. K., Hall, A. V., Wright, H. H., & O'Kane, J. M. (2017). A low-cost socially assistive robot and robot-assisted intervention for children with autism spectrum disorder: Field trials and lessons learned. *Autonomous Robots, 41*(3), 637–655. doi:10.1007/s10514-016-9554-4

Bosseler, A., & Massaro, D. W. (2003). Development and evaluation of a computer-animated tutor for vocabulary and language learning in children with autism. *Journal of Autism and Developmental Disorders, 33*(6), 653–672. doi:10.1023/B:JADD.0000006002.82367.4f

Bruckman, A., Bandlow, A., & Forte, A. (2009). HCI for kids. In A. Sears & J. A. Jacko (Eds.), *Human-computer interaction: Designing for diverse users and domains* (pp. 33–50). Boca Raton, FL: CRC Press.

Brunick, K. L., Putnam, M. M., McGarry, L. E., Richards, M. N., & Calvert, S. L. (2016). Children's future parasocial relationships with media characters: The age of intelligent characters. *Journal of Children and Media, 10*(2), 181–190. doi:10.1080/17482798.2015.1127839

Chen, Y., Zhou, D., Wang, Y., & Yu, J. (2017). Application of augmented reality for early childhood English teaching. *International Symposium on Educational Technology*, 111–115. doi:10.1109/ISET.2017.34

Cheng, K.-H., & Tsai, C.-C. (2014). Children and parents' reading of an augmented reality picture book: Analyses of behavioral patterns and cognitive attainment. *Computers & Education, 72*, 302–312. doi:10.1016/j.compedu.2013.12.003

Conti, D., Di Nuovo, S., Buono, S., & Di Nuovo, A. (2017). Robots in education and care of children with developmental disabilities: A study on acceptance by experienced and future professionals. *International Journal of Social Robotics, 9*(1), 51–62. doi:10.1007/s12369-016-0359-6

Conti, D., Di Nuovo, A., Cirasa, C., & Di Nuovo, S. (2017). A comparison of kindergarten storytelling by human and humanoid robot with different social behavior. *Proceedings of the Companion of the 2017 ACM/IEEE International Conference on Human-Robot Interaction* (pp. 97–98). doi:10.1145/3029798.3038359

Dalim, C. S. C., Dey, A., Piumsomboon, T., Billinghurst, M., & Sunar, S. (2016). TeachAR: An interactive augmented reality tool for teaching basic English to nonnative children. *IEEE International Symposium on Mixed and Augmented Reality* (pp. 82–86). doi:10.1109/ISMAR-Adjunct.2016.0046

Dore, R. A., Zosh, J. M., Hirsh-Pasek, K., & Golinkoff, R. M. (2017). Plugging into word learning: The role of electronic toys and digital media in language development. In F. Blumberg & P. Brooks (Eds.), *Cognitive development in digital contexts* (pp. 75–91). San Diego, CA: Academic Press.

Ebert, D., Gupta, S., & Makedon, F. (2016). Ogma: A virtual reality language acquisition system. *Proceedings of the 9th ACM International Conference on Pervasive Technologies Related to Assistive Environments* (pp. 1–5). New York, NY: ACM Press. doi:10.1145/2910674.2910681

Eden, S. (2014). Virtual intervention to improve storytelling ability among deaf and hard-of-hearing children. *European Journal of Special Needs Education, 29*(3), 370–386. doi:10.1080/08856257.2014.909177

Farr, W., Yuill, N., Harris, E., & Hinske, S. (2010). In my own words: Configuration of tangibles, object interaction and children with autism. *Proceedings of the 9th International Conference on Interaction Design and Children* (pp. 30–38). New York, NY: ACM Press. doi:10.1145/1810543.1810548

Farr, W., Yuill, N., & Raffle, H. (2010). Social benefits of a tangible user interface for children with autistic spectrum conditions. *Autism, 14*(3), 237–252. doi:10.1177/1362361310363280

Fridin, M., & Belokopytov, M. (2014). Acceptance of socially assistive humanoid robot by preschool and elementary school teachers. *Computers in Human Behavior, 33*, 23–31. doi:10.1016/j.chb.2013.12.016

Gordon, G., Spaulding, S., Kory Westlund, J., Lee, J. J., Plummer, L., Martinez, M., . . . Breazeal, C. (2016). Affective personalization of a social robot tutor for children's second language skills. *Proceedings of the 30th AAAI Conference on Artificial Intelligence* (pp. 3951–3957). Phoenix, Arizona, USA.

He, J., Ren, J., Zhu, G., Cai, S., & Chen, G. (2014). Mobile-based AR application helps to promote EFL children's vocabulary study. *IEEE 14th International Conference on Advanced Learning Technologies (IWALT)* (pp. 431–433). doi:10.1109/ICALT.2014.129

Hengeveld, B., Hummels, C., Overbeeke, K., Voort, R., van Balkom, H., & de Moor, J. (2009). Tangibles for toddlers learning language. *Proceedings of the 3rd International Conference on Tangible and Embedded Interaction* (pp. 161–168). doi:10.1145/1517664.1517702

Hoff, E. (2006). How social contexts support and shape language development. *Developmental Review, 26*(1), 55–88. doi:10.1016/j.dr.2005.11.002

Holmquist, L. E., Zuckerman, O., Ballagas, R., Ishii, H., Ryokai, K., & Zhang, H. (2019). The future of tangible user interfaces. *Extended Abstracts of the 2019 CHI Conference on Human Factors in Computing Systems*. doi:10.1145/3290607.3311741

Hong, Z. W., Huang, Y. M., Hsu, M., & Shen, W. W. (2016). Authoring robot-assisted instructional materials for improving learning performance and motivation in EFL classrooms. *Journal of Educational Technology & Society, 19*, 337–349.

Hourcade, J. P., Bederson, B. B., Druin, A., & Taxén, G. (2002). KidPad: Collaborative storytelling for children. *CHI '02 Extended Abstracts on Human Factors in Computing Systems*, 500–501. doi:10.1145/506443.506449

Hsu, T. C. (2017). Learning English with augmented reality: Do learning styles matter? *Computers & Education, 106*, 137–149. doi:10.1016/j.compedu.2016.12.007

Hunter, S., Kalanithi, J., & Merrill, D. (2010). Make a Riddle and TeleStory: Designing children's applications for the siftables platform. *Proceedings of the 9th International Conference on Interaction Design and Children* (pp. 206–209). doi:10.1145/1810543.1810572

Hyun, E., Kim, S., Jang, S., & Park, S. (2008). Comparative study of effects of language instruction program using intelligence robot and multimedia on linguistic ability of young children. *RO-MAN 2008: The 17th IEEE International Symposium on Robot and Human Interactive Communication* (pp. 187–192). doi:10.1109/ROMAN.2008.4600664

Iverson, J. M. (2010). Developing language in a developing body: The relationship between motor development and language development. *Journal of Child Language, 37*(2), 229–261. doi:10.1017/S0305000909990432

Jadan-Guerrero, J., Jaen, J., Carpio, M. A., & Guerrero, L. A. (2015). Kiteracy: A kit of tangible objects to strengthen literacy skills in children with down syndrome. *Proceedings of the 14th International Conference on Interaction Design and Children* (pp. 315–318). doi:10.1145/2771839.2771905

Kanero, J., Geçkin, V., Oranç, C., Mamus, E., Küntay, A. C., & Göksun, T. (2018). Social robots for early language learning: Current evidence and future directions. *Child Development Perspectives, 12*(3), 146–151. doi:10.1111/cdep.12277

Kennedy, J., Baxter, P., & Belpaeme, T. (2015). Comparing robot embodiments in a guided discovery learning interaction with children. *International Journal of Social Robotics, 7*(2), 293–308. doi:10.1007/s12369-014-0277-4

Kim, E. S., Berkovits, L. D., Bernier, E. P., Leyzberg, D., Shic, F., Paul, R., & Scassellati, B. (2013). Social robots as embedded reinforcers of social behavior in children with autism. *Journal of Autism and Developmental Disorders, 43*(5), 1038–1049. doi:10.1007/s10803-012-1645-2

Kleiman, J., Pope, M., & Blikstein, P. (2013). RoyoBlocks: An exploration in tangible literacy learning. *Proceedings of the 12th International Conference on Interaction Design and Children* (pp. 543–546). doi:10.1145/2485760.2485861

Kory Westlund, J. M., & Breazeal, C. (2015). The interplay of robot language level with children's language learning during storytelling. *Proceedings of the 10th Annual ACM/IEEE International Conference on Human-Robot Interaction* (pp. 65–66). https://doi.org/10.1145/2701973.2701989

Kory Westlund, J. M., Dickens, L., Jeong, S., Harris, P., DeSteno, D., & Breazeal, C. (2015). A comparison of children learning new words from robots, tablets, & people. In M. Heerink & M. de Jong (Eds.), *Proceedings of new friends: The*

1st international conference on social robots in therapy and education (pp. 26–27). Almere, Netherlands: Windesheim Flevoland.

Kory Westlund, J. M., Jeong, S., Park, H. W., Ronfard, S., Adhikari, A., Harris, P. L., . . . Breazeal, C. L. (2017). Flat vs. expressive storytelling: Young children's learning and retention of a social robot's narrative. *Frontiers in Human Neuroscience, 11*(295), 1–20. doi:10.3389/fnhum.2017.00295

Köse, H., Uluer, P., Akalın, N., Yorgancı, R., Özkul, A., & Ince, G. (2015). The effect of embodiment in sign language tutoring with assistive humanoid robots. *International Journal of Social Robotics, 7*(4), 537–548. doi:10.1007/s12369-015-0311-1

Linebarger, D. L., & Vaala, S. E. (2010). Screen media and language development in infants and toddlers: An ecological perspective. *Developmental Review, 30*(2), 176–202. doi:10.1016/j.dr.2010.03.006

Macedonia, M., Bergmann, K., & Roithmayr, F. (2014). Imitation of a pedagogical agent's gestures enhances memory for words in second language. *Science Journal of Education, 2*(5), 162–169. doi:10.11648/j.sjedu.20140205.15

Macedonia, M., Groher, I., & Roithmayr, F. (2014). Intelligent virtual agents as language trainers facilitate multilingualism. *Frontiers in Psychology, 5*(295). doi:10.3389/fpsyg.2014.00295

Marshall, P. (2007). Do tangible interfaces enhance learning? *Proceedings of the 1st International Conference on Tangible and Embedded Interaction* (pp. 163–170). doi:10.1145/1226969.1227004

Martínez, A. A., Benito, J. R. L., González, E. A., & Ajuria, E. B. (2017). An experience of the application of augmented reality to learn English in infant education. *International Symposium on Computers in Education* (pp. 1–6). doi:10.1109/SIIE.2017.8259645

Milgram, P., & Kishino, F. (1994). A taxonomy of mixed reality visual displays. *IEICE Transactions on Information and Systems, 77*(12), 1321–1329.

Moriguchi, Y., Kanda, T., Ishiguro, H., Shimada, Y., & Itakura, S. (2011). Can young children learn words from a robot? *Interaction Studies, 12*(1), 107–118. doi:10.1075/is.12.1.04mor

Newland, L. A., Roggman, L. A., & Boyce, L. K. (2001). The development of social toy play and language in infancy. *Infant Behavior and Development, 24*(1), 1–25. doi:10.1016/S0163-6383(01)00067-4

Nijholt, A. (2006). Human and virtual agents interacting in the virtuality continuum. In E. Miyares Bermúdez & L. Ruiz Miyares (Eds.), *Linguistics in the twenty first century* (pp. 205–214). Newcastle, England: Cambridge Scholars Press.

O'Malley, C., & Fraser, D. S. (Eds.). (2004). *Literature review in learning with tangible technologies.* Bristol, England: Nesta FutureLab Series. Retrieved from https://telearn.archives-ouvertes.fr/hal-00190328/document

Oranç, C., & Küntay, A. C. (2019). Learning from the real and the virtual worlds: Educational use of augmented reality in early childhood. *International Journal of Child–Computer Interaction, 21*, 104–111. doi:10.1016/j.ijcci.2019.06.002

Piirainen-Marsh, A., & Tainio, L. (2009). Collaborative game-play as a site for participation and situated learning of a second language. *Scandinavian Journal of Educational Research, 53*(2), 167–183. doi:10.1080/00313830902757584

Ploog, B. O., Scharf, A., Nelson, D., & Brooks, P. J. (2013). Use of computer-assisted technologies (CAT) to enhance social, communicative, and language development in children with autism spectrum disorders. *Journal of Autism and Developmental Disorders*, *43*(2), 301–322. doi:10.1007/s10803-012-1571-3

Pu, M., & Zhong, Z. (2018). Development of a situational interaction game for improving preschool children's performance in English-vocabulary learning. *Proceedings of the 2018 International Conference on Distance Education and Learning* (pp. 88–92). New York, NY: ACM Press. doi:10.1145/3231848.3231851

Radu, I. (2014). Augmented reality in education: A meta-review and cross-media analysis. *Personal and Ubiquitous Computing*, *18*(6), 1533–1543. doi:10.1007/s00779-013-0747-y

Raffle, H. S., Parkes, A. J., & Ishii, H. (2004). Topobo: A constructive assembly system with kinetic memory. *Proceedings of the SIGCHI Conference on Human Factors in Computing Systems* (pp. 647–654). New York, NY: ACM Press. doi:10.1145/985692.985774

Repetto, C. (2014). The use of virtual reality for language investigation and learning. *Frontiers in Psychology*, *5*(1280). doi:10.3389/fpsyg.2014.01280

Rizzo, A., Marti, P., Decortis, F., Rutgers, J., & Thursfield, P. (2018). Building narrative experiences for children through real time media manipulation: POGO World. In M. Blythe & A. Monk (Eds.), *Funology 2: From usability to enjoyment* (pp. 479–492). Cham, Germany: Springer. doi:10.1007/978-3-319-68213-6_31

Ryokai, K., & Cassell, J. (1999). StoryMat: A play space for collaborative storytelling. *CHI '99 Extended Abstracts on Human Factors in Computing Systems* (pp. 272–273). New York, NY: ACM Press. doi:10.1145/632716.632883

Ryokai, K., Vaucelle, C., & Cassell, J. (2003). Virtual peers as partners in storytelling and literacy learning. *Journal of Computer Assisted Learning*, *19*(2), 195–208. doi:10.1046/j.0266-4909.2003.00020.x

Schery, T., & O'Connor, L. (1997). Language intervention: Computer training for young children with special needs. *British Journal of Educational Technology*, *28*(4), 271–279. doi:10.1111/1467-8535.00034

Snow, C. E., Tabors, P. O., & Dickinson, D. K. (2001). Language development in the preschool years. In D. K. Dickinson & P. O. Tabors (Eds.), *Beginning literacy with language: Young children learning at home and school* (pp. 1–25). Baltimore, MD: Brookes.

Stanton, D., O'Malley, C., Bayon, V., Hourcade, J. P., Sunblad, Y., Fast, C., . . . Benford, S. (2004). The KidStory project: Developing collaborative storytelling tools for children, with children. In J. Siraj-Blatchford (Ed.), *Developing new technologies for young children* (pp. 75–93). Stoke-on-Trent, England: Trentham Books Ltd.

Tanaka, F., & Matsuzoe, S. (2012). Children teach a care-receiving robot to promote their learning: Field experiments in a classroom for vocabulary learning. *Journal of Human-Robot Interaction*, *1*(1), 78–95. doi:10.5898/JHRI.1.1.Tanaka

Tartaro, A., & Cassell, J. (2008). Playing with virtual peers: Bootstrapping contingent discourse in children with autism. *Proceedings of the 8th International Conference on International Conference for the Learning Sciences*, *2* (pp. 382–389). Utrecht, Netherlands.

Tellier, M. (2008). The effect of gestures on second language memorisation by young children. *Gesture*, *8*(2), 219–235. doi:10.1075/gest.8.2.06tel

Uluer, P., Akalın, N., & Köse, H. (2015). A new robotic platform for sign language tutoring. *International Journal of Social Robotics*, *7*(5), 571–585. doi:10.1007/s12369-015-0307-x van den Berghe, R., Verhagen, J., Oudgenoeg-Paz, O., van der Ven, S., & Leseman, P. (2019). Social robots for language learning: A review. *Review of Educational Research, 89*(2), 259–295. doi:10.3102/0034654318821286

Vogt, P., van den Berghe, R., de Haas, M., Hoffman, L., Kanero, J., Mamus, E., . . . Pandey, A. K. (2019). Second language tutoring using social robots: A large-scale study. *14th ACM/IEEE International Conference on Human-Robot Interaction* (pp. 497–505). doi:10.1109/HRI.2019.8673077

Vulchanova, M., Baggio, G., Cangelosi, A., & Smith, L. (2017). Language development in the digital age. *Frontiers in Human Neuroscience, 11.* doi:10.3389/fnhum.2017.00447

Whitehurst, G. J., & Lonigan, C. J. (1998). Child development and emergent literacy. *Child Development, 69*(3), 848–872. doi:10.1111/j.1467-8624.1998.tb06247.x

Yilmaz, R. M. (2016). Educational magic toys developed with augmented reality technology for early childhood education. *Computers in Human Behavior, 54,* 240–248. doi:10.1016/j.chb.2015.07.040

Yilmaz, R. M., Kucuk, S., & Goktas, Y. (2017). Are augmented reality picture books magic or real for preschool children aged five to six? Augmented reality picture books for preschool students. *British Journal of Educational Technology, 48*(3), 824–841. doi:10.1111/bjet.12452

Chapter 8

Designing apps to facilitate first and second language acquisition in children

Anja Starke, Juliane Leinweber,
and Ute Ritterfeld

Introduction

Due to their inherent features such as portability, built-in sensors, adaptability, and ease of use, mobile devices have become important learning tools in formal and informal educational settings (Giannakas, Kambourakis, Papasalouros, & Gritzalis, 2018; Sung, Chang, & Liu, 2016). The prevalent app platforms provide a great number of apps advertised as "educational"; yet, in most cases, there is little evidence to support the claim of educational impact (Kucirkova, Messer, Sheehy, & Fernández Panadero, 2014), for a number of reasons.

First, due to the rapidly evolving app market, it is practically impossible to evaluate every educational app. Second, evaluation is not necessarily in the interest of a producer because the outcome may not support the claim of educational value. Third, testing the impact of interactive media usage empirically is very challenging because all experiences are highly individualized (Klimmt, Vorderer, & Ritterfeld, 2004). Although some studies have attempted to identify generic principles for educational effects (Ritterfeld, Shen, Wang, Nocera, & Wong, 2009), it is highly questionable whether the insights gained generalize to other games that have not been investigated. Fourth, the ultimate question is rather whether it is the *game experience*, and not the game itself, that elicits educational effects (Ritterfeld, Cody, & Vorderer, 2009). Strictly speaking, an educational gaming experience can result from playing over-the-counter games that are not advertised as having pedagogical value; and, vice versa, so-called serious games may not fulfill the expectation at all (Jenkins et al., 2009). And fifth, as has been pointed out by Ritterfeld and Weber (2006), many effect studies that reveal positive outcomes used incentives to control usage.

The rationale behind gamification, however, lies in its inherent motivational realm. Educational games are supposed to prompt without coercion and encourage enduring and repeated usage (Ritterfeld et al., 2009). In other words, the game elements should drive high-frequency usage and deep processing of an educational content that would otherwise be less attractive for the target group. We do not propose that all educational exercises should be implemented in a game environment. Indeed, highly motivated students might even perceive serious games as time-consuming and distracting frills (Ritterfeld, 2011). The value of games lies mainly in their potential to attract those learners who are less drawn to the educational experience. Ideally, they play a game because it is fun to play it, and they process the educational content incidentally.

However, simply adding educational content to a game or game-like setting will not necessarily create an effective game for learning purposes (Ke, 2016). Instead, designing a game-based learning platform requires interdisciplinary collaboration to elicit and maximize its potential (Ke, Shute, Clark, & Erlebacher, 2019).

Game theorists, designers, and computer scientists understand how to develop enjoyable games and address their technical functionality. Pedagogical experts need to reflect upon the content and how it is best presented in a game format. Media psychologists are trained to bridge the gap between those two perspectives and look at the psychological functionality of the medium.

However, many of the available educational apps are still "just migrations of games and learning scenarios that already exist in non-digital form" (Hirsh-Pasek et al., 2015, p. 26). Not only do these products fail to integrate a reasonable didactic with their game design approach, but educational content and gamification elements are often totally unrelated (Falloon, 2013). Even if these gamification elements may be used for motivation or gratification, they do not assist the learning process (Ritterfeld & Weber, 2006). Instead of just adding gamification elements to some educational content, we need to blend the gaming with the learning experience and translate learning principles into a veritable game environment.

In this chapter, we exemplify such an integrated design process focusing on first and second language learning in children. We thereby recommend a three-step approach. In the first step, we ensure that content creation follows linguistic requirements. In the second step, we tap into the available knowledge on how to facilitate the learning process within an app. Finally, in the third step, we discuss how to build a game environment that elicits a motivating game experience.

Step 1: linguistic requirements

Many experts agree that language is a key factor for successful academic education and, as a consequence, for social participation (e.g., Conti-Ramsden, Durkin, Toseeb, Botting, & Pickles, 2018). Three groups of children are at risk for reduced language skills: those with a developmental language disorder (DLD), those who come from a lower socioeconomic status (SES) background and receive insufficient language input, and those from homes in which a language other than the society's main language is spoken (children learning a second language [L2]). DLD is a developmental disorder affecting around 7% of children (Tomblin et al., 1997) that is characterized by difficulties in the abilities to learn and use a language. Significant differences on a broad range of language measures are still present in adulthood and associated with lower academic and vocational qualifications (Conti-Ramsden et al., 2018). Children from families with low

SES do not present such a neurobiological disadvantage as children with DLD, but they are also at risk for language learning difficulties due to limited language learning experiences (e.g., Schwab & Lew-Williams, 2016). Because these experiences build decisively on the input provided, these children display rather small vocabulary knowledge compared to children from families with a higher SES (Qi, Kaiser, Milan, & Hancock, 2006). Finally, bilingualism is not necessarily a disadvantage for the child's (language) development. In general, children are able to learn two or more languages simultaneously (Serratrice, 2013), but success in acquiring an L2 depends on factors such as age at acquisition as well as the quality and quantity of the language input in the respective languages. The vocabulary size of bilingual children can differ considerably from monolingual children in any of the languages used (Bialystok, Luk, Peets, & Yang, 2010). For example, bilingual children showed comparable vocabulary knowledge in the mainstream language for words in the school context, but less word knowledge regarding words in the family and home setting (Bialystok et al., 2010). What all three groups – children with DLD, children from families with a low SES, and L2 learners – have in common is that they are in need of enriched linguistic input that may be provided within tailored apps. In order for apps to be effective, they need to be built on those learning principles that are relevant in the language learning process.

Taken together, six learning principles are shown to foster strong language skills: (1) frequency of input, (2) interest, (3) responsiveness, (4) focus on meaning, (5) clear information, and (6) vocabulary learning and grammatical development (see, e.g., Harris, Golinkoff, & Hirsh-Pasek, 2011; Parish-Morris, Golinkoff, & Hirsh-Pasek, 2013). Konishi, Kanero, Freeman, Golinkoff, and Hirsh-Pasek (2014) have modified these six principles for L2 development. Whereas five of the six principles focus on the same aspects, Principle 5, "be clear" (Harris et al., 2011), is replaced by "hearing diverse words and language structures" (Konishi et al., 2014). These authors stated that "these six principles incorporate multiple factors that impact language acquisition based on existing research on language development in monolingual children and children learning an L2" (Konishi et al., 2014, p. 405). In the following, we describe the six principles for application in the context of digital media.

Principle 1: children learn what they hear most

Research emphasizes that frequent language input matters, and that children learn what they hear most. Both the quantity and the quality of the input provided are important because children can extract statistical regularities and detect neighboring sounds. Redundancy in repeated input eases the incorporation of input into linguistic knowledge, especially in vocabulary learning. Mediated content embedded in reusable apps provides a superb opportunity for such redundant input – if the content is enjoyable. Because enjoyment serves as a motivational factor when using media content, it also influences repeated usage and thereby multiple exposure to the same or similar linguistic input (Ritterfeld, Klimmt, Vorderer, & Steinhilper, 2005). The effectiveness of any media input on the language learning experience will therefore depend strongly on the entertainment potential of the application.

Principle 2: children learn words for things and events that interest them

Children's interest plays an essential role in language acquisition, whereby perceptual (e.g., perceptual saliency) and social (e.g., joint attention) factors may promote language development. A gaming environment may not only simulate contexts including perceptual and social elements but may also address interesting content topics for the specific target group. Perceptual salience, for example, can be realized in an app context through attuning the audiovisual material to the specific learning goal (e.g., foregrounding the respective item or movement visually while accentuating the spoken word perceptually) and thereby guiding children's attention. Social attention might be realized by using a narrative character who joins the children's journey through the game and mimics joint attention.

Principle 3: interactive and responsive rather than passive contexts promote language acquisition

Children's vocalizations, gestures, and facial expressions evoke responses from an interactive environment. When types of interactions involve joint focus, positive affect, and appropriate scaffolding, they facilitate language acquisition. In contrast to most other media (TV, books), apps have the potential to be interactive and responsive. But technology is not yet able to thoroughly imitate human interactive behavior. There are still a lot of shortcomings in the available technology (such as smartphones, tablets, and robots) with regard to responsiveness to the complex multimodal behavior that characterizes human interaction (see Chapters 4 and 5 in this book).

Principle 4: children learn words best in meaningful contexts

Children need strategies that introduce them to new words. Their engagement in meaningful contexts has to be attained through semantically related activities. Research in the area of language, play, and memory indicates that children's background knowledge is deeper when novel words are presented in integrated and meaningful contexts. For example, toddlers benefit from a narrative context when learning prepositions (Rohlfing & Nachtigäller, 2016). The narrative formats typically used in games may provide the necessary meaningful context for word learning.

Principle 5: children need to hear diverse examples of words and language structures

Research demonstrates that children's phonological, semantic, syntactic, and literacy skills in their first language (L1) and L2 benefit from a diverse linguistic input through multiple sources. Whereas repetition in app usage provides the necessary redundancy to remember linguistic entities, variations in input allow children to deduce relevant knowledge on the usage of a word in different contexts, on morphological and syntactic rules, and even on pragmatics.

Principle 6: vocabulary and grammatical development are reciprocal processes

This principle is based on the evidence that children rarely learn new words and their meanings in isolation. Studies demonstrate that vocabulary and grammar develop simultaneously and interdependently (Konishi et al., 2014). This principle is best addressed in a context in which authentic interactions between the app user and the app, or when agents embedded in the app, are realized.

These six psycholinguistic principles should guide content creation for apps aiming to facilitate vocabulary and grammar development. Their implementation in a game environment requires another layer of guided learning that contextualizes the content in the ways indicated next.

Step 2: facilitating the learning process

With regard to language impairments, there are a few studies focusing on the effects of apps for children with broad communication handicaps, especially on the autism spectrum (e.g., King, Thomeczek, Voreis, & Scott, 2014; Pinto & Gardner, 2014). There is also evidence that tablet-based apps support a transfer of the learning process into the home setting and thereby increase practice frequency and, consequently, educational effects compared to nondigital interventions (Des Roches, Balachandran, Ascenso, Tripodis, & Kiran, 2015). Taken together, there is some evidence that game-based learning can be harvested in the domain of assisted language acquisition if reasonable didactic methods are incorporated.

Hirsh-Pasek et al. (2015) have compiled the essence of the past research on learning in children with the aim of incorporating this knowledge into mobile media-based learning. They propose that there are five pillars for creating an effective learning context: (1) active learning, (2) engagement, (3) meaningful learning, (4) social interaction, and (5) scaffolded exploration toward a learning goal.

1 Active learning

Refers to "minds-on" learning in contrast to mere physical activities. Minds-on is used for those activities requiring thinking and intellectual manipulation resulting in a new or deeper understanding. Active learning takes place in authentic learning environments in which children have the opportunity for meaningful experiences and interactions with respect to the learning content. One specific example in language acquisition is word learning through dialogic reading. A recent meta-analysis by Flack, Field, and Horst (2018) has demonstrated the overall effect of shared storybook reading on word learning in children. Dialogic reading, in which parents use open-ended questions, pointing, or repetition to encourage text-related talk during reading, was superior to nondialogic reading. These dialogic techniques encourage children to follow and think through the storyline, resulting in deeper learning.

Interactive media have the potential to mimic dialogic activities. Simple interactive activities in the app environment include, for example, touching the screen, moving the device, or taking pictures. Complex interactive activities, which have the potential to imitate simple social interactions, require talking into a microphone and getting an appropriate response. Such interaction can facilitate active learning if the respective activity is integrated into a meaningful learning context that requires a child's mental involvement. Including symbolic systems such as numbers, languages, visual icons, or geographic maps can contribute to such mental activity (Hirsh-Pasek et al., 2015).

2   Engagement

The authors differentiate three different kinds of engagement: behavioral, emotional (see also Chapter 2), and cognitive. Behavioral engagement refers to rule following or persistence; affective responses to a story, for example, indicate emotional engagement; and a cognitively engaged person is flexible in problem solving or is likely to invest in learning. Each kind of engagement supports staying on task as a crucial factor for effective learning.

One key barrier for engagement in children is distraction. For example, studies on picture books and interactive e-books have shown that children were more engaged and learned new content better with relatively plain books in contrast to books with manipulative features such as flaps (Chiong & DeLoache, 2013) or in multimedia enhanced e-books in contrast to traditional storybooks or e-books with interactive elements (Takacs, Swart, & Bus, 2015). Multimedia elements can be beneficial for learning by adding nonverbal information, but only if they are optimally attuned to the verbal information (Bus, Takacs, & Kegel, 2015). For instance, in the case of the complex process of learning a new verb, animations may help to illustrate the respective action.

In addition to preventing distraction, supporting extrinsic and intrinsic motivation in children is a key method for engagement. Extrinsic motivation arises mainly from anticipated rewards and incentives (Richter, Raban, & Rafaeli, 2015). Intrinsic motivation, on the other hand, originates inside of the individual and is more difficult to elicit. According to self-determination theory, individuals become intrinsically motivated if their fundamental psychological needs for competence, relatedness, and autonomy are addressed (Deci & Ryan, 2008). According to this theory, external rewards or social pressure are in conflict with the need for autonomy, resulting in a decrease of intrinsic motivation. To support intrinsic motivation, people need to have choices that matter.

Further, the learning challenge needs to target the optimal balance between being too simple or too complex, the so-called "Goldilocks principle". Because this sweet spot not only differs between individuals but also varies between situations and over time, the adaptivity of technology-based learning can be its most valuable asset (Ritterfeld, Shen et al., 2009). Adjusting the optimal level requires a previous outcome measure either as a pretask diagnosis or as an in-task learning result (see also Point 5, later in this chapter).

Feedback can trigger both extrinsic and intrinsic motivation, with the latter requiring it to be task-related, specific, and meaningful. Preschool children, who are generally more intrinsically inclined to solve problems and learn, tend to stay longer on a task when receiving causally rich feedback than those receiving causally weak information or simply stickers as a reward (Alvarez & Booth, 2014). Stickers or badges as rewards, unspecific feedback, or encouraging messages can facilitate extrinsic motivation and are easily embedded into a nonadaptive multimedia context.

3 Meaningful learning

The term "meaningful learning" was first coined by Ausubel (1968) as a foundation for motivation. He distinguished between rote learning and meaningful learning. Instead of merely recognizing and recalling facts, sustainable and useful – meaningful – learning results from personal relevance, a specific purpose, or from linking new material to existing knowledge (Hirsh-Pasek et al., 2015). In this capacity, meaningful learning is associated with problem solving. The two modes of learning – rote learning and meaningful learning – do not oppose each other. Instead, rote learning is also an essential prerequisite for meaningful learning because problem solving is often aligned with using existing knowledge in more complex tasks. In other words, rote learning is the means, whereas meaningful learning is the educational goal (Mayer, 2002). The concept of meaningful learning has been applied in various studies on multimedia-based learning, such as learning within the virtual environment Second Life (Keskitalo, Pyykkö, & Ruokamo, 2011) or for the evaluation of context-aware mobile learning (Huang & Chiu, 2015). Keskitalo et al. (2011), for example, created a virtual learning environment in Second Life in which students had to work together to solve a real-life scheduling and management problem and complete questionnaires on their learning experience in the same virtual environment. Results indicated that the virtual environment facilitated meaningful learning through active, self-directed, and goal-oriented, as well as constructive, study.

4 Social interaction

In the framework of self-determination theory, next to autonomy and competence, the third determinant for intrinsic motivation is relatedness. The basic assumption is that individuals are innately driven to internalize the ambient values and cultural practices of those to whom they feel or want to feel connected (Niemiec & Ryan, 2009). Cooperative and collaborative learning takes advantage of the benefits of social interaction within the learning process if individuals work together toward a common learning goal (see Ritterfeld, Weber, Fernandes, & Vorderer, 2004, for collaborative learning within media environments). Reviews and meta-analyses have confirmed the impact of such learning environments on academic achievement, socialization, motivation, and personal self-development (e.g. Gillies, 2016; Slavin, 2014). Five key components drive the cooperative learning effect: interdependence of group members, promotive interaction, individual responsibility, social skills, and group processing (Gillies, 2016). Collaborative learning within an app context can be realized in multiple ways. On one hand, a collaborative learning setting is created around one device while children work together on a project such as creating a digital book. On the other hand, the app itself can realize the collaborative learning context through, for instance, virtual agents, narrations, or multiplayer options while following a shared goal. Especially if reaching a goal requires social interaction, individuals are encouraged to process information more deeply, which in turn may result in better learning outcomes. In addition, social responsibility has proven to be effective in promoting deeper learning. Chase, Chin, Oppezzo, and Schwartz (2009) utilized a teaching agent to facilitate learning in fifth- and eighth-grade students. In one condition, the children were prompted to teach an agent; in the other condition, they were left to believe that they would learn for themselves. Teaching an agent made children spend more time on learning activities.

5   Scaffolded exploration toward a learning goal

Finally, guidance through the learning process toward a well-defined learning goal is of great importance for its success. Recent meta-analyses have focused on the effects of the level of control of a teacher on the learning outcomes of their students (Alfieri, Brooks, Aldrich, & Tenenbaum, 2011; Carolan, Hutchins, Wickens, & Cumming, 2014; Furtak, Seidel, Iverson, & Briggs, 2012). Alfieri et al. (2011) found that direct instruction was superior to unassisted discovery. However, teacher-assisted discovery resulted in better learning outcomes compared to highly controlled teaching methods. Although effect sizes vary considerably among the meta-analyses, ranging from small (Carolan et al., 2014) to medium effects (Furtak et al., 2012), they all suggest a benefit from assisted discovery compared to direct instruction or unassisted discovery.

Scaffolding, as one specific assisted discovery method, has received a great deal of attention in educational research. The method originates from Vygotsky's sociocultural theory and was first adopted by Wood, Bruner, and Ross (1976) to describe a specific type of guided learning toward a learning goal. Scaffolding describes an interactive process in which a teacher provides support that is fine-tuned to the student's current skill level. Consequently, a continuous diagnostic process is a key aspect in scaffolding. The support provided should be either at the same or a slightly increased skill level. The more competent the child becomes, the less support the teacher needs to provide (van de Pol, Volman, & Beishuizen, 2010) until the child is able to accomplish the task independently. Ke and Abras (2013) showed that struggling students tend to stop playing a game when tasks become too challenging. Hence, implementing artificial intelligence into an app can facilitate scaffolded explorations. Every action of the user can thereby be used as diagnostic information to adapt the system to a user's specific skills and needs. Adaptive input and tailored challenges based on the Goldilocks principle can lead to better engagement, motivation and – most importantly – to deep learning. Other authors have provided evidence for the importance of scaffolded guidance of game play through teacher or peer scaffolding. For example, Wong, Boticki, Sun, and Looi (2011) found positive effects of teacher scaffolding on overcoming obstacles or managing frustration, whereas peer scaffolding facilitated players' interaction and collaboration. However, Ke (2008) observed that peer tutoring was not very elaborated and was naturalistic. Especially for students with low prior knowledge, teacher guidance was most important for continuous gameplay and, as a consequence, for approaching a learning goal.

Sustainable learning results from active learning in a meaningful context. Social interactions can support such learning, for instance, through scaffolding toward a learning goal. There are various ways to address the five pillars of learning in a multimedia environment. But a simple translation of learning mechanisms into a multimedia environment will not necessarily result in an engaging game environment. Instead, the game environment needs to carefully merge principles of learning and entertainment.

Step 3: building the game environment

Mobile learning emerged from the integration of mobile devices into learning contexts (Giannakas et al., 2018). Mobile learning technologies enable learners to have access to learning content and collaborative activities independent from time and space. Thereby, mobile learning enables student learning in different contexts such as inside or outside of school, at different hours, and at their own pace. Moreover, it enables learners to repeat certain tasks. Instructors have the opportunity to interact with learners directly or indirectly through different communication channels such as messengers, e-mail, or video chat. Intelligent systems also permit adaptive learning. A recent meta-analysis by Sung et al. (2016) showed a medium overall effect of mobile devices on learning. Handhelds, such as smartphones, were associated with a medium effect size, compared to lower effect sizes resulting from laptop usage. Taken together, features such as portability or communicative functions seem to contribute positively to learning outcomes.

Mobile learning is often associated with game-based learning. Digital game-based learning is a concept that uses digital games to achieve a deep processing of educational content. According to Shute and Ke (2012), a well-designed game consists of seven core elements: interactive problem solving, specific goals/rules, adaptive challenges, control, ongoing feedback, uncertainty that evokes player engagement, and sensory stimuli (i.e., the combination of graphics, sounds, and/ or storyline).

The main reason for using game technology for learning is that games encourage motivation and deep engagement (Abdul Jabbar & Felicia, 2015) – two important aspects for effective learning. Additionally, the multimodal representation and visualization of information in games can enhance learning, similarly to the aforementioned learning of language via interactive storybooks (Takacs et al., 2015). Simulated problem solving and instant feedback also help to create an immersive and authentic context for active and meaningful learning. Therefore, integration of game elements within the learning environment is important.

From a psychological perspective, gaming is a truly voluntary and nonpurposeful activity that is enjoyed for its own sake (Oerter, 2013). The experience during gameplay is often described with the terms flow (Csikszentmihalyi, 2014) or immersion (Spiegel & Hoinkes, 2009), in which the game reality is more salient than the surrounding physical and social world. The enjoyment in gameplay is driven strongly by a combination of technical and psychological functionality. According to Ke (2016), gameplay consists of two layers: the game mechanics and the narrative, and these have to interact as meaningfully as possible. The game mechanics layer involves rules and actions associated with those rules. Rules determine the play behavior as well as the winning or losing state in the game. They frame player strategies and the means by which a player tries to attain a certain goal in the game. Usually, there is a core mechanism in the game, an activity that the player repeats to reach the end-game state. The narrative of a game is not always defined by a complex storytelling. Narratives can be integrated into games in three ways: (a) as a global goal (e.g., an adventure mission), (b) as a restricted instance or plot in game level(s), and (c) as a sandbox or an open-ended game world that permits players to state their own goals or stories via authoring- or construction-based play (Jenkins, 2004; Ke et al., 2019). Game designers use different formats to create these narratives. So-called environmental storytelling refers to a deliberate design of the game environment in which every detail can add something to the storyline. The technique of backdrop stories or missions introduces a main plot or main goal of a game that can be complemented by localized incidents or plots within a game level (localized narratives). Ke (2016) has characterized different learning game genres in terms of their core game mechanics and involvement of narrative, thereby providing an informed foundation for decision making while designing a learning game (see Table 8.1). Concerning speech, language, and communicative learning, every game type could be possible depending on the focused skill. Table 8.1 gives some examples for potential learning contents.

Table 8.1 Genres of learning games classified via core mechanics, narrative design (Ke, 2016, p. 222), and potential speech, language, and communication learning content (by the authors)

Game type	Core mechanics	Narrative				Examples of SLC content
		ES	BS	LN	OE	
Casual puzzle game	Logic and thought during puzzle solving	Maybe	Maybe	No	No	• Synthesis of words • Writing
Action	Quick thinking and reflexes (e.g., in jumping, shooting)	Yes	Maybe	No	No	• Fast retrieval of words
Adventure	Overcoming long-term obstacles, involving constant exploration, item collection, and puzzle solving	Yes	Yes	Maybe	No	• Word learning • Grammatical learning
Strategy	Strategic deployment via system and planning	Yes	Yes	Maybe	No	• Learning of strategies for word learning
Role playing	Interacting with characters, information collection, and decision making	Yes	Yes	Yes	Maybe	• Development of various communication skills
Simulation	Interaction with and discovering underlying simulated model or system	Yes	Maybe	No	No	• Describing observations
Construction	Designing, building, and resource management	Yes	Maybe	No	Yes	• Narrative skills

ES = Environmental storytelling; BS = Backdrop story or mission; LN = Localized narrative; OE = Open-ended; SLC = Speech, language, and communication

Various gaming elements, such as motivational elements, interactive elements, fun elements, and multimedia elements, influence cognitive and emotional engagement in gameplay (Abdul Jabbar & Felicia, 2015). Motivational elements involve factors that influence players' thoughts and behaviors with regard to meaningful gameplay and learning (e.g., rules, choices, rewards, or adaptation). Interactive elements describe elements allowing participation and involvement in gaming activities (e.g., role play, resources, conflicts). Fun elements trigger a player's sense of enjoyment and excitement (e.g., challenges, storytelling and narratives, characters). Multimedia elements constitute elements attracting a player's physical attention through sensory stimuli (e.g., visualization, animation, videos, audio, sound effects, or motion).

In their review, Abdul Jabbar and Felicia (2015) analyzed the impact of various gaming elements on emotional and cognitive engagement, as well as on learning and motivation. Creating motivating, engaging, and concurrently effective game environments for learning is extremely challenging. Moreover, the target group is often highly heterogeneous. Accordingly, studies reveal differential effects of multimedia elements such as graphics, animations, videos, text, or audio. Ke and Abras (2013), for example, analyzed the gaming behavior of students with different special needs. They found that some visualizations were too abstract for these students, leading to a high need for teacher support.

Narrative elements such as virtual characters and a storyline support emotional and cognitive engagement in game-based learning (Abdul Jabbar & Felicia, 2015). Including challenging tasks into a game also seems to motivate individuals and support engagement (Shu & Liu, 2019). However, as mentioned before, challenge has to be attuned to the player's skill level if it is to facilitate engagement and learning.

Implementing scaffolding methods into game-based learning platforms also showed positive effects. Sun, Wang, and Chan (2011) found that scaffolding decreases the time needed for task solving, and thereby also decreases frustration in students. However, the authors also point out that students often rely on the guidance of the technology to identify their mistakes and correct them. Role play seems to affect students' knowledge, skill, and motivation (Abdul Jabbar & Felicia, 2015) if it incorporates cooperative and collaborative learning and facilitates the need for relatedness. Abdul Jabbar and Felicia (2015) also found various cases of performance feedback in game-based learning settings. Praise and immediate feedback in the form of graphics or sounds seem to attract students and improve their self-efficacy.

With their learning mechanics and gaming mechanics model, Arnab et al. (2015) provide a framework for analyzing learning games in order to implement learning principles and game elements. They stress the thoughtful implementation of learning principles into games through distinct game mechanics, and they link game mechanics with thinking skills and associated learning mechanisms. For example, applying something is associated with learning mechanisms such as task execution, imitation, or demonstration, and it can be implemented into a game through capture elimination, time pressure, simulation, or movements. Understanding, on the other hand, is linked to objectifying or learning through tutorials and can be translated into game format via role play or imported directly through tutorial videos.

The following section summarizes the aforementioned principles and brings them together in a set of recommendations for designing a learning app.

From theory to practice: recommendations for designing a language learning app

Designing an app for language learning is a challenging task. Specific language learning principles as well as general learning mechanisms need to be considered and attuned to build a reasonable learning context with the necessary motivating entertainment potential. Solely translating learning principles into a multimedia format will not suffice to engage people in gaming, and consequently give them a learning experience. Supplemented interdisciplinary expertise is a key factor in the design of an app aiming to fulfill any educational purpose. However, that sounds easier than it is. In their development project *E-Rebuild*, Ke et al. (2019) described the problems that occur in interdisciplinary collaboration and communication and suggest a framework for the design process of game-based learning platforms from the perspective of the designer and the computer scientist. The authors also mention that developers have to initially decide which learning-gaming experience they want to create, and they suggest different basic questions for decision making at this starting point. Such questions include the specification of the learning content, the aesthetic experience, and the associated gaming mechanics. Our approach adds to the process in addressing the intertwining of content and game mechanisms that we consider necessary before the design process starts. Taken together, we propose six principles of app design (Table 8.2) based on the available research. These should facilitate language acquisition in children and incorporate multiple factors that affect the different learning strategies.

Table 8.2 Six principles of app design to facilitate language acquisition in children

Principle 1	*Specify your target group and the focused language structure*
Principle 2	*Determine key language learning methods*
Principle 3	*Include the target group in the design process*
Principle 4	*Fine-tune learning and gaming*
Principle 5	*Implement as many and as few game mechanisms as needed*
Principle 6	*Use an iterative process to fine-tune language and general learning principles within the game design*

Principle 1: specify your target group (including age and language background) and the focused language structure

The specification of the target group in terms of age, language background (bilingualism, developmental language disorders, etc.), and potential additional important factors such as comorbid phenomena (e.g., problems in phoneme discrimination, phonological working memory, as two frequent problems in children with DLD), is the basis for structuring the language learning content. At this point, experts from (special needs) education, linguistics, speech-language pathology, developmental psychology, or related disciplines should be included.

Principle 2: determine key language learning methods

The next principle requires a determination of evidence-based methods aiming to facilitate the focused language structure in the specified target group. The focus on the targeting language structure is the key element and has to trigger each step throughout the design process. Multiple factors such as the linguistic complexity of the word material, the number of repetitions (high frequency), and diverse examples of words and language structures have to be considered.

Principle 3: include the target group in the design process

The target group has to be involved actively in developing digital game-based learning approaches to improve the quality of learning by transferring knowledge and skills. Moreover, involving the target group in the design process supports engagement and motivation for players regardless of their age and abilities. This participatory design can be achieved by performing a series of participatory workshops using an evidence-based evaluation process (Nedopil, Schauber, & Glende, 2013). Within this process, learning content and gameplay can be evaluated formatively, and necessary modifications can be applied in due time.

Principle 4: fine-tune learning and gaming

The main challenge in the design process is to attune the chosen learning principles and methods with appropriate game mechanics. On the one hand, learning principles have to be translated into the game to allow for sustainable learning. On the other hand, there is a need for a proper game design to support engagement and motivation. Well-designed games provide ample features supporting important learning mechanisms.

Principle 5: implement as many and as few game mechanisms as needed

Game mechanics should be implemented wisely to scaffold learning to the focused learning goal. The game needs to provide as much information (e.g., learning material, hints, guidance through an adaptive system) to the user as needed for meaningful, deep learning. However, we advise against overdoing game mechanisms in order to avoid distraction.

Principle 6: use an iterative process to fine-tune language and general learning principles within the game design

Repetitive feedback loops for the fine-tuning between learning and gaming are necessary to facilitate not only a learning effect but also the engagement and motivation of the target group. As stated in Principle 3, a constant inclusion of the target group in the design process is an important aspect in order to gather feedback on acceptance, attraction, usability, and further aspects resulting in a tailored game for the focused group and learning content.

Summary and conclusion

We have introduced six principles that should be considered in an integrated process of designing a game to be used for a (second) language acquisition. These principles derive from a three-step approach: (1) game content follows linguistic principles, (2) knowledge facilitates the learning process within an app, and (3) the game design is discussed in order to deliver optimal motivation and engagement. All six principles cannot be viewed in isolation from each other, are mutually dependent, and can facilitate each other. Following these principles in the design process of games aiming at language learning is more likely to increase their efficacy and support children in their need to improve their language skills. Interdisciplinary collaboration is a key factor in the design process. The next step is to test whether and how the proposed approach assists this process.

The potential of language learning apps lies especially in the implementation of artificial intelligence and speech recognition to enable adaptive learning of not only receptive but also productive language skills. But to date, there are still a lot of shortcomings in the automatic recognition of child and disordered speech. The advantages of social partners for learning can be realized digitally through avatars or multiplayer settings. Avatars can serve not only as learning guides in the game environment but also as students to be taught. Research needs to focus on how to design and implement avatars into digital environments for children. Additionally, multiplayer settings are able to implement collaborative learning into a game environment. Research should accompany the implementation processes to clarify whether common collaborative learning methods need to be adapted for a digital environment. There are still a lot of limitations in the available technology and in the understanding of the implementation and concurrence of various (language) learning principles into an engaging and motivating game environment. Therefore, an interdisciplinary research-driven design process can help to improve recommendations for a reasonable design process toward creating an effective language learning app. In the end, apps cannot replace social interaction. But they can contribute to fostering first and second language learning by providing an entertaining learning environment that children use voluntarily and repeatedly, thereby resulting in sustainable learning.

Three key considerations for parents, educators, and producers

- Using apps or gaming does not have negative effects on child development per se. In fact, children's intrinsic motivation for playing can be utilized for learning.
- Reasonably designed apps can support educational processes because children can use them independently of location and time.
- Designing apps for language learning is a complex process that requires interdisciplinary collaboration.

References

Abdul Jabbar, A. I., & Felicia, P. (2015). Gameplay engagement and learning in game-based learning. *Review of Educational Research, 85*(4), 740–779. doi:10.3102/0034654315577210

Alfieri, L., Brooks, P. J., Aldrich, N. J., & Tenenbaum, H. R. (2011). Does discovery-based instruction enhance learning? *Journal of Educational Psychology, 103*(1), 1–18. doi:10.1037/a0021017

Alvarez, A. L., & Booth, A. E. (2014). Motivated by meaning: Testing the effect of knowledge-infused rewards on preschoolers' persistence. *Child Development, 85*(2), 783–791. doi:10.1111/cdev.12151

Arnab, S., Lim, T., Carvalho, M. B., Bellotti, F., de Freitas, S., Louchart, S., . . . de Gloria, A. (2015). Mapping learning and game mechanics for serious games analysis. *British Journal of Educational Technology, 46*(2), 391–411. doi:10.1111/bjet.12113

Ausubel, D. P. (Ed.). (1968). *Educational psychology: A cognitive view.* New York, NY: Holt, Rinehart and Winston.

Bialystok, E., Luk, G., Peets, K. F., & Yang, S. (2010). Receptive vocabulary differences in monolingual and bilingual children. *Bilingualism: Language and Cognition, 13*(4), 525–531. doi:10.1017/s1366728909990423

Bus, A. G., Takacs, Z. K., & Kegel, C. A. T. (2015). Affordances and limitations of electronic storybooks for young children's emergent literacy. *Developmental Review, 35*, 79–97. doi:10.1016/j.dr.2014.12.004

Carolan, T. F., Hutchins, S. D., Wickens, C. D., & Cumming, J. M. (2014). Costs and benefits of more learner freedom: Meta-analyses of exploratory and learner control training methods. *Human Factors*, *56*(5), 999–1014. doi:10.1177/0018720813517710

Chase, C. C., Chin, D. B., Oppezzo, M. A., & Schwartz, D. L. (2009). Teachable agents and the protégé effect: Increasing the effort towards learning. *Journal of Science Education and Technology*, *18*(4), 334–352. doi:10.1007/s10956-009-9180-4

Chiong, C., & DeLoache, J. S. (2013). Learning the ABCs: What kinds of picture books facilitate young children's learning? *Journal of Early Childhood Literacy*, *13*(2), 225–241. doi:10.1177/1468798411430091

Conti-Ramsden, G., Durkin, K., Toseeb, U., Botting, N., & Pickles, A. (2018). Education and employment outcomes of young adults with a history of developmental language disorder. *International Journal of Language & Communication Disorders*, *53*(2), 237–255. doi:10.1111/1460-6984.12338

Csikszentmihalyi, M. (Ed.). (2014). *Flow and the foundations of positive psychology: The collected works of Mihaly Csikszentmihalyi*. Dordrecht, Netherlands: Springer. doi:10.1007/978-94-017-9088-8

Deci, E. L., & Ryan, R. M. (2008). Self-determination theory: A macrotheory of human motivation, development, and health. *Canadian Psychology*, *49*(3), 182–185. doi:10.1037/a0012801

Des Roches, C. A., Balachandran, I., Ascenso, E. M., Tripodis, Y., & Kiran, S. (2015). Effectiveness of an impairment-based individualized rehabilitation program using an iPad-based software platform. *Frontiers in Human Neuroscience*, *8*, 1015. doi:10.3389/fnhum.2014.01015

Falloon, G. (2013). Young students using iPads: App design and content influences on their learning pathways. *Computers & Education*, *68*, 505–521. doi:10.1016/j.compedu.2013.06.006

Flack, Z. M., Field, A. P., & Horst, J. S. (2018). The effects of shared storybook reading on word learning: A meta-analysis. *Developmental Psychology*, *54*(7), 1334–1346. doi:10.1037/dev0000512

Furtak, E. M., Seidel, T., Iverson, H., & Briggs, D. C. (2012). Experimental and quasi-experimental studies of inquiry-based science teaching: A meta-analysis. *Review of Educational Research*, *82*(3), 300–329. doi:10.3102/0034654312457206

Giannakas, F., Kambourakis, G., Papasalouros, A., & Gritzalis, S. (2018). A critical review of 13 years of mobile game-based learning. *Educational Technology Research and Development*, *66*(2), 341–384. doi:10.1007/s11423-017-9552-z

Gillies, R. M. (2016). Cooperative learning: Review of research and practice. *Australian Journal of Teacher Education*, *41*(3), 39–54. doi:10.14221/ajte.2016v41n3.3

Harris, J., Golinkoff, R. M., & Hirsh-Pasek, K. (2011). Lessons from the crib to the classroom: How children really learn vocabulary. In S. B. Neuman & D. K. Dickinson (Eds.), *Handbook of early literacy research* (pp. 49–60). New York, NY: Guilford Press.

Hirsh-Pasek, K., Zosh, J. M., Golinkoff, R. M., Gray, J. H., Robb, M. B., & Kaufman, J. (2015). Putting education in "educational" apps: Lessons from the science of learning. *Psychological Science in the Public Interest*, *16*(1), 3–34. doi:10.1177/1529100615569721

Huang, Y.-M., & Chiu, P.-S. (2015). The effectiveness of a meaningful learning-based evaluation model for context-aware mobile learning. *British Journal of Educational Technology*, *46*(2), 437–447. doi:10.1111/bjet.12147

Jenkins, H. (2004). Game design as narrative architecture. In N. Wardrip-Furin & P. Harrigan (Eds.), *First person: New media as story, performance, and game* (pp. 118–130). Cambridge, MA: MIT Press.

Jenkins, H., Camper, B., Chisholm, A., Grigsby, N., Klopfer, E., Osterweil, S., . . . Chor Guan, T. (2009). From serious games to serious gaming. In U. Ritterfeld, M. Cody, & P. Vorderer (Eds.), *Serious games: Mechanisms and effects* (pp. 448–468). New York, NY: Routledge.

Ke, F. (2008). A case study of computer gaming for math: Engaged learning from gameplay? *Computers & Education, 51*(4), 1609–1620. doi:10.1016/j.compedu.2008.03.003

Ke, F. (2016). Designing and integrating purposeful learning in game play: A systematic review. *Educational Technology Research and Development, 64*(2), 219–244. doi:10.1007/s11423-015-9418-1

Ke, F., & Abras, T. (2013). Games for engaged learning of middle school children with special learning needs. *British Journal of Educational Technology, 44*(2), 225–242. doi:10.1111/j.1467-8535.2012.01326.x

Ke, F., Shute, V., Clark, K. M., & Erlebacher, G. (Eds.). (2019). *Interdisciplinary design of game-based learning platforms.* Cham, Germany: Springer. doi:10.1007/978-3-030-04339-1

Keskitalo, T., Pyykkö, E., & Ruokamo, H. (2011). Exploring the meaningful learning of students in second life. *Journal of Educational Technology & Society, 14*(1), 16–26. Retrieved from www.jstor.org/stable/jeductechsoci.14.1.16

King, A. M., Thomeczek, M., Voreis, G., & Scott, V. (2014). iPad® use in children and young adults with autism spectrum disorder: An observational study. *Child Language Teaching and Therapy, 30*(2), 159–173. doi:10.1177/0265659013510922

Klimmt, C., Vorderer, P., & Ritterfeld, U. (2004). Experimentelle Medienforschung mit interaktiven Stimuli: Zum Umgang mit Wechselwirkungen zwischen "Reiz" und "Reaktion". In W. Wirth (Ed.), *Forschungslogik und -design in der Kommunikationswissenschaft: Band 1: Einführung, Problematisierungen und Aspekte der Methodenlogik aus kommunikationswissenschaftlicher Perspektive* (pp. 142–156). Köln, Germany: Halem.

Konishi, H., Kanero, J., Freeman, M. R., Golinkoff, R. M., & Hirsh-Pasek, K. (2014). Six principles of language development: Implications for second language learners. *Developmental Neuropsychology, 39*(5), 404–420. doi:10.1080/8756564 1.2014.931961

Kucirkova, N., Messer, D., Sheehy, K., & Fernández Panadero, C. (2014). Children's engagement with educational iPad apps: Insights from a Spanish classroom. *Computers & Education, 71*, 175–184. doi:10.1016/j.compedu.2013.10.003

Mayer, R. E. (2002). Rote versus meaningful learning. *Theory Into Practice, 41*(4), 226–232. doi:10.1207/s15430421tip4104_4

Nedopil, C., Schauber, C., & Glende, S. (2013). *Guideline: The art and joy of user integration in AAL projects.* Retrieved from www.aal-europe.eu/wpcontent/uploads/2015/02/AALA_Guideline_YOUSE_online.pdf

Niemiec, C. P., & Ryan, R. M. (2009). Autonomy, competence, and relatedness in the classroom. Applying self-determination theory to educational practice. *Theory and Research in Education, 7*(2), 133–144. doi:10.1177/1477878509104318

Oerter, R. (Ed.). (2013). *Psychologie des Spiels. Ein handlungstheoretischer Ansatz* (2nd ed.). *Beltz-Taschenbuch Psychologie: Vol. 46.* Weinheim, Germany: Beltz Nikolo.

Parish-Morris, J., Golinkoff, R. M., & Hirsh-Pasek, K. (2013). From coo to code: Language acquisition in early childhood. In P. D. Zelazo (Ed.), *The Oxford handbook of developmental psychology* (Vol. 1, pp. 867–908). New York, NY: Oxford University Press.

Pinto, M., & Gardner, H. (2014). Communicative interaction between a nonspeaking child with cerebral palsy and her mother using an iPad™. *Child Language Teaching and Therapy, 30*(2), 207–220. doi:10.1177/0265659013518338

Qi, C. H., Kaiser, A. P., Milan, S., & Hancock, T. (2006). Language performance of low-income African American and European American preschool children on the PPVT-III. *Language, Speech, and Hearing Services in Schools, 37*(1), 5–16. doi:10.1044/0161-1461(2006/002)

Richter, G., Raban, D. R., & Rafaeli, S. (2015). Studying gamification: The effect of rewards and incentives on motivation. In T. Reiners & L. C. Wood (Eds.), *Gamification in education and business* (Vol. 60, pp. 21–46). Cham, Germany: Springer. doi:10.1007/978-3-319-10208-5_2

Ritterfeld, U. (2011). Beim Spielen lernen? Ein differenzierter Blick auf die Möglichkeiten und Grenzen von Serious Games. *Computer + Unterricht, 21*(84), 54–57.

Ritterfeld, U., Cody, M., & Vorderer, P. (Eds.). (2009). *Serious games: Mechanisms and effects.* New York, NY: Routledge.

Ritterfeld, U., Klimmt, C., Vorderer, P., & Steinhilper, L. K. (2005). The effects of a narrative audiotape on preschoolers' entertainment experience and attention. *Media Psychology, 7*(1), 47–72. doi:10.1207/S1532785XMEP0701_3

Ritterfeld, U., Shen, C., Wang, H., Nocera, L., & Wong, W. L. (2009). Multimodality and interactivity: Connecting properties of serious games with educational outcomes. *CyberPsychology and Behavior, 12*(6), 691–698. doi:10.1089/cpb.2009.0099

Ritterfeld, U., & Weber, R. (2006). Video games for entertainment and education. In P. Vorderer & J. Bryant (Eds.), *LEA's communication series. Playing video games: Motives, responses, and consequences* (pp. 399–414). Mahwah, NJ: Lawrence Erlbaum Associates.

Ritterfeld, U., Weber, R., Fernandes, S., & Vorderer, P. (2004). Think science! Entertainment education in interactive theaters. *Computers in Entertainment, 2*(1), 11. doi:10.1145/973801.973819

Rohlfing, K. J., & Nachtigäller, K. (2016). Can 28-month-old children learn spatial prepositions robustly from pictures? Yes, when narrative input is provided. *Frontiers in Psychology, 7.* doi:10.3389/fpsyg.2016.00961

Schwab, J. F., & Lew-Williams, C. (2016). Language learning, socioeconomic status, and child-directed speech. *WIREs Cognitive Science, 7*(4), 264–275. doi:10.1002/wcs.1393

Serratrice, L. (2013). The bilingual child. In T. K. Bhatia & W. C. Ritchie (Eds.), *The handbook of bilingualism and multilingualism* (2nd ed., pp. 87–108). Chichester, England: Blackwell.

Shu, L., & Liu, M. (2019). Student engagement in game-based learning: A literature review from 2008 to 2018. *Journal of Educational Multimedia and Hypermedia, 28*(2), 193–215. Retrieved from www.learntechlib.org/p/183934

Shute, V. J., & Ke, F. (2012). Games, learning, and assessment. In D. Ifenthaler, D. Eseryel, & X. Ge (Eds.), *Assessment in game-based learning: Foundations, innovations, and perspectives* (Vol. 38, pp. 43–58). New York, NY: Springer. doi:10.1007/978-1-4614-3546-4_4

Slavin, R. E. (2014). Cooperative learning and academic achievement: Why does groupwork work? *Anales de Psicología, 30*(3), 785–791. doi:10.6018/analesps.30.3.201201

Spiegel, S., & Hoinkes, R. (2009). Immersive serious games for large scale multi-player dialogue and cocreation. In U. Ritterfeld, M. Cody, & P. Vorderer (Eds.), *Serious games: Mechanisms and effects* (pp. 469–485). New York, NY: Routledge.

Sun, C.-T., Wang, D.-Y., & Chan, H.-L. (2011). How digital scaffolds in games direct problem-solving behaviors. *Computers & Education, 57*(3), 2118–2125. doi:10.1016/j.compedu.2011.05.022

Sung, Y.-T., Chang, K.-E., & Liu, T.-C. (2016). The effects of integrating mobile devices with teaching and learning on students' learning performance: A meta-analysis and research synthesis. *Computers & Education, 94*, 252–275. doi:10.1016/j.compedu.2015.11.008

Takacs, Z. K., Swart, E. K., & Bus, A. G. (2015). Benefits and pitfalls of multimedia and interactive features in technology-enhanced storybooks: A meta-analysis. *Review of Educational Research, 85*(4), 698–739. doi:10.3102/0034654314566989

Tomblin, J. B., Records, N. L., Buckwalter, P., Zhang, X., Smith, E., & O'Brien, M. (1997). Prevalence of specific language impairment in kindergarten children. *Journal of Speech Language and Hearing Research, 40*(6), 1245–1260. doi:10.1044/jslhr.4006.1245

Van de Pol, J., Volman, M., & Beishuizen, J. (2010). Scaffolding in teacher–student interaction: A decade of research. *Educational Psychology Review, 22*(3), 271–296. doi:10.1007/s10648-010-9127-6

Wong, L.-H., Boticki, I., Sun, J., & Looi, C.-K. (2011). Improving the scaffolds of a mobile-assisted Chinese character forming game via a design-based research cycle. *Computers in Human Behavior, 27*(5), 1783–1793. doi:10.1016/j.chb.2011.03.005

Wood, D., Bruner, J. S., & Ross, G. (1976). The role of tutoring in problem solving. *Journal of Child Psychology and Psychiatry, 17*(2), 89–100. doi:10.1111/j.1469-7610.1976.tb00381.x

Chapter 9

Digital children's literature in the interplay between visuality and animation

A model for analyzing picture book apps and their potential for children's story comprehension

Claudia Müller-Brauers, Jan M. Boelmann,
Christiane Miosga, and Ines Potthast

Introduction

Recent years have seen an enormous increase in digital media use (e.g., Wirth et al., Chapter 6 in this volume). Even very young children are now using digital devices such as smartphones or tablets (Bitkom, 2019; Chaudron, DiGioia, & Gemo 2018; Kucirkova & Littleton, 2016; Neumann & Neumann, 2017; Ofcom, 2018; Real & Correro, 2015). Book markets have also adapted to this trend. E-books (electronic books), enhanced e-books, and apps do not just represent new media that provide manifold opportunities to get involved with stories. They are also becoming more attractive to parents and practitioners working in the field of early childhood education (Ehmig & Reuter, 2013; Kucirkova & Littleton, 2016). However, at the same time, research confirms that parents and educators are uncertain about how to use digital media in order to foster children's learning development and reading motivation (Chaudron, DiGioia, & Gemo 2018; Howard & Wallace, 2016; Kucirkova & Littleton, 2016). Therefore, in this chapter, we suggest a model derived from narrative and media theory (Boelmann, 2019; Staiger, 2014; Thiele, 2000) for analyzing picture book apps in terms of their potential for children's story comprehension. We apply the model exemplarily to the picture book app *Sweet dreams, Howie Hare* (Schulmeyer, 2011), and discuss quality criteria that can help parents and educators make didactically reasonable choices. We assume that animations (visual and audio) serving a narrative function possess great potential for promoting story comprehension because they can highlight the information or narrative means integrated in the text or even complement the text by providing additional information (Thiele, 2000). To frame our assumptions theoretically, we first focus on current research on analogue and digital picture book reading, showing that a great challenge in digital conditions lies in how visual and audio animations should be embedded in the reading process. This is followed by general theoretical considerations from picture book analyses that we use as a basis for our media analysis. In the last section, we discuss our results didactically by relating them to practice and suggesting a set of criteria for selecting narrative picture book apps.

Analogue and digital picture book reading

Focusing on children's literature in the context of child development and education reveals multitudinous studies verifying that shared reading has an extremely positive effect on early literacy outcomes (e.g., Fletcher & Reese, 2005; Justice & Ezell, 2000). Numerous studies show positive effects in terms of vocabulary learning (e.g., Wasik, Hindman, & Snell, 2016), narrative skills (Grolig, Cohrdes, Tiffin-Richards, & Schroeder, 2019), or receptive language abilities (DeBaryshe, 1993). The effectiveness of shared book reading can be explained pragmatically through the specific interactive conditions under which picture book and storybook reading function. Based on cognitively and emotionally activating interaction formats such as *sustained shared thinking* (Siraj-Blatchford, Sylva, Muttock, Gilden, & Bell, 2002) or *shared attention* (Tomasello, 2009), adult readers ideally stimulate the cognitive and linguistic development of the child by using scaffolding processes to adapt interactive framing to the child's individual language level (Hildebrandt, Scheidt, Hildebrandt, Hédervári-Heller, & Dreier, 2016). When doing this, parents and early childhood professionals use *multimodal motherese* (cf. Gogate, Bahrick, & Watson, 2000; Jungmann, Miosga, Fuchs, & Rohlfing, 2009) or responsive strategies to support children's language acquisition processes by adapting their language, gestures, facial expressions, prosody, or gaze sensitively to the needs and interests of the child. In this way, they create *emotional attunement* (Miosga, 2019) as a prerequisite and condition for successful language and literary learning processes and model activities in the *zone of proximal development* (Vygotsky, 1987).

In the case of digital children's literature, the reader's task is even more complex. The literate reader is not only responsible for structuring the reading situation dialogically and, accordingly, adjusting it to the individual language development level of the child; the reader's task is also to steer the technical features of the app (visual and audio animation, touchscreen, etc.) interactively by linking them to the storyline. The complexity of this task is confirmed by various studies showing that parents involve their children more strongly in the story when reading conventional picture books (e.g., Parish-Morris, Mahajan, Hirsh-Pasek, Michnick Golinkoff, & Fuller, 2013). Furthermore, adult readers have proved to be distracted by technical features of the digital medium (e.g., hot spots, audio animations) if these are too dominant or nonsystematic. This, in turn, can reduce the activating interaction formats and might impact negatively on story comprehension (Krcmar & Cingel, 2014; Parish-Morris, Mahajan, Hirsh-Pasek, Michnick Golinkoff, & Fuller, 2013; Miosga, Chapter 2 in this volume). Children's attention can also be disturbed by audio animations such as music elements or noise; or they may focus on animated images and visualizations that are not connected to the content of the story (Bus, Takacs, & Kegel, 2015, p. 92). Moreover, games or gaming features, which are also available in electronic form, may interrupt activating interaction formats during reading (Bus, Takacs, & Kegel, 2015, p. 88). Nonetheless, digital children's literature also has a potential for developing receptive narrative skills. Verhallen, Bus, and de Jong (2006), for example, assessed how the early narrative and language skills of 60 preschoolers were affected by animated storybook images in comparison to static images. Findings from an experimental study showed that children with Dutch as their second language who came from low socioeconomic status (SES) backgrounds had a high learning outcome from a multiply presented digital animated version (audio + visual) of the story in terms of both story comprehension and linguistic skills. Brunsmeier and Kolb (2017) assessed how the reception of story apps influenced story comprehension in elementary school students attending English as a Foreign Language (EFL) classrooms in terms of story content and narrative means. Based on interview and video data, they found that students responded positively to story apps because the animation and sound effects not only got them emotionally involved in the story but also helped them to better understand its content and acquire new lexical forms. Therefore, the quality of features is an important factor: "[. . .] animations and sounds proved to be a decisive criterion for selecting appropriate story apps since these features could either support or distract from the understanding of the story" (Brunsmeier & Kolb, 2017, p. 11). Furthermore, it can be assumed that different app types (e.g., direct [e.g., animated Wimmelbooks] vs. open [narrative picture book apps]) not only initiate different forms of interaction and conversation styles, but also enhance literacy skills differently, including the development of digital and multimodal resources that provide divergent linguistic and visual input (Sandvik, Smørdal, & Østerud, 2012).

However, against the background of an increasing use of digital children's literature in preschool educational institutions, we have to ask how technical features of picture books or enhanced e-books are related to the structure of the story, and what can be deduced from this for children's early literacy development. Because clear quality criteria of enhanced e-books and apps for preschoolers are often lacking, this is of particular interest when it comes to implementing literacy environments in kindergarten and preschool and taking a learning-related approach to digital media in the context of early childhood education. As Henkel (2018) points out:

> Viewing children's literature from the perspective of materiality may help to identify levels and aspects involved when it is realized as apps, and, furthermore, it may capture some of the paradoxical conditions of the app, which arise in the relationship between materiality and immateriality and in the ambiguous movement between various formats, genres and media.
>
> (p. 339)

How to analyze picture books

Comprising manifold genres (Thiele, 2000), picture books are the first type of books with which children come into contact. From this stage onward, children's language development starts to proliferate massively, and around the age of 18 months, children enter the world of literature: "[. . .] the vocabulary spurt goes hand in hand with a picturebook spurt" (Kümmerling-Meibauer & Meibauer, 2015a, p. 16). Picture books differ from other children's books in that images set the mandatory condition (Thiele, 2000): they work without text, but not without images (Kurwinkel, 2017, p. 14). Nevertheless, in the case of picture books based on "narrative scripts" (Kümmerling-Meibauer & Meibauer, 2015a, p. 17), both images and text not only convey meaning but also have a narrative structure that can either overlap or also be inconsistent (Staiger, 2014, p. 17): "telling"/verbal storytelling (text) versus "showing"/visual storytelling (images) (Kurwinkel, 2017, p. 48). If a picture book contains text, the verbal and visual code is interwoven in a strong and mutually dependent interconnection (Staiger, 2014, p. 12) that generates meaning and "aesthetic experience" (cf. Thiele, 2000, p. 77): "In picture books, words and pictures invite reader [*sic*] to create literal realities in the world to correspond with them" (Wu, 2014, p. 1415). Accordingly, a large part of the research on picture books examines their multimodal level by reconstructing text–image relations (e.g., Nikolajeva & Scott, 2006; Wu, 2014). However, looking at the picture book multimodally – in the sense of a "multimodal, narrative text and a medium" (cf. Staiger, 2014, p. 12) – opens up further perspectives going beyond image–text relations. Staiger (2014, pp. 14–21) suggests five dimensions of picture books that are closely interlinked and functionally interconnected: the (1) narrative, (2) verbal, (3) pictorial, (4) intermodal, and (5) paratextual and material dimension. In line with our analytic focus, we shall highlight the narrative, intermodal, and material dimensions here.[1]

In the *narrative dimension*, the picture book is examined from two perspectives in its function as a narrative medium: the content and the presentation of a story. The content perspective, often referred to as the "*histoire*" (Todorov, 1966), comprises what is told in the story: plot, narrative theme, space, motifs, figures, and narrated time (Kurwinkel, 2017, p. 52). This also includes the content structure of the narrative, reflecting the distinctive course of action within the narrated text (Kurwinkel, 2017, p. 81) – "[. . .] a common macroschema which children recognise [*sic*] and reproduce after a couple of years of schooling [. . .]" (Stephens, 1995, p. 853). The classical structure consists of an onset or an orientation in which central information is presented on the narrative setting (e.g., place of action, characters, etc.). This is followed by an unexpected turn in action and a complication in which a problem is created that needs to be solved (Kurwinkel, 2017, p. 82). The narrative is completed by a resolution leading to a status of action in which the problem has been solved (Stephens, 1995, p. 854). The term "*discours*" (Todorov, 1966) refers to the narrative means chosen by the author in order to elaborate the narrative, such as the narrative perspective/ mode, figure speech, tense, or time sequence of events (chronological or non-chronological). In German narratology, theoretical works focusing on the narrative mode used to refer to the works of Stanzel (1986) by distinguishing three main narrative situations/perspectives: (1) authorial – displaying an omniscient "point of view" of the narrator with respect to action, character's emotions and intentions, time, space, and so forth; (2) personal – displaying a specific point of view of the narrator based on one figure's experiences and often marked by the use of the inner monologue or free indirect speech; and (3) first person – displaying a point of view representing the first-person singular (see also Kurwinkel, 2017, pp. 107–108).

The *intermodal dimension* highlights image–text relations from a semiotic perspective (Wu, 2014). Thiele (2000, pp. 78–79) suggests three different aspects of the text–image relation:[2] (1) "parallelism" – images and text are identical in relation to the allocation of information and refer to each other; (2) "contrapuntal" – the information provided by the text and images is negated and cannot be merged to a meaningful context (often used as a means to generate comical or irritating effects (in this way, images can show the opposite of what is in the text)) and (3) "plaited braid" – images and text can provide different information, but are closely interwoven and functionally related by complementing each other to form a coherent narrative (see also Kurwinkel, 2017, pp. 160–163).

The *paratextual and material dimension* addresses the material nature of a narrative picture book such as the book format, cover, endpapers, title, type of paper, binding, or motion elements. Staiger (2014, pp. 20–21) argues that the material nature of a picture book may enhance not only the popularity of a book for children but also reading motivation. This can also be assumed for digital picture books, whose materialities are more complex and diverse. Hence, the materiality of digital children's literature differs fundamentally from conventional books. E-books – usually read on electronic readers, tablets, or smartphones – are very similar to traditional books in that they use electronic techniques simply to recreate or simulate book pages. E-books used on e-book readers, computers, or tablet PCs enable the digital reception of books, but in an intermodal way. Picture book apps provide not only animations that may not just be controlled via the touchpad, but also include a read-aloud and recording function, as well as game and audio features such as background noises or music (Kurwinkel, 2017, pp. 38–39). Some picture book apps also have "hot spots": "[. . .] specific areas on the screen where readers can tap, swipe, or pinch across a device's surface to generate sounds, animations, or even additional content during the reading experience" (Serafini, Kachorsky, & Aguilera, 2016, p. 511). Additionally, words that are read out by the read-aloud function can simultaneously be highlighted in color (Fahrer, 2014). Thus, picture book apps, which can be operated with a smartphone or tablet, represent a technical evolution of enhanced e-books, allowing readers an interactive and multimodal immersion in stories (Serafini, Kachorsky, & Aguilera, 2016). However, due to their respective technical characteristics, picture book apps tend to loosen the media relation to the conventional book and have a stronger affinity to gaming or learning apps (Fahrer, 2014). Thus, materiality can be considered as a key component of digital picture books that can influence not only the effect of the text and the image but also the reception process (Kurwinkel, 2017, p. 80).

Analysis

In the following, we use the example of the picture book app *Sweet dreams, Howie Hare* by Heribert Schulmeyer (2011) to examine which kind of animations are integrated into digital picture books and how these are linked to the narrative structure of the story in order to highlight the potential of this app for story comprehension. We assume that if animations are attached closely to the narrative dimension, they have a strong potential for supporting the child's story comprehension. We chose this app because it (a) addresses children in infancy at a time when narrative skills are beginning to unfold (Peterson, Jesso, & McCabe, 1999) and (b) provides a wide range of animation types that can be used interactively to illustrate the potentials of picture book apps for children's story comprehension. This also allows us to adopt multiple analytic criteria that can be used to develop substantial quality criteria. In our analysis, we focus on two main questions: (1) What kind of animated effects are integrated in the digital representation of the picture book? (2) In which manner do animations correspond to the narrative dimension of the picture book?

To answer question 1, we examine animations in the digital version of the book in terms of their technical characteristics on the animative level. Technically speaking, we distinguish three different parameters:

1   *Form:* visual (e.g., movements), audio (e.g., noises), visual + audio
2   *Activation:* automatic (e.g., background music) or manual (on request after being clicked on) with manual animations being either hidden or controlled by hot spots
3   *Frequency:* once, repeatable, or constant

To answer question 2, we first analyze the picture book *Howie Hare* using Staiger's (2014) approach. This allows us to reconstruct its visual level and its literary and medial adaptation of the printed book. Second, we assess whether the animations have a narrative function. Here, we refer to the aforementioned work of Thiele (2000) and focus on three different types of text–image relations: (1) "parallel" (identical correlation of text and images), (2) "contrapuntal" (inconsistent, contradictory text–image relation), and (3) "plaited braid" (text and images complementary and deeply interwoven). We further distinguish between narrative animations and animations with an illustrative/atmospheric function such as making space vivid (visual) or evoking emotions (audio). Third, we also include the speaker in our analysis (Boelmann, 2019, p. 257), who transfers the written text into oral language and thereby adopts the role of the narrator or reader.

These considerations result in the following analysis model (see Figure 9.1) comprising three different, mutually interwoven levels of digital picture book analysis:

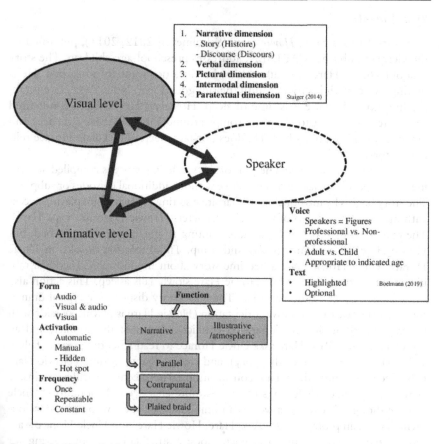

Figure 9.1 ViSA model for picture book app analysis

1   The *visual level* resulting from the interplay of the different dimensions of the picture book template (narrative, verbal, intermodal, material, etc.; see Staiger, 2014)

2   The *animative level* referring to animations (visual and audio) in both technical and functional terms

3   The *speaker dimension* comprising (a) voice: one speaker versus several speakers, vocal variation in order to imitate different voices or to highlight direct speech, adaptation of the speaker to different age groups (child vs. adult), interruptible or not (in terms of time breaks during receptive processing); and (b) text: presented optionally alongside the read-aloud function or words highlighted simultaneously to the read-aloud function.

Visual level

The story *Sweet dreams, Howie Hare* (Schulmeyer, 2012, 2011), published by the German publisher CARLSEN, addresses preschool-age children. The story is about Howie Hare, a small rabbit who does not want to go to bed. He is playing soccer with his friends until the sun goes down. Now, Papa Hare is taking him home because it is time to sleep. However, Howie Hare is not tired yet. Instead of going to sleep, he romps around the house. He grimaces and practices jumping on his bed. He does not fall asleep until Uncle Horace tells him a story.

The narrative dimension: The plot of the single-line story is compiled according to the specific structure of a narrative without additional episodes or subplots. The story begins by introducing the narrative setting (Howie Hare playing soccer with his friends) and two of the main characters (Howie Hare and Papa Hare). The conflict is depicted in Papa Hare wanting to put Howie Hare to bed, but Howie Hare still wanting to play and romp. The resolution unfolds in Uncle Horace telling Howie Hare a bedtime story about moon rabbits (fictional rabbits living on the moon) while Howie Hare slowly falls asleep. This action also depicts the closure of the narrative. Thus, the story displays the typical dramaturgical structure of a narrative: orientation (Howie Hare is playing outside with his friends), rising action (father–son conflict), climax of the conflict, and an unexpected turn (Papa Hare asks Uncle Horace to read a bedtime story), falling action (Uncle Horace tells the story), and closure/happy ending (Howie Hare falls asleep). The narrative is based on an authorial perspective providing an inside view of the character's feelings ("He was quite angry") and thoughts ("Uncle Horace thought it over") as well as an omniscient perspective on plot development. The main protagonists – Papa Hare, Howie Hare, and Uncle Horace – are represented as having human characteristics: a strict father, a son striving for autonomy, and a good-natured uncle who solves the conflict between son and father. The figures displayed are static in their conception; no figure changes in character or goes through a personal development. Indeed, the pictorial representation of father and uncle is quite similar. Instead, what are dynamic are the places in the narrative: the more Howie Hare romps, the more the places of action change (outside, living room, bathroom, nursery, etc.). In contrast, as soon as the action falls due to the intervention of the uncle, the place of action is only the nursery room. Just as multiple changes of place can be detected, there are also time adjustments. In the line of rising action, pace is increased via skipping steps in the sequence of events (time jumps), as soon as action-falls-narrated time equals narrative time. As in many other picture books as well (Kümmerling-Meibauer & Meibauer, 2015b), figurative speech is often used, as reflected in a high proportion of direct speech. Here, figurative speech in direct speech strictly takes the form of posing the speech itself, followed by a comment on the speaker. These acts of direct speech alternate with descriptive sentences embracing clauses containing statements, interrogative sentences, and exclamations.

The verbal dimension: The story is a classical bedtime story for young children and can be considered as appropriate for children 2–3 years of age due to its simple syntax and wording. The word choice stems mostly from the everyday-life register. Wording in this context includes specific subjectives (soccer, hare), action verbs (play), and a description in an active mode as well as adjectives in a descriptive manner (happy). A few composita (bedtime story) and metaphorical expressions (moon hares) enhance young children's lexical storage. The level of sentence structure provides rather short, mostly paratactic sentences. Elliptic expressions ("How boring") underline the everyday-life characterization of everyday speech in interaction. The construction along the visual dimension becomes tangible with a maximum of five sentences on a double page. Two narrative tenses – simple past to unfold the story itself, and simple present to depict direct speech – deliver a time framework for young children to orient themselves.

The intermodal dimension: The text-to-image ratio is dominantly parallel (10 of 12 double pages). In two pages, the text-to-image ratio comprises a "plaited braid" (Thiele, 2000, p. 79, see Figures 9.2 and 9.3).

On double page 5, the text refers to the main protagonist Papa Hare providing insight into his despair and exhaustion (Figure 9.2). In turn, the image shows

Figure 9.2 "Downstairs, the ceiling lights were wobbling. 'Won't the boy ever stop?' sighed Papa Hare."

Source: (Schulmeyer, 2012)[3]

Figure 9.3 "'Would you please tell him a bedtime story?' Papa Hare asked Uncle Horace. 'Oh dear,' Uncle Horace answered."

Source: (Schulmeyer, 2012)[4]

not only Papa Hare but also Uncle Horace, who is going to solve the conflict between Papa Hare and Howie Hare in the course of resolution by telling Howie Hare a bedtime story. In this way, the following action and the resolution of the narrative is initiated; text and image complement each other.

On double page 6 (Figure 9.3), text and image provide different information. The text refers to the situation in which Papa Hare is asking Uncle Horace to tell Howie Hare a bedtime story, whereas the image displays Uncle Horace going up the stairs. Nonetheless, both the verbal and the visual code are interlinked and generate a meaningful context, thereby making a story. However, because the text is kept linguistically simple, images dominate the picture book. Children can understand the story without listening to the text.

The material dimension: The digital version of *Howie Hare* represents a picture book app that is based 1:1 on the printed book. Users can download the app from the Android store, and from the Apple store. The individual versions differ slightly from each other. We base our analysis on the Apple version published in 2011. The app includes a read-aloud function, an optional noise function, a recording and playback function (which allows parents to record and play their own stories), an optional insertion of text, picture puzzles, and craft tips. Furthermore, the recording and playback function allow parents to record and read the story in different languages, with their own stories and in their own manner.

Animative level

In total, the picture book app contains 49 animations: 57% of them are visual, 18% audio, and 27% visual + audio. The majority of the animations are repeatable (73%); 14% can be activated only once; and 14% of the animations run constantly when the noise function is switched on. Only one animation is constant when the noise function is switched off (wobbling of the ceiling light). The majority of the animations (88%) are hidden manually. That means that they can be activated via trial and error. Hot spots, which accompany the reading process of the story, are not integrated. Except for the animated ceiling light, all constant animations are audio and can be switched off with the noise function. As can be seen from the numbers just mentioned, a considerable proportion of animations carry a narrative semantic function with some potential for supporting story comprehension.

The group of narrative animations contains predominantly animations (31%) that function as a "parallelism" to the text. That means that the animations highlight identical information such as "Howie Hare played soccer with his friend" (animation: football rotates in the air), and "Upstairs in bed he practiced big jumps" (animation: Howie Hare jumps with his stuffed animal on the bed). This is not surprising because "parallelism" or "symmetry" is a common pattern for the text–image relation in picture books for young children (Kurwinkel, 2017, p. 160). A considerable proportion of animations evoke a complementary relation to the text by assigning additional meaning to the text ("plaited braid"). For example, Howie Hare runs toward Uncle Horace in order to listen to the story; or a beetle sits in a tree, picks up one of its legs, and makes a "sh" sound when Howie Hare is falling asleep. In addition, 33% of the animations also highlight narrative means by displaying conflicts, emotions, figure speech, or plot development. Examples are:

- "After supper, you'll brush your teeth and go to bed," said Papa sternly. (animation: Papa Hare shakes the door of the living room and raises his hand)
- "We could sit at the window and look at the moon," he suggested. (animation: Uncle Horace moves his lips)
- "'Sweet dreams, Howie Hare!' he murmured happily." (animation: duvet raises and lowers, snoring sounds are audible, happy ending)

The climax of the narrative is particularly marked by a constant and automatic animation (audio + visual). This animation initiates the resolution of the conflict between father and son by Uncle Horace telling Howie a bedtime story: "Downstairs, the ceiling lights were wobbling" (animation: ceiling light wobbles back and forth).

Furthermore, there is only one animation that can be interpreted as "contrapuntal". On double page 1, clicking the sun twice leads to a renewed sunrise; on page 2, the sun reappears, thereby breaking the timeline of the narrative because every sunrise represents one day and this indicates unintentionally the passing of several days. Interactively, this inconsistency can become hard to elaborate. Here, both reader and child can become distracted.

Beside animations with a narrative–semantic function, a larger number of animations (55%) carry illustrative and atmospheric functions such as an owl sitting outside in the trees hooting, a sunset with a dimming effect, beetles sitting in the gutter making music, or leaves of a tree rustling and moving. These animations are not linked directly to the storyline.

Audio atmospheric animations can be considered as appropriate with respect to the target age group. They do not overload the reception process because they play noises in a controlled manner and do not start automatically – with one exception, when the noise function is switched off in order to mark the climax of the story (wobbling ceiling lights). Musical elements are integrated only once (beetles playing music). Moreover, audio animations consist mostly of one or two audio elements (noises) when being activated. The same applies to visual animations.

Speaker

The speaker of a story claims a central authority for herself or himself through translating a text – which may be ambiguous and interpretable in many ways – into a supposedly correct auditory version through a specific vocal and prosodic realization (Boelmann & Radvan, 2019).

When the optional reader function is activated in the English version, there are two different children's speakers. This allows a strong connection to children's everyday lives and can be motivating (Real & Correro, 2015). At the same time, some factors might complicate the reception in the child. On the one hand, the young speakers do not alternate regularly in the sense of clearly defined roles, and they do not offer an orientation to the narrative structure. This might hinder connecting with the narrator(s). On the other hand, the young speakers try to characterize dialogues in their own manner as in a role play. Häusermann calls this engaged and playful telling (Häusermann, 2010b, p. 210). In general, it should be noted that nonprofessionals often show deficits in melodic accentuation, syllabic stress, and articulation (Häusermann, 2010a, p. 195) that, in turn, might also lead to a problematic interpretation of the text. Strong accentuation can also limit the manifold interpretation of the text by the listening child. In the app *Sweet dreams, Howie Hare*, the speech patterns of the English speakers are in parts very expressive and dominating in their interpretation. Hence, the father who tells Howie Hare to go to bed is likely to be interpreted as being a very strict father due to the specific intonation. Text can be inserted optionally. However, words are not highlighted parallel to the speaker's reading.

Discussion

Theoretically, it can be assumed that story book apps enhance story comprehension by presenting literature in an animated and attractive way, particularly when older literate children are able to use the features of the app autonomously in order to explore details of the story or even modify the story, or use the read-aloud function that can strengthen understanding of the written text (Brunsmeier & Kolb, 2017). There are also reasons to assume that even in infancy, digital picture books provide great potential for narrative learning – on the condition that animations refer to the storyline, clarify the contents of the story, or underline narrative means such as dramatization or emotionality (Miosga, Chapter 2 in this volume). Based on our analysis, we assume that visual animations based on "parallelism" or "plaited braid" may particularly support children's story comprehension because they underline or complement content-based aspects that are elaborated in the text. The additional visual illustrations may particularly support children with low-level language skills and less language input within family literacy practices. Thus, we assume that a reduction of visual animations that have no direct narrative function or are not attached coherently to the narrative dimension of the book could help children to focus on the story. Miosga (see Chapter 2), for example, shows that when children were asked about the narrative plot and content of the story in a digital condition, they listed irrelevant but animated characters. On the other hand, animations may also help to draw a child's attention to the core elements of a story (Smeets & Bus, 2013) or highlight narrative means and patterns – and this may support the acquisition of narrative skills. However, there is also evidence that story comprehension and word learning do not depend on the extent to which irrelevant or relevant information is animated (Etta & Kirkorian, 2019). Hence, there are still gaps in research when it comes to the relation between medium, interaction, and early literacy competence. For example, future research could assess in which way children refer to different types of animations (narrative ["parallel," "contrapuntal," or "plaited braid"] or illustrative/atmospheric) when retelling the content of the digital picture book.

However, research does indicate the significance of the interactive context and the adult's role in using digital literature (Kumpulainen & Gillen, 2017). Hiniker, Sobel, Hong, Suh, Irish, Kim, & Kientz (2015) showed that children under 3 years of age were able to interpret and follow audio or visual animations as instructions only when they were initiated by an adult reader. Further, integrating the animations in the reading process in a language-supportive and cognitively stimulating way depends on the interactive competence of the reader. If readers are aware of the form, activation, frequency, and function of animations, it is more likely that they can also use illustrative and even contrapuntal animations to engage the child in the story by reacting to the child's response or resolving logical discrepancies (see Chapter 2). In the app *Sweet dreams, Howie Hare*, the adult reader could clarify the inconsistent animated sunset or use the animated owl for a conversational, narratively interlinked impulse within a "sustained shared thinking" format: *Look, even the owl is so tired that it falls from the tree, but now it's time for Howie Hare to go home, the sun is going down again. . . . Has the sun not just risen? Now, Howie Hare wakes up again, doesn't he? What do you think? Shall we let the sun go down again? So that Howie Hare can go home.*

Animations, music, and background noises that serve only an illustrative/atmospheric function can also be used to involve the dialogue partner emotionally or to link the story to everyday experiences if the reader is able to attach them

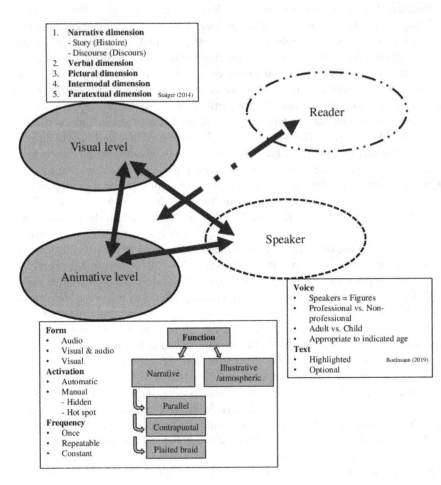

Figure 9.4 ViSAR model for picture book app interaction analysis

to the story. For example: *Look, the beetles in the gutter are playing good night music for Howie Hare and Uncle Horace! Do the beetles make music in our garden too? What do you think?*

This points to the significance of the context and the adult's role in using digital literature and framing the reading process with the child interactively: Interactive guidance is key (Kumpulainen & Gillen, 2017). Thus, when discussing the animative quality of a picture book app, it is also crucial to reconsider the interactive reading process in which the animations are situated. This results in a modified model (see Figure 9.4) that can be operationalized empirically in the future.

Practical implications

However, a wide range of apps and e-books on the market differ in the way they integrate visual and audio animations in order to support and frame the story. Thus, different animations can complicate or facilitate the establishment of interactive scaffolding processes. Animations, music, and background noises that serve only an illustrative/atmospheric function can additionally distract children and lead to cognitive overload (Bus, Takacs & Kegel, 2015). The hot spots that are often integrated into narrative apps to display figure speech can engage and motivate the child, but also distract by steering the learner's attention not to the story but to the clicking process (Willoughby, Evans, & Nowak, 2015). On the other hand, if the reader is given no visual cues indicating which animation is to be operated at which point, this can also impede the digital reading process and the connection to the structure and content of the narrative. Therefore, it is not only important for practitioners to know the quality criteria for picture book apps, but also to be aware of animations that require more or less interactive elaboration. This also includes knowledge about the interactive formats in which digital children's literature can be read in a didactically coherent and meaningful way, and a didactic understanding of how technical features can be used in a reflective, guided, and inclusive way when using apps and e-books in early educational settings.

In summary, in terms of early childhood education and family literacy, the quality of the app and the quality of interactivity are crucial factors. Thus, a material and interaction-oriented approach to picture book analysis as suggested here is not just relevant in terms of technical developments and interactive guidelines for parents. It also delivers practical implications for early childhood education, such as raising preschool caregivers' and educators' awareness and sensitization for app qualities and interactive formats in which digital children's literature can be integrated in a didactically coherent and meaningful way. This particularly comprises didactic knowledge about how technical features can be used in a reflective, guided, and inclusive way when using apps and e-books in early educational settings.

Three key considerations for parents, educators, and producers

Based on our analysis, when selecting, applying, or producing narrative picture book apps in early childhood education settings, educators and developers should:

- Watch out for a high proportion of narrative animations and, at the same time, a low proportion of illustrative or atmospheric animations
- Be aware of the amount of distractive hot spots
- Use animations dialogically as a trigger to support story comprehension

Notes

1 The *verbal dimension* refers to the language input provided by the text: wording, syntax, tense, linguistic style, text composition, and so forth. Basically, it is about how coherence is established on the basis of linguistic means and forms. This level of picture book analysis is particularly relevant for language promotion in kindergarten (von Lehmden, Porps, & Müller-Brauers, 2017). *The visual dimension* refers to the "visual code" of the picture book such as its visual design, color symbolism, picture space, typography, page layout, pictorial composition, and style (Staiger, 2014).
2 International research often refers to Nikolajeva and Scott's (2006) categorization here.
3 Heribert Schulmeyer, Schlaf gut, Hansi Hase © Carlsen Verlag GmbH, Hamburg 2012.
4 Heribert Schulmeyer, Schlaf gut, Hansi Hase © Carlsen Verlag GmbH, Hamburg 2012.

References

Bitkom. (Eds.). (2019). *Kinder und Jugendliche in der digitalen Welt*. Retrieved from www.bitkom.org/sites/default/files/2019–05/bitkom_pk-charts_kinder_und_jugendliche_2019.pdf

Boelmann, J. M. (2019). Hörspiele. In T. von Brand & F. Radvan (Eds.), *Handbuch Lehr- und Lernmittel für den Deutschunterricht. Bestandsaufnahmen, Analysen, didaktische Reflexionen* (pp. 249–261). Hannover, Germany: Klett Kallmeyer.

Boelmann, J. M., & Radvan, F. (2019). Grundlagen–Methoden–Anwendungen. Empirische Zugänge zum Hörbuch. In C. Rosebrock & L. Grimm (Eds.), *Spielarten der Populärkultur–ästhetische und didaktische Perspektiven* (pp. 255–277). Baltmannsweiler Hohengehren, Germany: Schneider.

Brunsmeier, S., & Kolb, A. (2017). Picturebooks go digital: The potential of story apps for the primary EFL classroom. *Children's Literature in English Language Education, 5*(1), 1–20.

Bus, A. G., Takacs, Z. K., & Kegel, C. A. T. (2015). Affordances and limitations of electronic storybooks for young children's emergent literacy. *Developmental Review, 35*, 79–97.

Chaudron, S., DiGioia, R., & Gemo, M. (2018). *Young children (0–8) and digital technology, a qualitative study across Europe*. EUR 29070. doi:10.2760/294383. Retrieved from https://core.ac.uk/download/pdf/159629895.pdf

DeBaryshe, B. D. (1993). Joint picture-book reading correlates of early oral language skill. *Journal of Child Language, 20*(2), 455–461.

Ehmig, S. C., & Reuter, T. (2013). *Vorlesen im Kinderalltag. Bedeutung des Vorlesens für die Entwicklung von Kindern und Jugendlichen und Vorlesepraxis in den Familien. Zusammenfassung und Einordnung zentraler Befunde der Vorlesestudien von Stiftung Lesen, DIE ZEIT und Deutsche Bahn 2007–2012*. Retrieved from www.stiftunglesen.de/download.php?type=documentpdf&id=951

Etta, R. A., & Kirkorian, H. L. (2019). Children's learning from interactive eBooks: Simple irrelevant features are not necessarily worse than relevant ones. *Frontiers in Psychology, 9*, 2733. doi.org/10.3389/fpsyg.2018.02733

Fahrer, S. (2014). Bilderbuch und digitale Medien: E-Books, Apps & Co. In J. Knopf & U. Abraham (Eds.), *BilderBücher. Theorie* (pp. 117–124). Baltmannsweiler Hohengehren, Germany: Schneider.

Fletcher, K. L., & Reese, E. (2005). Picture book reading with young children: A conceptual framework. *Developmental Review, 25*(1), 64–103.

Gogate, L. J., Bahrick, L. E., & Watson, J. D. (2000). A Study of multimodal motherese: The role of temporal synchrony between verbal labels and gestures. *Child Development, 71*(4), 878–894.

Grolig, L., Cohrdes, C., Tiffin-Richards, S. P., & Schroeder, S. (2019). Effects of preschoolers' storybook exposure and literacy environments on lower level and higher level language skills. *Reading and Writing, 32*(4), 1061–1084.

Häusermann, J. (2010a). Die sprecherische Gestaltung. In J. Häusermann, K. Janz-Peschke & S. M. Rühr (Eds.), *Das Hörbuch. Medium–Geschichte–Formen* (pp. 185–196). Konstanz, Germany: UVK Verlagsgesellschaft mbH.

Häusermann, J. (2010b). Hörbücher als Produkt der sprecherischen Umsetzung. In J. Häusermann, K. Janz-Peschke, & S. M. Rühr (Eds.), *Das Hörbuch. Medium–Geschichte–Formen* (pp. 197–218). Konstanz, Germany: UVK Verlagsgesellschaft mbH.

Henkel, A. Q. (2018). Exploring the materiality of literary apps for children. *Children's Literature in Education, 49*(3), 338–355.

Hildebrandt, F., Scheidt, A., Hildebrandt, A., Hédervári-Heller, É., & Dreier, A. (2016). "Sustained shared thinking" als Interaktionsformat und das Sprachverhalten von Kindern. *Frühe Bildung, 5*(2), 82–90.

Hiniker, A., Sobel, K., Hong, S. R., Suh, H., Irish, I., Kim, D., & Kientz, J. A. (2015). Touchscreen prompts for preschoolers: Designing developmentally appropriate techniques for teaching young children to perform gestures. *Proceedings of the 14th International Conference on Interaction Design and Children* (pp. 109–118). Boston, MA: ACM.

Howard, V., & Wallace, M. (2016). Today's tech literacy tools: Parental perceptions of apps for preschoolers. *Children and Libraries, 14*(1), 3–9.

Jungmann, T., Miosga, C., Fuchs, A., & Rohlfing, K. (2009). Konzeption und Evaluation eines Elterntrainings auf der Grundlage der Befunde der Multimodalen Motherese-Forschung. In U. De Langen-Müller, M. Hielscher-Fastabend, & B. Kleissendorf (Eds.), *Sprachtherapie lohnt sich?! Zum aktuellen Stand der Evaluations- und Effektivitätsforschung in der Sprachtherapie* (p. 234). Köln, Germany: ProLog.

Justice, L. M., & Ezell, H. K. (2000). Enhancing children's print and word awareness through home-based parent intervention. *American Journal of Speech-Language Pathology, 9*(3), 257–269. doi:10.1044/1058-0360.0903.257

Krcmar, M., & Cingel, D. P. (2014). Parent–child joint reading in traditional and electronic formats. *Media Psychology, 17*(3), 262–281. doi:10.1080/15213269.2013.840243

Kucirkova, N., & Littleton, K. (2016). *The digital reading habits of children: A national survey of parents' perceptions of and practices in relation to children's reading for pleasure with print and digital books.* Retrieved from www.booktrust.org.uk/globalassets/resources/research/digital_reading_survey-final-report-8.2.16.pdf

Kümmerling-Meibauer, B., & Meibauer, J. (2015a). Picturebooks and early literacy. How do picturebooks support early conceptual development? In B. Kümmerling-Meibauer, J. Meibauer, K. Nachtigäller, & K.R. Rohlfing (eds.), Learning from picturebooks. Perspectives from child development and literacy studies. London: Routledge, 13–32.

Kümmerling-Meibauer, B., & Meibauer, J. (2015b). Vorlese-Input und Redewiedergabe. In E. Gressnich, C. Müller, & L. Stark (Eds.), *Lernen durch Vorlesen. Sprach- und Literaturerwerb in Familie, Kindergarten und Schule* (pp. 15–33). Tübingen, Germany: Narr Francke Attempto.

Kumpulainen, K., & Gillen, J. (2017). *Young children's digital literacy practices in the home: A review of the literature.* Retrieved from http://digilitey.eu/wp-content/uploads/2017/01/WG1LR_with-amends-JG.pdf

Kurwinkel, T. (2017). *Bilderbuchanalyse. Narrativik–Ästhetik–Didaktik.* Stuttgart, Germany: UTB.

Miosga, C. (2019). "Come together"–Multimodale Responsivität und Abstimmung im Spracherwerb und in der Sprachförderung. In I. Bose, K. Hannken-Illjes, & S. Kurtenbach (Eds.), *Kinder im Gespräch–mit Kindern im Gespräch* (pp. 149–174). Berlin, Germany: Frank & Timme.

Neumann, M. M., & Neumann, D. L. (2017). The use of touch-screen tablets at home and pre-school to foster emergent literacy. *Journal of Early Childhood Literacy, 17*(2), 203–220. doi:10.1177/1468798415619773

Nikolajeva, M., & Scott, C. (2006). *How picture-books work.* London, England: Routledge.

Ofcom. (2018). *Children and parents: Media use and attitudes report.* Retrieved from www.ofcom.org.uk/__data/assets/pdf_file/0024/134907/Children-and-Parents-Media-Use-and-Attitudes-2018.pdf

Parish-Morris, J., Mahajan, N., Hirsh-Pasek, K., Michnick Golinkoff, R., & Fuller Collins, M. (2013). Once upon a time: Parent–child dialogue and storybook reading in the electronic era. *Mind, Brain, and Education, 7*(3), 200–211.

Peterson, C., Jesso, B., & McCabe, A. (1999). Encouraging narratives in preschoolers: An intervention study. *Journal of Child Language, 26*(1), 49–67.

Real, N., & Correro, C. (2015). Digital literature in early childhood: Reading experiences in family and school contexts. In M. Manresa & N. Real (Eds.), *Digital literature for children: Texts, readers and educational practices* (pp. 173–189). Brussels, Belgium: Peter Lang.

Sandvik, M., Smørdal, O., & Østerud, S. (2012). Exploring iPads in practitioners' repertoires for language learning and literacy practices in kindergarten. *Nordic Journal of Digital Literacy, 7*(3), 204–221.

Schulmeyer, H. (2012). *Schlaf gut, Hansi Hase!* Hamburg, Germany: Carlsen.

Schulmeyer, H. (2011). *Sweet dreams, Howie Hare!* Hamburg, Germany: Carlsen.

Serafini, F., Kachorsky, D., & Aguilera, E. (2016). Picture books in the digital age. *The Reading Teacher, 69*(5), 509–512.

Siraj-Blatchford, I., Sylva, K., Muttock, S., Gilden, R., & Bell, D. (2002). *Researching effective pedagogy in the early years. Research report 356.* London, England: DfES. Retrieved from www.327matters.org/docs/rr356.pdf

Smeets, D., & Bus, A. (2013). Picture storybooks go digital: Pros and cons. In S. B. Neuman & L. B. Gambrell (Eds.), *Quality reading instruction in the age of common core standards* (pp. 176–189). Newark, DE: International Reading Association. Retrieved from http://digilitey.eu/wp-content/uploads/2015/09/Picture-Storybooks-Go-Digital.pdf

Staiger, M. (2014). Erzählen mit Bild-Schrifttext-Kombinationen. Ein fünfdimensionales Modell der Bilderbuchanalyse. In J. Knopf & U. Abraham (Eds.), *Bilder-Bücher. Band 1 Theorie* (pp. 12–23). Baltmannsweiler Hohengehren, Germany: Schneider.

Stanzel, F. K. (1986). *A theory of narrative*. Cambridge, England: Cambridge University Press.

Stephens, J. (1995). Writing by children, writing for children: Schema theory, narrative discourse and ideology. *Revue belge de philologie et d'histoire, 73*(3), 853–863. Retrieved from www.persee.fr/doc/rbph_0035-0818_1995_num_73_3_4041

Thiele, J. (2000), Das Bilderbuch. In J. Thiele & J. Steitz-Kallenbach (Eds.), Handbuch Kinderliteratur Grundwissen für Ausbildung und Praxis (pp. 70–98).

Todorov, T. (1966). Les catégories du récit littéraire. *Communications, 8*, 125–151.

Tomasello, M. T. S. deJang (2009). *Why we cooperate*. Cambridge, MA: MIT Press.

Verhallen, M. J. A. J., Bus, A. G., & de Jong, M. T. S. (2006). The promise of multimedia stories for kindergarten children at risk. *Journal of Educational Psychology, 98*(2), 410–419.

von Lehmden, F., Porps, L., & Müller-Brauers, C. (2017). Grammatischer Sprachinput in Kinderliteratur–eine Analyse von Genus-Kasus-Hinweisen in input- und nicht inputoptimierten Bilderbüchern. *Forschung Sprache, 5*(2), 44–61.

Vygotsky, L. S. (1987). Thinking and speech. In R. W. Rieber & A. S. Carton (Eds.), *The collected works of L.S. Vygotsky* (Vol. 1), *Problems of general psychology* (pp. 39–285). New York: Plenum Press.

Wasik, B. A., Hindman, A. H., & Snell, E. K. (2016). Book reading and vocabulary development: A systematic review. *Early Childhood Research Quarterly, 37*(4), 39–57.

Willoughby, D., Evans, M. A., & Nowak, S. (2015). Do ABC eBooks boost engagement and learning in preschoolers? An experimental study comparing eBooks with paper ABC and storybook controls. *Computers & Education, 82*, 107–117.

Wu, S. (2014). A multimodal analysis of image–text relations in picture books. *Theory and Practice in Language Studies, 4*(7), 1415–1420. Retrieved from https://pdfs.semanticscholar.org/0e39/ed036fc924ba547b8d411f147c9ac1ee524a.pdf

Chapter 10

DAZonline.ch

A gallery of annotated interactive pictures for cross-situational language learning

Susanne Grassmann

Introduction

Children understand pictures as symbols at around the age of 2 years (e.g., DeLoache, 1991), and they can learn a language through looking at pictures that are described or labeled for them at an even younger age (e.g., Smith & Yu, 2008). Using pictures as an educational resource dates back at least to the seventeenth century, when Comenius (1658) published his famous book *Orbis Sensualium Pictus*. This book contains about 150 pictures with numbers pointing to words below printed in boldface in short paragraphs. These pictures are drawings of natural landscape scenes, still lifes, schemes, and so forth. The book was used for language learning for centuries (Gutek, 1995).

Inspired by this seventeenth-century picture book, we designed a web platform with which learners of all ages can explore a language through annotated pictures (which are called *Lernbild* on the platform). The platform combines Comenius's idea with Web 2.0 technology and state-of-the-art knowledge about multimedia and language learning. It also features different perspectives and contexts – a property of pictures that can be utilized for cross-situational learning. That is, beyond the intentional construction of Lernbild-series for cross-situational learning, the growing number of Lernbilds – contributed by parents, teachers, and our experts – naturally leads to partial overlap and repetition of content both in language and depicted situations across various Lernbilds. Adaptive algorithms assist learners in developing their individual learning path, maximizing learning outcome by optimizing repetition and variation across Lernbilds suggested for a learner.

At the time of writing this chapter, a prototype was already up and running (Lernbild, 2019). The platform is free of charge. Users can browse through and explore both pictures and picture-related language, either by themselves or in a joint interaction similar to joint picture book reading. The Web 2.0 technology enables teachers and caregivers to contribute to the picture collection and create personalized content for the children in their care. Thus, the picture gallery naturally optimizes itself for cross-situational learning (see the section *The Design of DAZonline* later in this chapter).

Figure 10.1 A digital version of one of Comenious' images

Source: (https://dazonline.ch/stundent-lesson/92)

The goal of this chapter is first, to show that it is possible to develop digital learning environments for language and literacy promotion that implement many aspects and features of natural language learning in children's daily interactions with parents and teachers – including joint picture book reading. The scientific foundation of DAZonline will briefly be reviewed. Second, the development process and the design principles of the gallery are described. The chapter concludes by suggesting that Lernbild-Galleries such as DAZonline might be tomorrow's picture books.

Theoretical background

Language development

Children learn most of their language through interaction with other people (e.g., Golinkoff, Hoff, Rowe, Tamis-LeMonda, & Hirsh-Pasek, 2019). Language learning is boosted when the child and the interlocutor share a joint focus of attention – thereby helping the child to infer the meaning of the accompanying language (e.g. Tomasello & Farrar, 1986), especially when such interaction occurs frequently and in various contexts (Hills, Maouene, Riordan, & Smith,

2010; Johns, Dye, & Jones, 2016; Weisleder & Fernald, 2013). Furthermore, children learn novel words best when their interlocutor is responsive to their interest and talks about objects and events that are in the children's focus of attention (e.g., Farrant & Zubrick, 2012; Tomasello & Farrar, 1986). Even young children indicate their interests through pointing gestures designed to make their parents provide either object labels (e.g., Wu & Gros-Louis, 2015) or action demonstrations (e.g., Begus, Gliga, & Southgate, 2014). Pointing is a very powerful way to indicate and interpret someone's focus of attention (Kita, 2008), and children already understand its communicative function when they are as young as 12 to 18 months (e.g., Hollich, Hirsh-Pasek, & Golinkoff, 2000).

When providing their children with novel words for something in the joint focus of attention, caregivers tend to first label the objects that their children point to and then, subsequently, to provide additional information about these objects: for example, their properties, their taxonomy, or further aspects (e.g., Wong & Clark, 2002). When doing this, parents tend to produce variation sets and series of utterances in which neighboring utterances share lexical elements (Küntay & Slobin, 1996; Moran et al., 2019; Tal & Arnon, 2018).

Children, on the other hand, tend to interpret novel words as whole object labels and interpret subsequent references to the same object as being labels for its properties, its taxonomy, and further aspects (e.g., Markman, 1989). Moreover, when learning novel words, children profit from immediate repetition (Schwab & Lew-Williams, 2017) and continuous discourse interaction with multiple references to the same object (Horowitz & Frank, 2015; Schwab & Lew-Williams, 2017). In addition to this, variation sets might also enhance children's language learning. Up to now, however, this has been demonstrated only for adults learning an artificial language (Onnis, Waterfall, & Edelman, 2008).

Children also learn from verbal expressions being repeated across different situations (Smith & Yu, 2008). In fact, most topics – be it vocabulary development in a certain area or grammatical development – require multiple exposures to be learned (Johns et al., 2016; Lieven, 2006; Saji et al., 2011; Unger, Vales, & Fisher, 2018) and bring about the ability to transfer a word to new contexts. However, such cross-situational learning depends on memory; and older children as well as children with better memories and prediction skills are able to do this better (Suanda, Mugwanya, & Namy, 2014; Vlach & DeBrock, 2017; Vlach & Johnson, 2013). Nonetheless, such demands on memory can be decreased by increasing predictability. Indeed, enhanced predictability supports children's word learning both within a situation (Benitez & Saffran, 2018) and across encounters with the same word in different contexts (Benitez & Smith, 2012; Zettersten, Wojcik, Benitez, & Saffran, 2018).

Joint picture book reading

The potential of book reading. One particularly important way to interact with children in order to promote their language development is joint picture book reading. This reveals reliably positive effects on first language, second language, and literacy development (e.g., Ennemoser, Kuhl, & Pepouna, 2013; Ludwig, Guo, & Georgiou, 2019; but see Noble et al., 2018 for a critical review). The reason for this may be at least partially that joint picture book reading is a prime example of responsive interaction with a joint focus of attention (see Degotardi, 2017). Furthermore, it has been suggested that book reading fosters language because books provide challenging experiences and present children with highly diverse contexts and fairly complex language (Cameron-Faulkner & Noble, 2013; Montag, 2019). Various contexts are imported for language development, because a corollary of this diversity of contexts is linguistic diversity and the repetition of the same words in different contexts – thereby allowing for cross-situational learning. For example, the information in a visual display can provide important additional information for concept development and may aid cross-situational learning (Unger et al., 2018; Zettersten et al., 2018).

However, children love reading the same book repeatedly (Leavitt & Christenfeld, 2011) and this very practice enhances their word learning (e.g., Horst, Parsons, & Bryan, 2011; Wilkinson & Houston-Price, 2013). Horst et al. (2011) suggest that repeated reading of the same book facilitates word learning due to a contextual cueing effect – which makes it easier to recognize the referred-to objects than is the case when contexts change (see Horst, 2013). However, it is also possible that exact repetitions of sentences through repeatedly reading the same story drive the child's advanced learning.

Several design aspects influence children's language learning from joint picture book reading. They do not just do this in good ways, but also in bad ways; for example, highly salient design features such as pop-ups hinder children's word learning from books (Tare, Chiong, Ganea, & Deloache, 2010). Furthermore, irrelevant design details are particularly harmful to learners with lower executive function skills who have difficulties in allocating attention to relevant information while ignoring extraneous information (e.g., Kaminski & Sloutsky, 2013; McEwen & Dubé, 2015) – difficulties that might disrupt learning (Horst, Scott, & Pollard, 2010). Therefore, reducing details can avoid cognitive overload and distraction (see Rey, 2012; Sweller, Ayres, & Kalyuga, 2011). For example, Flack and Horst (2018) demonstrated that children learn words better when presented with one book page at a time. However, oversimplification is not good for learning either because learning is increased by a certain degree of (desirable) difficulty (Bjork, 1994; Zosh, Brinster, & Halberda, 2013).

Book design is also relevant for the ease of transfer to the real world. Research has shown that books with realistic photographs lead to better transfer than books with drawings (Ganea, Pickard, & DeLoache, 2008; Simcock & DeLoache, 2006). This suggests that the additional details in the photograph can promote some aspects of learning.

The potential of touchscreens. Manually touching a screen is almost identical to pointing at a book page; and receiving a contingent immediate response from the touchscreen device is similar to caregivers' replies to such pointing gestures in joint book reading. Therefore, it is not surprising that researchers have been exploring the potential of touchscreen devices for language learning (Xie et al.,

2018). Empirical studies have demonstrated that even toddlers can learn words when interacting with touchscreen devices all by themselves (Dore et al., 2018; Walter-Laager et al., 2017). In addition, caregivers have been found to engage in joint app use and joint reading of interactive books in similar ways to their joint reading of printed books (Strouse & Ganea, 2017; Takacs, Swart, & Bus, 2014). However, and also rather like the way things are with books, the design of digital content can also influence learning negatively (Takacs, Swart, & Bus, 2015). Therefore, particular care needs to be taken when designing digital learning environments for children.

The design of DAZonline

Starke, Leinweber, and Ritterfeld (see Chapter 8) suggest that digital educational media need to be developed by interdisciplinary teams made up of game theorists, designers, computer scientists, and pedagogical experts. These teams should follow six design principles: (1) specify your target group and the focused language structure; (2) determine key language learning methods; (3) include the target group in the design process; (4) fine-tune learning and gaming; (5) implement as many and as few game mechanisms as needed; and (6) use an iterative process to fine-tune language and general learning principles with game design.

When developing DAZonline, we worked with the user-centered design approach. Our starting point was that many teachers in Switzerland complain that children lack verbal and literacy skills across grades from preschool to high school. Our goal was to provide teachers and other pedagogical staff with an easy-to-use tool for language and literacy promotion. Indeed, a review of the language and literacy promotion programs for children and youth from non-German speaking families revealed that the offerings may not be sufficient for effective and enduring language learning. We then summarized the research on language and literacy development and identified the most important activities and how they are optimally structured. We then "translated" these activities and their characteristics into a concept of digital activities. Thus we developed DAZonline similar to Stracke et al.'s six principles.

Principle 1: target group and content

The target group for DAZonline, the first platform for picture-based language learning, comprises language learners of all ages coming from all backgrounds, and their caregivers. There is almost no restriction on the minimum age for using annotated interactive pictures. Research has shown that even 2-year-olds can learn words when interacting alone with an interactive image on a touchscreen (Walter-Laager et al., 2017; Xie et al., 2018). Furthermore, research has demonstrated that caregivers engage in high-quality interaction with children when co-reading not only printed books but also interactive e-books (Strouse & Ganea, 2017; Takacs et al., 2014). Therefore, it seems likely that such interaction will also occur around annotated interactive pictures. Especially for preschoolers, this is likely to lead to the best learning outcomes compared to solitary interaction with a screen device (see Dore et al., 2018; Walter-Laager et al., 2017).

The linguistic focus is also very broad: both vocabulary and grammatical and morphological structures can be acquired from exploring Lernbilds. Importantly, everyday words of both open-class (nouns and verbs occur in all Lernbilds; adjectives: e.g., Lernbild, 2019, p. 190), and closed-class words (e.g., prepositions: ibid., pp. 232–234), as well as academic (e.g., ibid., pp. 157–159) and professional vocabulary (e.g., ibid., pp. 119–121), are possible content for Lernbilds. The same is true for grammatical structures. Lernbilds can be used to introduce colloquial, simpler spoken-language forms as well as academic and more complex forms (e.g., ibid., p. 192). To foster learning the latter, they are available also for everyday content (e.g., passive: ibid., p. 95; relative clause: ibid., p. 98). Lernbilds can comprise rhymes (e.g, ibid., p. 133), poetry, and humor (e.g, ibid., p. 126). The wide focus compares to books and makes the annotated interactive pictures particularly valuable for language learning and promotion. Indeed, this solves one big problem with existing educational media: that these rarely include sophisticated language (see Danielson, Wong, & Neuman, 2019).

Principle 2: learning method

As described previously, the goal is to get as close as possible to natural language acquisition. Therefore, to some extent, the interaction with the content on the platform simulates responsive interaction with a joint focus of attention. When opening the platform, users browse and explore the gallery, and miniature previews may spark the initial selection of certain pictures. When selecting a miniature, the corresponding annotated picture is shown full screen, and the user can touch the hot spot in the image and listen to and read related utterances.

When learners browse through the annotated interactive picture gallery, they will encounter unknown words and structures. Over time and with repeated browsing through various annotated interactive pictures, words and phrases will repeat and contrast with one another across the annotated interactive pictures. Therefore, the platform provides users with the possibility of cross-situational learning. Across the annotated interactive pictures, the users will encounter a variety of verbal expressions related to different contexts – each of which might partially overlap with preceding content that the user has explored already.

For example, in the series *"im Garten"* [in the garden], the full variation set comprises seven sentences. First, in the picture *"im Garten 1"* (see Lernbild, 2019, p. 94), the following utterances form a variation set:

- *Ein Velo* [A bike]
- *Das Velo steht auf der Wiese* [The bike is standing on the grass]
- *Ein Rasenmäher* [A lawnmower]
- *Der Rasenmäher steht auf der Wiese* [The lawnmower is standing on the grass]

The variation set is further expanded in the other two Lernbilds (*"im Garten 2"* and *"im Garten 3"*) in the series:

- *Ein Junge* [A boy]
- *Der Junge schiebt das Velo* [The boy is pushing the bike]
- *Der Rasenmäher wird vom Jungen geschoben* [The lawnmower is pushed by the boy]

The content designers at Lernbild are advised to first provide the label of an object and add an expansion utterance containing the object label. This expansion is presented to the user, who "requests" more information by touching the flashcard providing the label. This two-step mini-variation set simulates how parents introduce novel labels to their children (e.g., Wong & Clark, 2002). However, as shown in the earlier example, variation sets can (and should) spread across both the utterances included in each Lernbild, as well as the Lernbilds in a series.

The implementation of Web 2.0 technology allows teachers to create content. There is some evidence that personalized content can support language learning (Kucirkova, Messer, & Sheehy, 2014). However, to ensure quality, the user-generated pictures need to be reviewed by an expert team. One of the biggest challenges for untrained designers is the fact that experts see and process pictures differently from novices (De Groot, 1978). The most relevant difference for language learning and instruction is that experts attend to details much more than novices do (Hoffman & Fiore, 2007; Vaidyanathan, Pelz, Alm, Shi, & Haake, 2014). The effect of this can be seen in many picture-based language learning applications; images are annotated with a single sentence about a tiny detail in the image – that the learner is highly unlikely to attend to.

Our professional content designers use several methods to ensure that the learner's attention is directed to the right spot in a complex picture. For example, they can blur the irrelevant elements in the picture or highlight the important elements by using color, placing them at the center of the image, or having a person in the image who directs attention to where the learner should look (Axelsson, Churchley, & Horst, 2012; Flack, 2018; Fletcher-Watson, Findlay, Leekam, & Benson, 2008; Wilkinson & Light, 2011). Importantly, beyond the hot spots that respond to the user's indication of interest by providing related utterances, DAZonline does not use animations because they may potentially interfere with learning (see Starke et al., Chapter 8 in this volume; Takacs et al., 2015).

In addition to exploring Lernbilds online, teachers can use cross-media activities and blend learning in the real world and in the digital world. For example, teachers can make quick response (QR) codes that contain the URL of certain pictures, and then place them at relevant real-world locations. This nicely blends digital and real-world activities and could potentially even enhance learning and transfer. Another possibility for blended learning activities around the picture gallery is to adapt the procedure used by Charitonos and Charalampidi (2015) and Wong, Chin, Tan, and Liu (2010). These authors asked learners to take pictures related to certain linguistic expressions. Together with their caregivers, learners can then upload such pictures to the platform and form new content – thereby providing children with personalized, annotated, interactive pictures. We are planning to investigate the learning in digital-only and blended learning settings in the near future.

Principle 3: include the target group in the design process

Currently, the prototype of DAZonline.ch is online and subject to testing. Teachers and parents of preschool and elementary school children as well as social workers, volunteers, and teachers of immigrants (including refugees) are providing us with feedback on both their experience with creating Lernbilds and using them in classroom. The primary goal of the prototype testing is to determine additional functionality that could improve interaction quality.

Principle 4: fine-tune learning and gaming

As of February 2020, the feedback from our test-users will be analyzed and prioritized for the second iteration of software development. Preliminary analyses suggest focusing on additional functionality, increasing user experience in the classroom, and maybe implementing some gaming element.

Principle 5: game elements

Up to now, no gamification elements have been implemented. This is mainly to ensure that users focus attention on the content and not on game mechanics. We prefer to suggest creating real-world games around the use of the picture gallery. For example, the previously described cross-media learning scenario of placing QR codes[1] at relevant real-world locations could be transformed further into paper chases and various other games. In the 2020 software development iteration, some minigames might be included as an additional activity.

Principle 6: iterative process to further fine-tune

Today, software development is an iterative process. For DAZonline, we are planning further iterations to keep increasing usability and learning with Lernbilds.

Discussion and future directions

Annotated interactive pictures are easy to access and have a high potential for fostering and promoting language and literacy development in all children. Most importantly, because pictures are everywhere, an annotated interactive picture gallery such as DAZonline might provide us with a way to "languagize" (Golinkoff et al., 2019) children's lives and increase their chances of academic success and quality of life. Annotated interactive pictures enable the users not just to relate new expressions, rare words, and academic language to everyday situations; they can also broaden horizons and show situations (both fantastic and real) that are not part of the learner's life, open up new perspectives, and show the world from diverse angles. Annotated interactive pictures can also be used to promote academic language and relate it to real-world situations. Nonetheless, future research has to establish how effectively annotated interactive pictures actually promote language development.

With the growing number of annotated interactive pictures at DAZonline, the diversity will not only grow but also reveal structures that can be used by AI algorithms to provide recommendations to the learner. Until the algorithms are implemented, the designers must strive to ensure an optimal balance between variation and repetition: the larger the picture gallery, the more natural the variation and repetition that drives cross-situational, and thus robust, learning. To provide learners with an optimal mix of variation and repetition on the platform, we plan to implement a multidimensional recommendation system. Multidimensional recommendation algorithms are optimal because (1) the learner maintains navigational control to choose from a variety of suggestions and retains a sense of autonomy while receiving optimal guidance; (2) it is notoriously difficult to recommend a single optimal picture with which to continue because learners differ in both their interests and their prior knowledge (Hasnine et al., 2018; Hasnine et al., 2019); and (3) algorithms must also consider that the relevance of repetition and variation across successive learning situations varies as a function of age, memory capacity, and mastery of language (Vlach & DeBrock, 2017).

Annotated interactive pictures might be tomorrow's picture books – not least because sharing and viewing pictures is ubiquitous. If designed properly, I suggest that annotated interactive pictures are as valuable for language and literacy development as picture books; and perhaps even more so because even less literate parents will enjoy exploring them together with their children, and learners can explore them even when they are alone without the presence of an interlocutor. Last but not least, annotated interactive pictures can be used in various blended learning situations that will potentially increase transfer to real-world language use.

Three key considerations for parents, educators, and producers

Annotated interactive pictures might outperform joint book reading in promoting language and literacy development – particularly when they are collected together in a gallery with adaptive filters and recommendation algorithms. They are something for parents, educators, and producers to consider when using or producing digital media for language promotion.

- A gallery of annotated interactive pictures provides a unique and easy-access language learning resource. Because teachers and caregivers can upload their content to the gallery, the platform fits in well with today's habit of online picture sharing while exploiting this habit for educational purposes. Indeed, even parents with lower language and literacy skills might use such a platform and explore the images together with their children – with the quality of interaction being supported by the software.

- Most of the activities that foster language development in joint book and e-book reading (joint attention, responsive interaction, elaborated conversation about the content) are also possible in the joint exploration of annotated interactive pictures. The gallery allows users to explore the content on the basis of their interest while nonetheless profiting from tailored progression over time. The gallery provides a diverse vocabulary in diverse contexts.

- The additional implementation of filters and recommendation algorithms allows the user to select overlapping or constant vocabulary (same words) or contexts (same pictures). This makes individualized and cross-situational learning possible. Filtering and recommendation systems can enhance language uptake by optimizing variability across situations in line with the learner's skill – something rather difficult to accomplish with books.

Note

1 QR Code is registered trademark of DENSO WAVE INCORPORATED.

References

Axelsson, E. L., Churchley, K., & Horst, J. S. (2012). The right thing at the right time: Why ostensive naming facilitates word learning. *Frontiers in Psychology, 3*, 88.

Begus, K., Gliga, T., & Southgate, V. (2014). Infants learn what they want to learn: Responding to infant pointing leads to superior learning. *PLoS One, 9*(10), e108817.

Benitez, V. L., & Saffran, J. R. (2018). Predictable events enhance word learning in toddlers. *Current Biology, 28*(17), 2787–2793.e4.

Benitez, V. L., & Smith, L. B. (2012). Predictable locations aid early object name learning. *Cognition, 125*(3), 339–352.

Bjork, R. A. (1994). Institutional impediments to effective training. In D. Druckman & R. A. Bjork (Eds.), Learning, remembering, believing: Enhancing human performance (pp. 295–306). Washington, DC: National Academy Press.

Cameron-Faulkner, T., & Noble, C. (2013). A comparison of book text and child directed speech. *First Language, 33*(3), 268–279.

Charitonos, K., & Charalampidi, M. (2015). Designs for heritage language learning: A photography project in the UK supplementary education. In T. H. Brown & H. J. van der Merwe (Eds.), *The mobile learning voyage: From small ripples to massive open waters*. Communications in Computer and Information Science (Vol. 560, pp. 198–216). Cham, Germany: Springer.

Comenius, I. (1658). *Orbis sensualium pictus*. Retrieved January 27, 2020, from www.hs-augsburg.de/~harsch/Chronologia/Lspost17/Comenius/com_o000. html

Danielson, K., Wong, K. M., & Neuman, S. B. (2019). Vocabulary in educational media for preschoolers: A content analysis of word selection and screen-based pedagogical supports. *Journal of Children and Media, 13*(3), 345–362.

Degotardi, S. (2017). Joint attention in infant–toddler early childhood programs: Its dynamics and potential for collaborative learning. *Contemporary Issues in Early Childhood, 18*(4), 409–421.

De Groot, A. D. (Ed.). (1978/1965). *Thought and choice in chess*. The Hague, Netherlands: Mouton.

DeLoache, J. S. (1991). Symbolic functioning in very young children: Understanding of pictures and models. *Child Development, 62*(4), 736–752.

Dore, R. A., Hassinger-Das, B., Brezack, N., Valladares, T. L., Paller, A., Vu, L., Golinkoff, R. M., & Hirsh-Pasek, K. (2018). The parent advantage in fostering children's e-book comprehension. *Early Childhood Research Quarterly, 44*(3), 24–33.

Ennemoser, M., Kuhl, J., & Pepouna, S. (2013). Evaluation des dialogischen Lesens zur Sprachförderung bei Kindern mit Migrationshintergrund. *Zeitschrift für Pädagogische Psychologie, 27*, 229–239.

Farrant, B. M., & Zubrick, S. R. (2012). Early vocabulary development: The importance of joint attention and parent–child book reading. *First Language, 32*(3), 343–364.

Flack, Z. M. (2018). *The role of attention in word learning from shared storybook readings* (PhD Thesis, University of Sussex). Retrieved January 27, 2020, from http:// sro.sussex.ac.uk/id/eprint/72703/

Flack, Z. M., & Horst, J. S. (2018). Two sides to every story: Children learn words better from one storybook page at a time. *Infant and Child Development, 27*(1), e2047.

Fletcher-Watson, S., Findlay, J. M., Leekam, S. R., & Benson, V. (2008). Rapid detection of person information in a naturalistic scene. *Perception, 37*(4), 571–583.

Ganea, P. A., Pickard, M. B., & DeLoache, J. S. (2008). Transfer between picture books and the real world by very young children. *Journal of Cognition and Development, 9*(1), 46–66.

Golinkoff, R. M., Hoff, E., Rowe, M. L., Tamis-LeMonda, C. S., & Hirsh-Pasek, K. (2019). Language matters: Denying the existence of the 30-million-word gap has serious consequences. *Child Development, 90*(3), 985–992.

Gutek, G. L. (Ed.). (1995). *A history of the Western educational experience* (2nd ed.). Prospect Heights, IL: Waveland Press.

Hasnine, M. N., Flanagan, B., Akcapinar, G., Ogata, H., Mouri, K., & Uosaki, N. (2019). Vocabulary learning support system based on automatic image captioning technology. In N. Streitz & S. Konomi (Eds.), *Distributed, ambient and pervasive interactions* (pp. 346–358). Cham, Germany: Springer.

Hasnine, M. N., Mouri, K., Flanagan, B., Akcapinar, G., Uosaki, N., & Ogata, H. (2018). Image recommendation for informal vocabulary learning in a context-aware learning environment. *Proceedings of the 26th International Conference on Computers in Education* (pp. 669–674). Manila, Philippines: Asia-Pacific Society for Computers in Education.

Hills, T. T., Maouene, J., Riordan, B., & Smith, L. B. (2010). The associative structure of language: Contextual diversity in early word learning. *Journal of Memory and Language, 63*(3), 259–273.

Hoffman, R. R., & Fiore, S. M. (2007). Perceptual (re)learning: A leverage point for human-centered computing. *IEEE Intelligent Systems, 22*(3), 79–83.

Hollich, G., Hirsh-Pasek, K., & Golinkoff, R. M. (2000). What does it take to learn a word? *Monographs of the Society for Research in Child Development, 65*(3), 1–16.

Horowitz, A. C., & Frank, M. C. (2015). Young children's developing sensitivity to discourse continuity as a cue for inferring reference. *Journal of Experimental Child Psychology, 129*, 84–97.

Horst, J. S. (2013). Context and repetition in word learning. *Frontiers in Psychology, 4*, 149.

Horst, J. S., Parsons, K. L., & Bryan, N. M. (2011). Get the story straight: Contextual repetition promotes word learning from storybooks. *Frontiers in Psychology, 2*, 17.

Horst, J. S., Scott, E. J., & Pollard, J. A. (2010). The role of competition in word learning via referent selection. *Developmental Science, 13*(5), 706–713.

Johns, B. T., Dye, M., & Jones, M. N. (2016). The influence of contextual diversity on word learning. *Psychonomic Bulletin & Review, 23*(4), 1214–1220.

Kaminski, J. A., & Sloutsky, V. M. (2013). Extraneous perceptual information interferes with children's acquisition of mathematical knowledge. *Journal of Educational Psychology, 105*(2), 351–363.

Kita, S. (Ed.). (2008). *Pointing: Where language, culture, and cognition meet* (2nd ed.). New York, NY: Taylor & Francis.

Kucirkova, N., Messer, D., & Sheehy, K. (2014). Reading personalized books with preschool children enhances their word acquisition. *First Language, 34*(3), 227–243.

Küntay, A., & Slobin, D. I. (1996). Listening to a Turkish mother: Some puzzles for acquisition. In D. I. Slobin, J. Gerhardt, A. Kyratzis, & J. Guo (Eds.), *Social interaction, social context, and language: Essays in honor of Susan Ervin-Tripp* (pp. 265–286). Hillsdale, NJ: Lawrence Erlbaum Associates.

Leavitt, J. D., & Christenfeld, N. J. S. (2011). Story spoilers don't spoil stories. *Psychological Science, 22*(9), 1152–1154.

Lernbild. (2019). *DAZonline* [Web application]. Retrieved from https://dazonline.ch.

Lieven, E. (2006). How do children develop syntactic representations from what they hear? In P. Vogt, Y. Sugita, E. Tuci, & C. Nehaniv (Eds.), *Symbol grounding and beyond* (pp. 72–75). Berlin, Germany: Springer.

Ludwig, C., Guo, K., & Georgiou, G. K. (2019). Are reading interventions for English language learners effective? A meta-analysis. *Journal of Learning Disabilities, 52*(3), 220–231.

Markman, E. M. (Ed.). (1989). *Categorization and naming in children: Problems of induction.* Cambridge, MA: MIT Press.

McEwen, R. N., & Dubé, A. K. (2015). Engaging or distracting: Children's tablet computer use in education. *Journal of Educational Technology & Society, 18*(4), 9–23.

Montag, J. L. (2019). Differences in sentence complexity in the text of children's picture books and child-directed speech. *First Language, 39*(5), 527–546.

Moran, S., Lester, N. A., Gordon, H., Küntay, A., Pfeiler, B., Allen, S., & Stoll, S. (2019). Variation sets in maximally diverse languages. *Proceedings of the 43rd Boston*

University Conference on Language Development (pp. 427–440). Somerville, MA: Cascadilla Press.

Noble, C., Sala, G., Peter, M., Lingwood, J., Rowland, C. F., Gobet, F., & Pine, J. (2018). The impact of shared book reading on children's language skills: A meta-analysis [Preprint]. *Educational Research Review, 28,* 100290.

Onnis, L., Waterfall, H. R., & Edelman, S. (2008). Learn locally, act globally: Learning language from variation set cues. *Cognition, 109*(3), 423–430.

Rey, G. D. (2012). A review of research and a meta-analysis of the seductive detail effect. *Educational Research Review, 7*(3), 216–237.

Saji, N., Imai, M., Saalbach, H., Zhang, Y., Shu, H., & Okada, H. (2011). Word learning does not end at fast-mapping: Evolution of verb meanings through reorganization of an entire semantic domain. *Cognition, 118*(1), 45–61.

Schwab, J. F., & Lew-Williams, C. (2017). Discourse continuity promotes children's learning of new objects labels. *Proceedings of the 39th Annual Conference of the Cognitive Science Society* (pp. 3101–3106). Seattle, WA: Cognitive Science Society.

Simcock, G., & DeLoache, J. (2006). Get the picture? The effects of iconicity on toddlers' reenactment from picture books. *Developmental Psychology, 42*(6), 1352–1357.

Smith, L., & Yu, C. (2008). Infants rapidly learn word-referent mappings via cross-situational statistics. *Cognition, 106*(3), 1558–1568.

Strouse, G. A., & Ganea, P. A. (2017). Toddlers' word learning and transfer from electronic and print books. *Journal of Experimental Child Psychology, 156,* 129–142.

Suanda, S. H., Mugwanya, N., & Namy, L. L. (2014). Cross-situational statistical word learning in young children. *Journal of Experimental Child Psychology, 126,* 395–411.

Sweller, J., Ayres, P., & Kalyuga, S. (Eds.). (2011). *Cognitive load theory.* New York, NY: Springer.

Takacs, Z. K., Swart, E. K., & Bus, A. G. (2014). Can the computer replace the adult for storybook reading? A meta-analysis on the effects of multimedia stories as compared to sharing print stories with an adult. *Frontiers in Psychology, 5,* 1366.

Takacs, Z. K., Swart, E. K., & Bus, A. G. (2015). Benefits and pitfalls of multimedia and interactive features in technology-enhanced storybooks: A meta-analysis. *Review of Educational Research, 85*(4), 698–739.

Tal, S., & Arnon, I. (2018). SES effects on the use of variation sets in child-directed speech. *Journal of Child Language, 45*(6), 1423–1438.

Tare, M., Chiong, C., Ganea, P., & Deloache, J. (2010). Less is more: How manipulative features affect children's learning from picture books. *Journal of Applied Developmental Psychology, 31*(5), 395–400.

Tomasello, M., & Farrar, M. J. (1986). Joint attention and early language. *Child Development, 57*(6), 1454–1463.

Unger, L., Vales, C., & Fisher, A. (2018, August 2). *The role of co-occurrence statistics in developing semantic knowledge.* Retrieved January 27, 2020, from https://doi.org/10.31234/osf.io/qmy2n. Version of January 9, 2020.

Vaidyanathan, P., Pelz, J., Alm, C., Shi, P., & Haake, A. (2014). Recurrence quantification analysis reveals eye-movement behavior differences between experts and novices. *Proceedings of the Symposium on Eye Tracking Research and Applications–ETRA '14* (pp. 303–306). New York, NY: ACM.

Vlach, H. A., & DeBrock, C. A. (2017). Remember dax? Relations between children's cross-situational word learning, memory, and language abilities. *Journal of Memory and Language, 93*, 217–230.

Vlach, H. A., & Johnson, S. P. (2013). Memory constraints on infants' cross-situational statistical learning. *Cognition, 127*(3), 375–382.

Walter-Laager, C., Brandenberg, K., Tinguely, L., Schwarz, J., Pfiffner, M. R., & Moschner, B. (2017). Media-assisted language learning for young children: Effects of a word-learning app on the vocabulary acquisition of two-year-olds. *British Journal of Educational Technology, 48*(4), 1062–1072.

Weisleder, A., & Fernald, A. (2013). Talking to children matters: Early language experience strengthens processing and builds vocabulary. *Psychological Science, 24*(11), 2143–2152.

Wilkinson, K. M., & Light, J. (2011). Preliminary investigation of visual attention to human figures in photographs: Potential considerations for the design of aided AAC visual scene displays. *Journal of Speech, Language, and Hearing Research, 54*(6), 1644–1657.

Wilkinson, K. S., & Houston-Price, C. (2013). Once upon a time, there was a pulchritudinous princess . . . : The role of word definitions and multiple story contexts in children's learning of difficult vocabulary. *Applied Psycholinguistics, 34*(3), 591–613.

Wong, A., & Clark, E. V. (2002). Pragmatic directions about language use: Offers of words and relations. *Language in Society, 31*(2), 181–212.

Wong, L.-H., Chin, C.-K., Tan, C.-L., & Liu, M. (2010). Students' personal and social meaning making in a Chinese idiom mobile learning environment. *Journal of Educational Technology & Society, 13*(4), 15–26.

Wu, Z., & Gros-Louis, J. (2015). Caregivers provide more labeling responses to infants' pointing than to infants' object-directed vocalizations. *Journal of Child Language, 42*(3), 538–561.

Xie, H., Peng, J., Qin, M., Huang, X., Tian, F., & Zhou, Z. (2018). Can touchscreen devices be used to facilitate young children's learning? A meta-analysis of touchscreen learning effect. *Frontiers in Psychology, 9*, 2580.

Zettersten, M., Wojcik, E., Benitez, V. L., & Saffran, J. (2018). The company objects keep: Linking referents together during cross-situational word learning. *Journal of Memory and Language, 99*, 62–73.

Zosh, J. M., Brinster, M., & Halberda, J. (2013). Optimal contrast: Competition between two referents improves word learning. *Applied Developmental Science, 17*(1), 20–28.

Index

Printed in the United States
By Bookmasters